The European Union

ECONOMICS TODAY
Edited by Andrew Leake

The *Economics Today* series surveys contemporary headline topics in applied economics. Each book in the series is written by an expert in the field in a style that is fluently readable. It serves the student of introductory economic principles while also making the subject accessible to a more general reader. The series embraces the problem-solving skills of the new generation of students and stresses the importance of real-world issues and the significance of economic ideas.

Published

Andrew Leake: **The Economic Question**
Jean-Louis Barsoux and Peter Lawrence: **The Challenge of British Management**
Andy Beharrell: **Unemployment and Job Creation**
Frank Burchill: **Labour Relations**
Mark Cook and Nigel M. Healey: **Growth and Structural Change**
Kenneth Durham: **The New City**
S. F. Goodman: **The European Union** (3rd edition)
Ian Hodge: **Environmental Economics**
Kent Matthews: **Macroeconomics and the Market**
Charles Smith: **Economic Development, Growth and Welfare**
Jenny Wales: **Investigating Social Issues**
John Wigley and Carol Lipman: **The Enterprise Economy**
Margaret Wilkinson: **Taxation**

THE EUROPEAN UNION

Third Edition

S. F. Goodman

MACMILLAN

First edition (*The European Community*) 1990
Reprinted 1991, 1992
Second edition 1993
Reprinted 1993
Third edition (*The European Union*) 1996

Published by
MACMILLAN PRESS LTD
Houndmills, Basingstoke, Hampshire RG21 6XS
and London
Companies and representatives
throughout the world

ISBN 0-333-66266-0

A catalogue record for this book is available from the British Library.

10 9 8 7 6 5 4 3 2 1
05 04 03 02 01 00 99 98 97 96

Printed in Great Britain by
Antony Rowe Ltd
Chippenham, Wiltshire

For Helen

Contents

List of Tables and Figures

Tables

Figures

Preface

This third edition of *The European Community* is renamed *The European Union* and the change of title is more than symbolic. The Treaty on Union signed at Maastricht represents a watershed in the history of Western Europe because it shifts the emphasis of the European Community away from economic matters towards political affairs. Whilst there has been continued progress in economic, financial and social matters over the last three years, the stress has been on foreign and security policy and on justice and home affairs.

This edition contains detailed discussions of the most important economic, financial and social developments of recent years. The proposals for monetary union and a single currency are examined and the work of the new European Monetary Institute is explained. We now have the benefit of several new reports and decisions on monetary union. There is an analysis of the problems faced by the Exchange Rate Mechanism and of Britain's position in relation to it.

The book also includes analysis of the new regional policies, the Cohesion Fund and the Trans-European Networks that will transform the face of Europe over the next twenty years. Progress on social policies is also dealt with in the context of the Social Chapter reforms of the Treaty and the United Kingdom's opt-out. The environmental context of industrial change is of increasing importance and this section of the book has been expanded.

The future route taken by the European Union depends to a great extent on its success in tackling unemployment so this edition deals at length with the Delors White Paper on 'Growth, Competitiveness and Employment' and its implications.

There have been various reforms put in place since the last edition so the progress of the reforms of the Common Agricultural Policy and of the 1992 Single Market are discussed in detail. The issue of fraud is also examined. The issues raised by the Schengen Agreements are of very great importance for the future of Europe and are dealt with in detail.

The Treaty on Union included attempts to increase the democratic element in the Union, particularly in the role of the European Parliament. Much heat is generated by the concept of national sovereignty and by the question of majority voting in Council. A discussion of these themes appears throughout the book partly in the context of the future enlargement of the European Union to include Central and Eastern European states. The significance of the various agreements with these states is surveyed. There is also an examination of the effects of the enlargement in 1995 to include Austria, Finland and Sweden and of the European Economic Area.

Developments in these areas, and in social policy, together with the enlargement of the Union will make the Europe of the twenty-first century very different from that of the late 1950s when the European Economic Community was conceived.

There are topics that are not covered in the detail that some might wish. These include the extremely complex Common Fisheries Policy which is now largely about conservation, or should be, and has become very divisive. There is also little coverage of the Small and Medium Sized Enterprise initiatives being fostered so keenly by the Union. The main area of omission, however, is the scientific research field which has produced a large number of ever-changing initiatives.

The European Community has an exceptionally good statistical office (Eurostat). Its publications are available in all good reference libraries. Eurostat produces an excellent illustrated book called 'Europe in Figures', first published in 1988 and revised every two years. This is an ideal publication for the general reader who wants an easily assimilated and comprehensive coverage of the Community in statistical terms. It is superbly presented as is the more comprehensive A Social Portrait of Europe which contains magnificent coloured maps, charts and statistics. Its superb 142 pages at ECU 10, or £7.25 via HMSO bookshops, throws into sharp relief the tax on knowledge imposed by our own United Kingdom authorities in pricing works such as the annual Social Trends at £34. Recent European Union statistics present some problems because of German reunification and because of the impact of the Single Market from 1 January 1993 on trade statistics. The new system run by Intrastat has suffered from the failure of businesses to make returns.

The European Union also has a first-class information service. The Information Office of the Commission of the European Communities at 8 Storey's Gate, London SW1P 3AT, provides a wide range of free material as well as subscription matter. Some is in the form of Background Reports and some are periodicals in the *European Documentation* series. These periodicals, of which there are a large number, cover specific topics in great detail. They are an excellent starting point from which to begin the study of a given subject. The European Parliament has its own information service at 2 Queen Anne's Gate, London SW1H 9AA. Their material too is up to date and well presented.

Since these largely free sources of up-to-date information about the Union are readily available, I have tried in this book to concentrate on ideas, trends and developments rather than upon creating a factual reference book. By far the best single-volume reference book about the European Communities is *The European Community: A Practical Guide for Business, Media and Government* by Morris, Boehm and Geller (Macmillan). It contains excellent flow charts of all the main institutions and policies and an explanatory dictionary of all the main terms and bodies connected with the Community. It also lists all the legislation applicable to different areas of Community activity. The reader who wants a much more detailed analysis of the economic theory underlying the Community should read Edward Nevin's *The Economics of Europe* (Macmillan, 1990).

Jean Monnet, the 'father of the Community', said 'we are not forming coalitions between states, but union among people'. In other words, European integration is aimed at the hearts and minds of ordinary people. He concluded his memoirs by saying 'and the Community itself is only a stage on the way to the organised world of tomorrow'.

This great vision of Monnet, who was an extremely practical man, can only be fully appreciated against a historical background. This is why this book has a section evaluating the historical context of the progress of the Community. The Anglo-Saxon experience of modern history has been markedly different from that of the continental European. In this difference lies the explanation of our alternative views of the Community, of the European Union, its institutions and its future.

S. F. GOODMAN

List of Abbreviations

ACP	African, Caribbean and Pacific
AFTA	ASEAN Free Trade Area
AOSIS	Alliance of Small Island States
ASEAN	Association of South-East Asian Nations
B	Belgium
BENELUX	Belgium, The Netherlands and Luxembourg
CAD	Capital Adequacy Directive
CAP	Common Agricultural Policy
CCT	Common Customs Tariff
CEE	Central and Eastern Europe
CEFTA	Central European Free Trade Association
CFP	Common Fisheries Policy
CFSP	Common Foreign and Security Policy
CIS	Commonwealth of Independent States (ex-USSR)
COREPER	Committee of Permanent Representatives
CPI	Consumer Price Inflation (see also RPI)
CSCE	Conference on Security and Cooperation in Europe
D	Germany
DGs	Directorates-General
DK	Denmark
E	Spain
EAGGF	European Agricultural Guidance and Guarantee Fund
EC	European Community
ECB	European Central Bank
ECOFIN	Council of Economic and Finance Ministers
ECSC	European Coal and Steel Community
ECU	European Currency Unit

EEA	European Economic Area
EFTA	European Free Trade Association
EIB	European Investment bank
EIS	European Information System
EMCF	European Monetary Cooperation Fund (now run by EMI)
EMI	European Monetary Institute
EMS	European Monetary System
EMU	Economic and Monetary Union
EPC	European Political Cooperation
EPP	European People's Party
EPU	European Payments Union
ERDF	European Regional Development Fund
ESCB	European System of Central Banks
ESF	European Social Fund
EU	European Union
EUA	European Unit of Account
EURATOM	European Atomic Energy Community
EUROPOL	European Police
F	France
FIFG	Financial Instrument for Fisheries Guidance
FIN	Finland
FTA	Free Trade Area
GATS	General Agreement on Trade in Services
GATT	General Agreement on Tariffs and Trade
GDP	Gross Domestic Product
GNP	Gross National Product
GR	Greece
I	Italy
IBRD	International Bank for Reconstruction and Development
IGC	Intergovernmental Conference
ILO	International Labour Organisation
IMF	International Monetary Fund
IMP	Integrated Mediterranean Programmes
INF	Intermediate Range Nuclear Forces
IPC	Integrated Pollution Control
IRENE	Irregularities, Enquiries, Exploitation
IRL	Ireland
JCC	Joint Consultative Council

JHA	Justice and Home Affairs
L	Luxembourg
LFA	Less Favoured Areas
MCA	Monetary Compensatory Amount
MEP	Member of the European Parliament
MFN	Most Favoured Nation
MGQ	Maximum Guaranteed Quantity
NAFTA	North American Free Trade Association
NATO	North Atlantic Treaty Organisation
NL	Netherlands
OCA	Optimum Currency Area
OECD	Organisation for Economic Cooperation and Development
OEEC	Organisation for European Economic Cooperation
OSCE	Organisation for Security and Cooperation in Europe
P	Portugal
PCA	Partnership and Cooperation Agreement
PPP	Purchasing Power Parity
PPS	Purchasing Power Standards
QMV	Qualified Majority Vote
RPI	Retail Price Index (also CPI)
RPIX	Retail Price Index excluding mortgage interest payments
S	Sweden
SEA	Single European Act
SDR	Special Drawing Rights
START	Strategic Arms Limitation Talks (Treaty)
STV	Single Transferable Vote
TARGET	Trans-European Automated Real-Time Gross Settlements Express Transfer System
TENS	Trans-European Networks
UA	Unit of Account
UAA	Utilised Agricultural Area
UK	United Kingdom
VAT	Value Added Tax
VSTF	Very Short Term Facility
WEU	Western European Union
WTO	World Trade Organisation

Acknowledgements

The author and publishers wish to thank the following for permission to reproduce copyright material:

The Controller of Her Majesty's Stationery Office for extracts from *European Community Finances*, Cm 2824, Tables 4.4, 4.5, 4.6, 4.8 and Figure 4.4, and, from *Agriculture in the United Kingdom 1994*, Table 5.1. Crown Copyright is reproduced with the permission of the Controller of HMSO.

The Central Statistical Office for permission to reproduce Table 4.7 from *Social Trends 1995*.

The European Monetary Institute for permission to reproduce Table 8.1.

The Office for Official Publications of the European Communities for their generous help and for permission to reproduce tables, data and figures from their publications, particularly from *Basic Statistics of the European Union*, 1994 and 1995, from *Frontier Free Europe* and from the European Documentation and Europe on the Move series.

The author would like to thank the Information Services Unit of the European Commission for its help and unfailing courtesy and the Information Office of the European Parliament for providing so much valuable material. The Public Enquiries Group of the Bank of England were extremely helpful in answering queries and providing information. The German Embassy and the European Free Trade Association also gave considerable help. I would like to thank my wife, Lindsay, for her help with the index and bibliography and for her encouragement.

S.F.G.

Contemporary Issues 1

Revision of the Treaty on Union

The Maastricht Treaty on Union, agreed in December 1991 and finally put into force ten months behind schedule in November 1993, is a very important landmark in the development of Europe. It is a compromise between conflicting interests and is therefore imperfect and contains some inbuilt contradictions and sources of confusion. Its faults were partly recognised during the negotiations leading to the agreement. The Treaty, therefore, contains the requirement that an Intergovernmental Conference (IGC) be held in 1996 to review the working of the Treaty and to prepare for amendments. Chancellor Kohl of Germany, in September 1995, referred to 'Maastricht II' as the name of the amended treaty or as the name of a completely new treaty which would codify and restate all European Community and Union laws from the Treaty of Paris and the Treaty of Rome onwards. His choice of name is significant because it implies that the agreement on a new treaty will be postponed until the second half of 1997 when The Netherlands again hold the six-month rotating Presidency of the Union. That would be after a British general election and the implication is that Germany hopes for a change of British government to one that is less obstructionist in its approach to European union. This hope undoubtedly reflects the views of most of the other member states.

The Chancellor's speech reflects the belief held by the German Christian Democratic Party and its allies, and by many other political groupings in Europe, that the logical solution of the conflict between the need for greater democracy and greater efficiency in the conduct of Union affairs is a federal one. Thus one of the most important issues over the next few years is how to create a structure of government and administration for an enlarged and deeper European Union. The system created at Maastricht is not suited to further enlargement from the existing fifteen members, and is not appropriate for a Union which includes deeper economic and monetary union because it relies too heavily on intergovernmental cooperation that allows a dissident member to block proposals for change or to emasculate policies.

The period from 1994, through 1996 and beyond, will be dominated by the issues raised in preparation for the 1996 Intergovernmental Conference. Its meetings will, we are promised, be conducted with much greater openness or 'transparency' than those which led to the Treaty on Union. The secrecy and lack of public discussion over the Maastricht negotiations is usually quoted as the source of the problems in ratification of the Treaty. It is alleged that a large gap of comprehension developed between governments and the governed and that this allowed the anti-European populists and right-wing groups to play on fears of loss of identity, self-determination and democratic control, as well as on potential personal economic loss.

The legal basis of the European Union has become exceedingly complex and there is a strong case to be made for a completely new treaty to simplify the overlapping Treaties of Paris, Rome, Maastricht and the Single European Act together with assorted other legislation. In the process the relationships between the main power centres of the Union, that is the Commission, the Council, the European Parliament and the European Court, may be modified. If membership of the Union is to be extended after the IGC to about thirty nations there is a very strong case for a more formalized, essentially federal structure, to be created probably along the lines of the German model of very powerful member states with certain policies in common, rather than like the United States model of a very powerful, central, federal authority and relatively weak states. This issue is considered in some depth particularly in Chapter 4.

Economic Issues

There are many issues that have emerged over the years which will continue to cause conflict. The Common Agricultural Policy (CAP) and the Common Fisheries Policy (CFP) both cause major problems with regard to public expenditure, employment and national self-interest. The Commission began a new initiative in 1994 to introduce further reforms of the CAP. All previous reforms of the CAP have caused deep divisions between members. There are still loose ends to tie up in the implementation of the single market and the free movement of persons, goods and capital, especially in the first case where national sovereignty has to be pooled if borders are to be open. In this context there is a serious debate about the methods of control over the new European Police (Europol). Most members want the European Court of Justice to act as a final court of appeal in conflicts with, or about, Europol but the United Kingdom in particular strongly resists this sacrifice of sovereignty. The control of Europol is an issue of profound importance to the maintenance of civil liberties. There is a probability that any revision of the Treaty on Union will contain a statement of human rights for citizens of the Union although that may cause difficulties for the United Kingdom.

On the economic front there are also important issues to be resolved on the way to a single currency and monetary union after 1999. There is no longer any real conflict over the importance of the social aspects of the Union and the Social Chapter of the Treaty on Union in particular, but the United Kingdom's opt-out from the Social Chapter has created an administrative anomaly which needs resolution in any new treaty. In practical terms it is the other 14 members who have opted out into their own Social Chapter protocol while the United Kingdom remains within the old European Community structure. There are, of course, differences of opinion about the detail of social policies but not on the need to maintain the social dimension. President Mitterrand of France said, 'Europe will be for workers as well as for bankers', and most European political parties accept that.

Three other economic aspects are still at issue. The first is the level of fraud within the Union although most of the identified fraud takes place under the aegis of the member states' financial systems and not those of the Union. The second is whether the regional funds and the new Cohesion Fund will be sufficient to achieve the stated aim of greater economic convergence in time for monetary union. Linked to this is whether the richer nations are willing to continue with their contributions to these funds on a sufficient scale, and whether they will be able to extend similar generosity to new Central European entrants. The third aspect is that of reducing the excessively high levels of unemployment in the European Union. The divisions here revolve around the 1993 Delors White Paper on 'Growth, Competitiveness and Employment' which presented proposals for creating 15 million new jobs by the year 2000. The European Council accepted the plan but many members are dissatisfied with progress so far. As a result, Sweden has proposed an amendment to the Treaty on Union that would commit member governments to giving priority to full employment. The amendment would give the European Council the direct authority to lay down economic policy guide-lines on employment. The proposed amendment has already aroused the opposition of the more free-market oriented governments.

Old Issues Persist

Another area where old issues will continue to divide is in the field of security and foreign policy and the future of NATO and the Western European Union (WEU). The Maastricht system of inter-governmental cooperation has not worked well, especially in Bosnia. There is also a need for a fundamental review of the future of NATO in the light of the desire of many members to create a European defence force and a common foreign policy and in view of the gradual withdrawal of the USA from direct European involvement.

Deepening and Widening the Union

Some still fear that a 'fortress Europe' will emerge, devoted to economic and political self-interest and impervious to the needs of the rest of the world. They believe that France in particular retains a 'fortress Europe' attitude because of its strong support for its own economic self-interest. Others, mainly European socialists or social democrats, fear that a Europe fit only for capitalists will emerge although the Social Chapter protocol of the Union Treaty makes this very unlikely. Some others are frightened of the prospect of the development of an interventionist bureaucracy trying to foist its ideas of a social market on to unwilling victims.

There is an anxiety about loss of national sovereignty in key areas of decision-making. In contrast, others extol the virtues of the pooling of sovereignty. The few visionaries who, in the 1980s, foresaw the creation of a federal state of Europe with federal institutions such as a single currency, a central bank, a European police force and eventually a European defence and foreign policy are being joined by many others who have accepted the inexorable logic of the creation of a Single Market. They argue that a genuine, unified market creates an imperative for a more coordinated and centralised system of decision-making, and that this is best achieved by an approach from first principles. Some see themselves in the same position as the fathers of the Constitution of the United States, in a place of destiny shaping the world of the future. Others, perhaps more practically, see a slow but inexorable pressure building up towards the establishment of more institutions in common. They expect to see greater uniformity of policies and the setting up of joint facilities and cooperation procedures, such as common defence and foreign policies, alongside, but not initially completely replacing, existing national policies. They are willing to wait to allow the economic and political pressures involved in the realisation of a single European market to show the logical inevitability of their ideas. The bitter debates in the aftermath of the Maastricht agreement and during the various referendum campaigns on its ratification represented a major set-back to those proposing a deepening of the Union. A rift has developed between the beliefs of a pro-European élite and those further away from the centre of European Union decision-making.

Not all European political parties or governments are entirely happy about the deepening of the Union, especially into defence, foreign affairs and social policy, although some governments are very keen on such trends. Enthusiasm tends to vary in inverse proportion to the perceived adverse effects. Germany's government, for example, has been in the forefront of the moves to a single European currency, but the closer it gets to realisation the greater has been the opposition of the German public. Within the United

Kingdom, the government under Mrs Thatcher's personal direction began a policy that contributed to her downfall in 1990, of waging an active campaign against any extension of Community powers into the social, political and economic spheres beyond those strictly necessary to implement the achievement of the single internal market. The same basic policy has been pursued by the government formed under Mr Major and resulted in a special opt-out protocol on monetary union's third stage for the United Kingdom in the Treaty on Union, and on the extraordinary device of the other eleven (now 14) members opting out with their own protocol on the Social Chapter. In contrast, the 'New' Labour Party in the United Kingdom has reversed its traditional antagonism to the Union and has discovered new delights in the European proposals for a social market. They hope to derive all sorts of benefits from Europe that they have failed to obtain within the United Kingdom. There are still deep divisions in the Labour party over Europe but it pays the party to minimise them and to concentrate on the deeper fissures in the Conservative party.

To some extent the success of deepening will depend on the outcome of the efforts to create 'cohesion' within the Union, that is greater uniformity of prosperity throughout the membership and the reduction of regional disparities in the quality of life. Some members have only supported some of the changes in the Treaty on Union in return for greater financial assistance and the creation of a 'Cohesion Fund'. Regional policies will assume much greater importance over the next twenty years, especially if the Union's membership is broadened. It is, in any case, essential to achieve greater cohesion if the introduction of a single currency is not to create economic chaos.

The Single European Act

The main catalyst for recent change has been the Single European Act which is referred to throughout this book. In brief, the Act was an attempt to realise the original objective of the creation of the European Economic Community under the Treaty of Rome in 1957. The intention then was to have a single market without barriers of any kind between the six countries that made up the original Community. As the Community enlarged to 12 members it became increasingly clear that many physical and technical barriers remained to prevent the free movement of goods, services and people. Internal customs barriers had gone but Europe was not a single market. As a result, in 1985, the heads of government of the Twelve agreed to complete the single internal market progressively by 31 December 1992. The Single European Act which implemented their agreement was signed in February 1986 and came into force on 1 July 1987. The establishment of the truly frontierless single market has involved the passing of 282 measures. Most have been transposed into members' domestic law although at very different rates. A few areas of dispute remain. The last areas under discussion have been direct taxation, financial services, transport and company law and the detail of some schemes such as the systems of collecting VAT. A problem that is not yet fully resolved is that of free movement of people across frontiers despite the attempt to solve them via the Schengen Agreement (see below in Chapter 12). Social measures were a source of dispute although strictly speaking they are not a direct part of the single market programme, but the Commission is keen to press ahead and cater for what they call the 'social dimension' of the single market.

The Pillars of the Treaty on Union

Until the Maastricht Treaty on Union, the growth of the European Community was usually likened to the organic growth of a tree with a single root system and spreading, sheltering branches. In other words the administrative and decision-making processes were embodied in a single system via the Council, the Commission, Parliament and Court of Justice. The Maastricht Treaty was a compromise that resulted in what is called a pillar system which attempts to add two new areas of policy, a Common Foreign and Security Policy (CFSP) and Justice and Home Affairs (JHA), to the original three Communities – Coal and Steel (ECSC), Economic (EEC) and Atomic Energy (Euratom). Figure 1.1 illustrates this pillar concept of the European Union. The pillars of the CFSP and JHA operate by intergovernmental cooperation through the administrative machine of the Commission, but it is obvious that the machinery is not working properly.

FIGURE 1.1

The Pillar Concept of the European Union

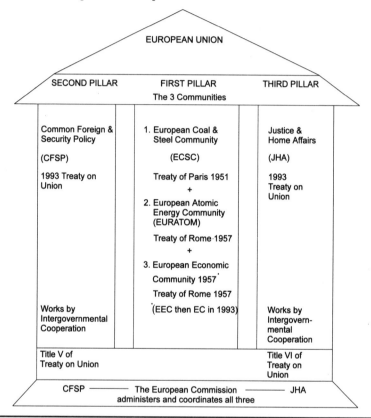

Pillar 1 consists of the three European Communities, the ECSC, the EC and Euratom which were created by the Treaties of Paris 1951 and Rome 1957. The Treaty on Union made official the dropping of the word 'economic' from the European Economic Community so it now named the European Community.

Pillar 2 deals with cooperation between the member states' governments in foreign and security policy. This builds on a long-standing degree of cooperation in security policy. The Treaty on Union specifies the details of cooperation procedures in Title V.

Pillar 3 is concerned with cooperation between members in justice and home affairs and the details are in Title VI of the Treaty on Union.

The creation of the European Union presents us with a problem of nomenclature. It would usually be inaccurate to refer to activities under the second and third pillars as those of 'the Community'. It has, incidentally, long been the habit of writers to refer to the 'European Community' in the singular when technically it should be 'Communities'. Most writers resolve the problem by referring to the 'European Union' or the 'Union'. Apparently, to say 'Union' is always correct whereas 'Community' is sometimes wrong. There are, of course, anomalies. Ambassadors remain accredited to the European Community because the European Union has no legal personality. In this book the term 'Community' is normally used to refer to pre-Treaty on Union events, and 'European Union' or 'Union' is used for post-1993, but it is very difficult to be consistent. One thing is clear, if you are a citizen of one of the member states you are also now a citizen of the European Union not of the European Community although it has not yet made much practical difference.

Decision-making in the European Union

Before discussing these areas of controversy, it will help if an outline is drawn of the Union's institutions and the process of decision-making. Details of these are discussed in subsequent chapters, especially in Chapters 4 and 11.

The Union has five main institutions: the Commission, the Council, the European Parliament, the European Court of Justice and the European Court of Auditors. Figure 1.2 shows a simplified outline of decision-making and institutional relationships in the European Union.

The Commission

This consists of twenty members who are appointed for five years. It proposes policy and legislation which is submitted to a variety of channels of consideration, mainly via the Council and the European Parliament. The Commission also executes the Council's decisions and supervises the daily running of the Union. Finally, the

FIGURE 1.2

A Simplified Version of the European Union's Decision-Making Procedure

The process of making decisions in the European Union is a complicated one. The procedures differ according to subject and type of measure. In general the procedure is as follows

The COMMISSION proposes new measures

The COUNCIL OF MINISTERS negotiates on the basis of the proposal, with the aim of reaching an agreed position. It may have to consult the two committees, Economic and Social, and of the Regions

The PARLIAMENT scrutinises the proposals and, depending on what they are about, has rights to put forward amendments. The EP also has joint decision-making procedures with the Council in some areas. It may also initiate legislation to a very limited extent. It may reject the budget.

The COUNCIL OF MINISTERS negotiates on the basis of the proposal, with the aim of reaching an agreed position. It is advised by COREPER, a committee of permanent officials

The COUNCIL OF MINISTERS then makes the decisions whether or not to adopt the measure

The COMMISSION ensures that it is put into action. National laws may need to be altered

The EUROPEAN COURT OF JUSTICE considers infringements of Union law, or questions of interpretation

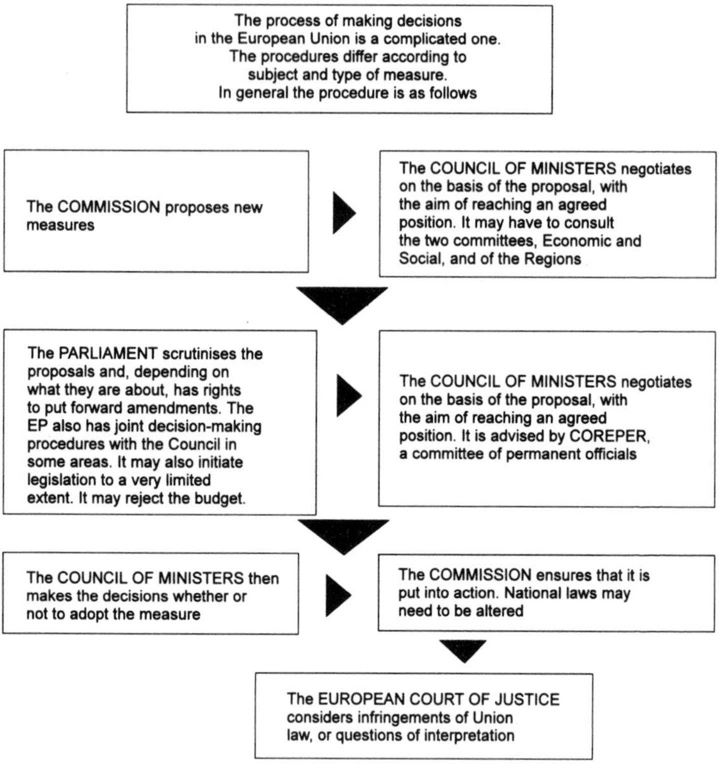

SOURCE   Adapted by the author from *Europe Today*, London Offices of the Commission of the European Communities and the European Parliament in cooperation with the Department of Education. November 1994

Commission acts as the guardian of the treaties and can take legal action against members who do not comply with European Union rules.

The Council

This body makes the decisions for the Union, sometimes in conjunction with the European Parliament. The Council sometimes comprises meetings of ministers for a subject (Council of Ministers)

or Council Working Groups who are officials from member states. The term Council also includes the Committee of Permanent Representatives of the members (COREPER). The meetings of ministers are held each April, June and October with extra meetings as required. At least twice a year the Heads of Government meet in what is called the European Council. Do not confuse this with the Council of Europe which is an organisation which had 39 members in 1996 after Russia joined. Some decisions can be made by a simple majority of eight of the 15 members, but some are made under a Qualified Majority Vote (QMV) of the Council. Some decisions still have to be unanimous. Which type of procedure is followed may be of great practical importance. See Chapter 4.

The European Parliament

It consists of 626 members directly elected for five years. There were elections in June 1994 so the next are due in 1999. Under the 'cooperation procedures' adopted by the Single European Act its opinion is required on many of the Commission's proposals before the Council can adopt them. Under the Treaty on Union a new codecision procedure with the Council is required and this has proved a significant increase in the Parliament's powers. The European Parliament is not a legislative body in the usual sense of the word in that it does not normally directly initiate legislation, although the Treaty on Union permits it to request the Commission 'to submit any appropriate proposal on matters on which it considers that a Community act is required for the purpose of implementing this Treaty'. It may also obtain legislative action by producing its own initiative reports, through the annual legislation programme and through joint declarations with the other institutions. The Parliament's activities are based in three locations. It meets in plenary session in Strasbourg and holds other meetings in Brussels. Its committee meetings are held in Brussels and its secretariat operates in Luxembourg. It has made a brave, and so far fruitless, attempt to locate all its activities in Brussels. The Treaty on Union contains several changes in the role and powers of the European Parliament, particularly the codecision procedure. Its power over the budget is explained in detail in Chapter 11 but remains that of giving advice, attempting amendment with Council and Commission approval, and rejection. The changes arising from the new treaty have increased the importance and effectiveness of the European Parliament. They are discussed in detail in Chapter 11.

The European Court of Justice

This court which meets in Luxembourg has 15 judges and nine advocates-general. It includes, since 1988, a Court of First Instance. It rules on the interpretation and application of Community law and its judgments are binding in member states. It has been extremely important in the development of the European Union, and its role is fully discussed in Chapter 11. It should not be confused with the European Court of Human Rights in Strasbourg which is an offspring of the Council of Europe.

The European Court of Auditors

The European Court of Auditors in Luxembourg, consisting of 15 members, was established in 1975 and has been working since 1977. The word 'European' was added to its title in 1994. The Treaty on Union strengthened the role of the Court in the fight against fraud and raised it to the status of an institution of the Union. It examines whether all revenue has been received and whether it has been spent legally. It also comments on the soundness of the financial management. It has no power to enforce its control measures or to investigate suspicions of irregularity. Its effectiveness lies in its ability to publicise its findings through its official publications. The Treaty requires the Court to provide the Council and Parliament with 'a statement of assurance as to the reliability of the accounts and the legality and regularity of the underlying transactions'. The question of fraud is discussed later in Chapter 4.

There are in addition to these five institutions, two 222 member advisory committees, an Economic and Social Committee and a Committee of the Regions. The Council or Commission must consult the relevant committee in seven areas: education, cultural 'incentive measures', public health, trans-European networks, the report on social and economic cohesion, basic rules governing all the structural funds, and implementing the rules for the regional fund. The Economic and Social Committee has a membership of representatives of employers, trade unions and consumers. The

Treaty on Union established the Committee of the Regions whose membership is mainly local and regional representatives nominated by their governments. On the financial side there is a very important European Investment bank (EIB) which provides loans and guarantees. Most of its assistance goes to less-developed regions, but it is also important in providing finance for the trans-European networks' (TENS) programmes aimed at improving cross-border power, energy and communication links. The Treaty on Union also set up the European Monetary Institute (EMI) which began work in 1994 on the second stage of monetary union. It will eventually give way to a European System of Central Banks (ESCB) and a European Central Bank (ECB) if and when the third stage of monetary union is reached after 1999 (see Chapter 8).

The Trialogue

The Trialogue is the name given to the negotiations between the three institutions that have to consult on various matters, especially the budget, the Council, the Commission and the European Parliament.

European Union Legislation

It will also be helpful to see in what forms the Union passes legislation or indicates its will. The European Coal and Steel Community unfortunately has a different designation from the other two members of the European Communities, the European (Economic) Community and Euratom. The classification provided for in the relevant Articles of the Treaty of Rome is as shown in Table 1.1.

TABLE 1.1
Classification of Legislation of the Treaty of Rome

ECSC	European Community	Euratom
(Article 14)	(Article 189)	(Article 161)
Decisions (general)	Regulations	Regulations
Recommendations	Directives	Directives
Decisions (individual)	Decisions	Decisions
—	Recommendations	Recommendations
Opinions	Opinions	Opinions

The following refers to the European Community and Euratom. The Council and Commission may make regulations, issue directives, take decisions, make recommendations or deliver opinions.

Regulations

These are applicable in full to all member states and do not need to be approved by national parliaments. The regulation takes legal precedence if there is any conflict with national law (see Chapter 11). In the ECSC the Decision (general) is the equivalent measure.

Directives

These state the result that must be achieved within a given period and it is up to each member to introduce or amend laws to bring about the desired effect. If the member fails to implement the directive the Commission may refer the matter to the Court of Justice if other approaches fail. Some parts of the directive may come into direct effect even if the member has not embodied the required changes into its national law. Directives are binding upon members as regards the objective to be achieved but the member state decides the form and method used to incorporate it into national law. Some members are very slow to make the necessary changes. The ECSC equivalent is its Recommendation.

Decisions

These are the normal means by which the Community orders something to be done in an individual case. They are addressed to member states, companies or individuals and are completely binding on them. If they impose financial obligations they are enforceable in the member's courts. The ECSC equivalent is its Decision (individual).

Recommendations and opinions

These simply state the views of the institution that issues them and are not binding. They are issued to member states and sometimes to individuals. In this context the ECSC equivalent is an Opinion. (Unfortunately the ECSC Recommendation is the equivalent of a binding European Community or Euratom Directive).

Delegated legislation

Although the legislative power of the Union lies in the Council it delegates some of its power to the Commission. This delegation is usually of routine and technical matters and is subject to the advice and assistance of committees composed of people from each member state.

How are Decisions Reached in the Council?

Under the EEC Treaty of Rome most Council decisions from 1958 to the end of 1968 had to be unanimous. It was intended to extend majority voting from 1966 but a row developed on whether a member state should be overruled when one of its essential interests was at stake. French objections to Common Agricultural Policy (CAP) changes were at the root of the conflict. A compromise called the Luxembourg compromise was reached in 1966 and it led to nearly 20 years where majority decisions were limited to budgetary and administrative matters. New members began to plead that they had special or very important interests and insisted on unanimity. The 1983 Solemn Declaration on European Union confirmed the compromise. Thus until the Single European Act of 1986 most decisions of the Council had to be unanimous. As a result the Community began to suffer from what was called 'Eurosclerosis', that is it crawled along at the pace of the most reluctant or intransigent. Since its passage decisions in some areas of policy still have to be unanimous. But one of the most significant changes to the principles of the Community has been to end an individual country's power of veto in areas where the Qualified Majority Vote (QMV) applies. Thus in areas directly associated with the creation of the single market it is possible to proceed with a qualified majority of 62 votes out of a total of 87. The United Kingdom, France, Germany and Italy have 10 votes each; Spain has 8; Belgium, Greece, the Netherlands and Portugal 5 each; Austria and Sweden 4 each; Denmark, Finland

and Ireland 3 each and Luxembourg 2. A blocking minority is 26 and requires the support of at least three states. In 1994 the Council took 48 decisions by QMV. Decisions in the Council may also on rare occasions be made in some circumstances with a simple majority of eight members. The details of voting are not published and this is a source of grievance to the media and to democrats although a new code of conduct was published in October 1995 that has increased the transparency of Council decision-making.

The process of decision-making under the cooperation procedure adopted in the Single European Act and the codecision procedure under the Treaty on Union is very complex and creates a great range of opportunities for pressure groups and lobbyists. The Commission has listed 22 main decision-making procedures in the Treaty on Union relating to the European Community treaties, four relating to the Common Foreign and Security policy and a further three for Justice and Home Affairs. Figures 4.2 and 4.3 in Chapter 4 are flow charts which show the cooperation procedure and the codecision procedure. Such charts do not, of course, show where the real power of decision lies.

In the Union the location of final decision-making will usually be the Council but those decisions are based upon a long series of discussions, meetings and lobbying in Brussels and Strasbourg and in members' own corridors of power. Some commentators attribute most power to the permanent officials of the Commission, to COREPER and to those Commissioners who are active and well versed in power broking. In the background there is always a tension between the national representatives working in Europe who tend to develop a wider European vision, and their departments back home who tend to have a more constricted view. The truth is that the power of decision-making is shared and also shifts between and within groups according to personalities, subject matter and national perceptions of their self-interest. There is a welcome growth of interest shown by political scientists, writing in English, in the Union's power structures but it falls short of that shown in national structures such as those of the United States or Britain. The question of the process of decision-making is worth bearing in mind when we return to consider the issues currently arising in the Union, particularly in Chapter 11.

What Sort of Union is Emerging?

A 'fortress Europe'

There has been and is a persistent fear among some people that a fortress Europe will emerge. They feared that it might evolve as a result of the changes in progress for establishing the single internal market, although that was definitely not the stated intention of the Heads of Government or Community officials. The phrase 'fortress Europe' has several interpretations and it is used, essentially, as a term of abuse. It means, in principle, that the Union will be setting up a unified market of 370 million relatively affluent people which will be able to fix an external tariff barrier to protect itself against competition from Japan, the Far East, Central and Eastern Europe and the United States and be detrimental to developing nations. The expansion of the European Union has bolstered the economic bargaining strength of western Europe against the individual nations of the world to obtain raw materials, primary products and energy at low cost. It might, in theory, be able to use its establishment, or harmonisation, of standards to place external suppliers at a disadvantage (see Chapter 3; Trade Theory). Some observers argue that it acted in a selfish and self-centred manner during the Uruguay Round of GATT talks that broke down in December 1990, staggered into life through 1991, resumed in 1992 and finally reached an agreement in December 1993. The Union spoke with a unified voice at the GATT talks but some national divisions of interest and emphasis were revealed in the discussions that established a common bargaining position. Divisions were particularly obvious on agricultural policy.

It can be argued, fairly convincingly, that the eventual agreement under the Uruguay Round and the setting up of the World Trade Organisation (WTO) shows that the European Union is not in danger of becoming a restrictionist trading fortress. Indeed, the opposite appears to be the case in that it has adopted a very liberal approach to the removal of trade barriers whilst trying to safeguard itself against unfair competition. The attitudes of the USA and Japan have been greater obstacles to free trade.

It is also possible, if the 'fortress Europe' approach were adopted, that the banking, monetary and financial systems might be used to discriminate against non-members. This would, of course, be easier if and when the Union adopts a single currency and forms a European Central Bank possibly after 1999. Such discrimination would presumably not find favour with all members, especially those most heavily dependent on foreign trade. When the European Union does establish a single currency, especially if it includes sterling, it would be the most important financial unit in world markets. A financial fortress Europe is almost an impossibility in the light of what is called the globalisation of world financial markets, that is the removal of barriers to financial transfers. There are some Europeans, and others, however, who would like to see some reimposition of controls on capital movements in order to reduce currency speculation and instability. (See Chapters 7 and 8 for an elaboration of this discussion.)

Another aspect of the potential 'fortress Europe' which worries some observers is that the European Union might become less accessible or even inaccessible to some groups of outsiders. Within the members' boundaries there should have emerged, by 1993, complete freedom of movement of citizens to work, live and set up enterprises. This is one area, however, where the aims of the single market have not yet been achieved, partly as a result of obstructions raised by the United Kingdom and also by Denmark. One of the debates at the Maastricht summit concerned immigration and the fear that the rules and regulations used to establish the mobility of Union citizens would be constructed in such a way as to exclude non-Union nationals. There is no doubt, on the one hand, that entry for tourism by non-nationals would be easier with only a single visa required for travel in all 15 states. On the other hand, however, there has been great concern about the fate of those seeking asylum. The 12 ministers responsible for immigration agreed, in 1989, and the three new entrants have also agreed, to the principle that a refugee will be able to apply once to enter the Union. If one country rejects the request they all will. Once accepted by one country the refugee will be accepted by all. They will also work out harmonisation procedures to deal with those seeking asylum. The ministers reaffirmed their support for the United Nations Convention on Refugees. This means that they will not return refugees to a country in which they have a well-founded expectation of persecution. The Union will, therefore, become a single entity for the purpose of seeking asylum. This, in itself, may not be cause for too much concern though a great deal depends on the detail of the harmonisation regulations. It also necessitates intergovernmental agreements on policing of the system and a very good computer system.

The Maastricht agreement provided for unanimous agreement until 1996 on a list of nations whose citizens will require a visa to enter the Union. After 1 January 1996 the list can be agreed by qualified majority. There is also a provision to deal with unforeseen emergencies such as a sudden potential inflow of refugees. Germany and Austria are particularly concerned about the possible influx of economic refugees from the Central and Eastern European states as they adjust to free market mechanisms or dissolve into political chaos. The United Kingdom has the potential flood of refugees from Hong Kong at the forefront of its desire for a strong exclusion policy. France is concerned about North African migrants and Italy about refugees from the old Yugoslavia. The various agencies which deal with refugees have expressed grave concern about the proposed new system. They are probably right to be concerned because the new system is almost bound to cause entry requirements of each country to be geared up towards the toughest. The country which admits the refugee will take responsibility for him or her under the proposals. The new system will, however, put an end to asylum seekers 'country hopping' in order to find one that will accept them. It is, of course, often very hard to tell the difference between genuine asylum seekers and those who simply want a better economic environment. There will be a common system for short-term visas of six-months' duration and a tightening up of regulations on family members who are allowed to join relatives already legally settled within the Community. The United Kingdom expressed great concern on both issues because it fears short-term refugees will stay permanently.

The agreements in principle that are discussed in the paragraph above have proved exceptionally difficult to apply in practice. The areas covered, immigration and asylum, are in Title VI of the Treaty on Union where the system of intergovernmental cooperation and unanimity is supposed to apply, but they are also subject to the original Treaties of Rome. The Commission, in its 1995 report on the working of the Treaty for the Intergovernmental Conference in 1996, is extremely critical of the failure to achieve reasonable progress in the area of cooperation in justice and home affairs. The intergovernmental cooperation procedures had scarcely been used and progress was reliant on the use of the old methods requiring unanimity. The Commission says that Article VI has proved ineffective and that 'the unanimity rule has proved to be the major source of paralysis, either preventing any action or decision at all, or reducing the decision taken to the lowest common denominator'.

There have been various responses to the threat of the creation of 'fortress Europe'. One response has been from the Japanese who have increased the rate at which they have been investing in new manufacturing plants in Europe. A high proportion, about 40 per cent, of their total European investment has been in the United Kingdom. The United Kingdom has been attractive to the Japanese because of the government's financial inducements, commitment to free trade, the relatively cheap labour force, the favourable tax system, improving labour relations, the absence of foreign-exchange controls and the English language. There was also the very important factor of the favourable experience of the large number of already established Japanese firms. The existence of plenty of good golf courses may also be a consideration!

One aspect of the threatened 'fortress' is the effect it might have on Third World countries. The Union has an assortment of programmes to help such countries and is, on the whole, generous. Through the four Lomé Conventions it has allocated large sums to helping African, Caribbean and Pacific (ACP) countries. The Fourth Lomé Convention will run from 1990 to 2000 and in the first five years to 1995 the Union will have provided 12 billion ECU in aid in the form of grants, soft loans and subsidies on interest rates, a 20 per cent increase in real terms compared with Lomé 3. Lomé 4 is already being reviewed to prepare for Lomé 5. The money is paid through the European Development Fund. The ACP countries in the Lomé Convention have free access to the Union for most of their agricultural and manufactured goods. There is a special system called Stabex to help stabilise their export earnings, and another called Sysmin to stabilise earnings from mining products. The fear is that Third World countries that are not favoured by the Lomé Conventions or by bilateral agreements will suffer from European Union competition in world markets. They may also be deprived of fair competition for their goods within Europe although the Uruguay Round agreement will eventually remove most barriers against them. The effects of the Uruguay Round agreement are uncertain but some predict that the overall effect will be to harm the poorest nations whilst the richest will benefit most. World Bank studies in 1995 contradict this view. Some experts allege that the European Union has already damaged developing countries by subsidising exports of food and by undercutting their embryo manufacturing industries. The Lomé Convention is undoubtedly an excellent and generous scheme but, like all such schemes, it is not perfect. Although it gives aid in what seems to be a relevant, specific and well-balanced manner aimed at self-sufficiency and independence, it is possible to criticise the perpetuation of over-dependency on the European market and a reduced ability for the beneficiaries to diversify their economies. A major concern is for those nations who are not signatories, especially Asian countries.

A free market for capitalists

There has been, and remains, a stark contrast between the attitude of the United Kingdom Conservative governments and most of the other governments of the European Union over the type of Union they want. The United Kingdom government was an enthusiastic supporter of the Single European Act and used its House of Commons majority, with a three-line whip and procedural guillotine, to ensure its swift ratification. It seems to have been somewhat carried away by its own propaganda about its own success in sweeping away regulations, controls and bureaucracy in creating the British 'economic miracle'. It seems to have deluded itself that its simple acceptance of an updated version of Adam Smith's idea of free market forces was also intended by the other members. It is, of course, possible to debate the existence and reality of the alleged British 'economic miracle' of the mid-1980s and of the real nature of cause and effect of change. The extent, for example, of the reduction of controls and bureaucracy in the United Kingdom was usually exaggerated. The concept of an 'economic miracle' leads to what are essentially semantic arguments. The stated growth rates of the United Kingdom economy depended upon the criteria for growth that were adopted and the base years chosen.

At the time, the other eleven members, and particularly the original six, were in favour of the single market because they saw it as a logical necessity if further economic growth and the reduction of unemployment were to be achieved. A detailed analysis of the costs of a 'non-Europe,' the Cecchini Report, showed that all members would benefit from extra growth, a lower rate of inflation and rising employment. They realised that the new breeze of competition would carry with it some degree of social consequence in terms of the restructuring of industry, commerce and employment. They supported the proposed controls on agricultural spending in order to leave more money available for the Social and Regional Funds of the Community. These motives· led them to expect and support proposals to add new social provisions to the Community alongside the economic changes required to create the single market.

The Single European Act permitted qualified majority decisions on measures to implement the single internal market. These included transport and environmental matters but excluded items relating to taxation, the free movement of persons and the interests of employees. It came as a shock to some British politicians, and even apparently to some members of the government, that the Community was producing binding regulations which affected everyday life in the United Kingdom to a marked extent. Many of these applied to the environment in areas such as the decision to enforce catalytic converters on vehicles to control exhaust emissions, or to control the quality of public water supplies and the quality of beaches. Mrs Thatcher, in early 1989, decided that her ministers were giving too much away in some areas. She appeared to regard this as a threat to national sovereignty and as bureaucratic control and, therefore, took personal charge of supervising the outcome of departmental discussions in the Community, hoping thereby to withstand the tide of change. Inevitably she was likened to King Canute, although we all know that King Canute was an exceptionally able king who was teaching his sycophantic courtiers a lesson by proving that he could not stem the tide as they had suggested. The outcome has been much the same. The powers were assigned by the Single European Act and it was already too late to be squawking about them. There are regular reports of changes that will be imposed against the British government's wishes – transport regulations, speed limiters for heavy goods vehicles, tobacco advertising controls, metric labelling of goods, for example.

A deregulated market

The real fear of the pro-free marketeers has been that the single market will turn out to be overregulated, bureaucratic and protectionist. Mrs Thatcher made this plain in her famous Bruges speech in 1988. Her views were restated by Mr Lawson, at that time Chancellor of the Exchequer, in 1989. He had a vision of 'a deregulated, free market, open Europe, driven by consumer choice . . . by transferring power not to Brussels but to the people'. These views were a potent force in the formation of British policy in the negotiations for the Treaty on Union and the general position has been maintained ever since, for example in Mr Major's speech at Leiden in September 1994. The United Kingdom government has managed to glean some support for the view that there is too much regulation and a committee, called the Molitor committee after its chairman, has been working on ways of reducing bureaucracy and regulation.

The Molitor committee was set up in 1994 by the German Presidency of the Union to see how European Union laws could be simplified in the interests of increasing growth and competitiveness and reducing unemployment. It reported to the European Council at Cannes in 1995. The report concentrated heavily on controversial areas such as the environment and health and safety. The European Parliament gave it a vote of no confidence partly for 'operating in secret without using normal democratic procedures'. Even the President of the Commission criticised parts of its report on the grounds that it should have looked at a much wider range of internal market legislation. It is clear from the report that many of the problems of overregulation stem from national laws and not from the European Union's. The issue of deregulation is one that will continue to cause dissension in the future mainly because there is nearly always a demand for more regulation whenever one or more member state thinks that there is not a level playing field in a particular area of competition.

The United Kingdom's opposition to proposals for a stronger Union has been fiercest in the field of monetary union, the adoption of a single currency, sterling's membership of the Exchange Rate Mechanism (although it did join the ERM between October 1990 and September 1992), merger and competition policy, the Social Charter, and the relaxation of border controls. In all these areas the

United Kingdom Conservative governments argued that too much regulation, harmonisation and loss of sovereignty were involved. Its wish to retain border controls is in contradiction to its general policy of removing restrictions. The details are discussed in Chapters 4 and 7.

A multi-speed or variable-geometry Europe

There is a very real danger that a multi-speed Europe will develop with the United Kingdom relegated to the sidelines of European decision-making. Another version of this idea is a 'variable-geometry' Europe referred to in Mr Major's Leiden speech. The Commission, in its report on the working of the Treaty on Union, expresses strong disquiet over the precedent created by the United Kingdom's opt-out from the Social Chapter and is concerned that other members, especially new entrants, will also want special treatment beyond the normal five or so years phasing in of common policies. There was some expectation among some Conservative politicians that the fall of Mrs Thatcher, largely over the strident tone of her anti-monetary union approach as well as the poll-tax fiasco, would create a significant shift of attitude in the party leadership. Indeed the new leader talked about being at the 'heart of Europe' but this sentiment was not borne out by the negotiating position adopted at Maastricht. On many issues, the United Kingdom stood alone. On others, it alienated opinion by its doctrinaire intransigence. Its opposition had been ineffective where majority decision-making applied although the qualified majority system was not often invoked. Moreover, the other members sometimes found ways of circumventing British opposition in areas where a majority was required. In 1990, for example, Germany, France and the Benelux countries, later joined by Italy, made their own 'Schengen' group agreement, outside the Community's structures, on removing border controls on the basis of an earlier 1985 scheme. This was eventually implemented, with several hiccups, in 1995 with the United Kingdom outside. See Chapter 12 for a full discussion of the Schengen Agreements.

The British government also excluded itself, by choice, from some areas of scientific research, from the Lingua programme to teach further foreign languages in schools, from proposals to cut cardiovascular disease by discouraging smoking and from some training grants. It was also against a Community-wide pensioners' identity card to give them access to cheaper fares and facilities. It proved particularly obdurate over attempts under the Social Charter to improve working conditions for the low-paid, women and the young. It continues to object resolutely to proposals to improve maternity-leave conditions for working women. There is a fear among the other members that this British attitude, which they regard as obstructionist, will be repeated during the Intergovernmental Conference of 1996. There are strong indications that their fears will be realised if United Kingdom statements about the conference and the Treaty review are accepted at their face value. The problem of the United Kingdom's intransigence may be overcome if, as Chancellor Kohl suggests, the IGC carries over into 1997, after a British general election.

The variable-geometry concept relates mainly to monetary union where two or three groups may form. The full details of this are discussed in Chapter 8. The possibility exists of the United Kingdom, although it itself will probably meet the criteria except for membership of the Exchange Rate Mechanism (ERM), forming a focus for those nations who are unable by 1999 to meet the convergence criteria required for movement to Stage 3 of the monetary union when a single currency and central bank will be formed. If the Cohesion Fund and regional policies fail to work to raise living standards in countries such as Greece, Portugal and Ireland, Britain could find itself leading the 'second division' nations in an inferior economic league. The United Kingdom is now in receipt of regional funds, under Objective 1 of the Regional Fund, for Merseyside and the Highlands and Islands where Gross Domestic Product per head is less than 75 per cent of the Union average. Alternatively, the United Kingdom could be leading a third division of itself and Greece completely outside any new managed monetary system.

After the 1996 review of the Treaty on Union there will be a number of new members of the Union from central Europe and the variable geometry concept could expand from its application to monetary union, and in the case of the United Kingdom the social chapter, to agricultural and regional policies. The Commission and its President M. Santer are very strongly opposed to what they call an 'à la carte' Europe. They say that 'allowing each country to pick and choose the policies it takes part in would inevitably lead to a negation of Europe'.

Federalism and Subsidiarity

These two words and their interrelationship are at the core of a very divisive issue in the European Union. Federalism is discussed in Chapters 2 and 4 but it will be helpful to explain the principle of 'subsidiarity' here because its adoption prevents the centralising tendency that many people, especially in the United Kingdom, associate with what they call federal government. The Treaty on Union agreed at Maastricht starts with the following phrases:

> By this Treaty, the High Contracting Parties establish among themselves a European Union. This Treaty marks a new stage in the process creating an ever closer Union among the peoples of Europe, where decisions are taken as closely as possible to the citizens.

The words 'ever closer Union' replaced the original draft phrase of 'Union with a federal goal' which created such a furore among certain anti-Community elements in Britain. The Treaty went on, in Article 3b, to define the principle of subsidiarity for the first time although Jacques Delors, President of the Commission defined it in a speech to the French Bishops at Lourdes in 1989. He said:

> Finally, the fourth principle is subsidiarity. I would say that, solely from the view of political effectiveness (I could quote de Tocqueville and others here), it is important not to concentrate too much power at the top, to be able to combine decision-making from the top and from the bottom and, wherever possible, to leave responsibility for solving a problem at the level closest to that problem.

The Treaty says:

> The Community shall act within the limits of the powers conferred upon it by this Treaty and of the objectives assigned to it therein. In the areas which do not fall within its exclusive jurisdiction, the Community shall take action in accordance with the principle of subsidiarity, only if and insofar as the objectives of the proposed action cannot be sufficiently achieved by the member states and can therefore, by reason of the scale or effects

of proposed action, be better achieved by the Community. Any action by the Community shall not go beyond what is necessary to achieve the objectives of the Treaty.

The Commission, in its assessment of the operation of the Treaty on Union, in May 1995, says that the principle of subsidiarity has begun to change the attitude of the institutions and there is more regular debate on the grounds for introducing each new proposal and about the distribution of powers relating to it. It goes on to warn, however, that the concept of subsidiarity is put forward for specific or short-term ends as a way of diluting the Union. It obviously has the United Kingdom in mind. As a warning, it adds that the principle can equally be used to justify measures which are better taken collectively rather than in isolation.

Conclusion

There will probably not be a 'fortress Europe' on the economic front because of the Uruguay Round agreement on the relaxation of many trade restrictions, but there may be one in terms of stricter controls over migration into the Union of both asylum seekers and economic migrants. Neither will there be a 'market for bankers and not workers'. The likelihood is that there will be a free single internal market, sensibly regulated and with a strong 'Social Charter' to maintain the rights of workers and consumers, pensioners, women and minorities. Some of this will impinge on the United Kingdom despite its opt-out from the Social Chapter. The European Parliament will continue to become more effective and probably more unpopular as a result, and there will be greater democratic participation. Most people will stop regarding national sovereignty as indivisible and will be prepared to see it as pooled in the European Union for mutual benefit rather than as being sacrificed. The addition of members such as Sweden, Austria and Finland will continue to tilt the balance even further in favour of a social market rather than a market for capitalists. There may develop a European Union of two or more divisions, or of variable geometry, if the Commission fails to prevent it and if economic and monetary union are not accompanied by greater cohesion. As the Union's membership expands, there will probably be much greater openness in the conduct of the debate about the steps to be taken to improve on the Treaty on Union and to create a new balance between the institutions, Council, Commission and Parliament. The pillar system incorporated in the Maastricht Treaty on Union may eventually be replaced by a more positive, federal structure but probably not by the 1996 Intergovernmental Conference.

Ideas into Institutions – How the European Community Began

Many of those who witnessed the appalling slaughter and destruction of the First World War realised that only some form of unification of the states of Europe could prevent further conflict. The Great Powers' struggle of the nineteenth century, the competition for empire and the arms race had culminated in a great cataclysm. Yet the nineteenth century had shown, in the case of the unification of Germany and Italy, that wars could be reduced by political and economic union. Further afield, the success of the American federal system, despite the supreme test of the Civil War, gave hope to the European democrat. The immediate aftermath of the First World War saw the creation of several new nation states and the resurrection of old states as the Austro-Hungarian empire collapsed and the Baltic states achieved temporary independence, since regained. Many boundaries were redrawn or established and we know, with the benefit of hindsight, that the Treaty of Versailles in 1919 contained the seeds of the Second World War. Perceptive critics of the time recognised that fact. The years 1919–39 can be regarded as an extended armistice.

It was against this background that the League of Nations was formed. It is fashionable to scoff cynically at the naïvety of those who thought that the League would ensure that the Great War would be 'the war to end all wars'. Admittedly, the League got off to a very bad start when the American President, Woodrow Wilson, one of its chief architects, failed to get the endorsement of the American people for his policies at Versailles and for the League. Yet millions saw in it a great hope for the future. The League did have some achievements. Disarmament agreements were reached. Naval building programmes were curtailed. Millions joined the Peace Pledge Union or its equivalent in other countries. The fact that these people's hopes were destroyed by the demonic forces of national socialism and deranged nationalism is for the whole of mankind to regret.

It was within this context of post-First World War reconstruction that a Pan-European Movement was launched in the 1920s. It called, in 1923, for a United States of Europe based mainly on the model of the United States. A few years later, in 1929, the League of Nations' Assembly in Geneva was the forum for an attempt to form a European Union within the context of the League of Nations. This was proposed by the French and German foreign ministers. The objective was very limited. It was to leave the separate states fully sovereign but would promote closer cooperation. The great depression in industry, commerce and finance which followed prevented this scheme from being adopted. The slump also created a breeding ground for the extension of versions of fascism from Italy to Germany and the Far East. Hopes for European unity were lost until after the Second World War.

The United Kingdom and Early Ideas for European Unity

The United Kingdom and Commonwealth had suffered a great loss of life during the First World War. The United Kingdom also lost its economic pre-eminence in several fields to the United States and new producers had sprung up, especially in the Far East. Despite this, Britain had not suffered the extensive physical war damage of France, Belgium, Northern Italy, and parts of Germany. There was not the same imperative for the British to seek European unity. Britain could still find comfort in the Victorian and Edwardian visions of Empire. Although the war had enabled the independent Dominions to reach maturity, the emotional ties of imperial grandeur lingered. They persisted until it became blatantly obvious, with the independence of India, Pakistan and Ceylon and then the flight from colonialisation in Africa after 1957, that Britain's future no longer lay outside, but within, Europe. The transition from imperial power to becoming a partner in a European Community was to prove slow, painful and erratic. Some would say that it has not yet been achieved in the hearts of many British people and a conference in March 1995 on 'Britain and the World' indicated that the Foreign Office was still heavily committed to the concept of Britain as the nation state 'punching above its weight' in the world.

The New Ideas After 1945

As the tide of war turned in the Allies' favour after 1943 they began to plan for the peace. Many lessons had been learned from the aftermath of the First World War. The need to have carefully worked out schemes to deal with the inevitable postwar chaos was fully understood. There was also a strong determination to try to avoid the perceived causes of the Second World War – namely, cyclical unemployment, protectionism, poverty and deprivation. These, and other similar factors, were seen as a breeding ground for fascism. There was also a fear in some quarters that postwar dislocation of society would enable communism to flourish. In Britain, this planning for the postwar years included the Beveridge Report 'Full Employment in a Free Society'. This was published in November 1944 but several parts of it had received a public airing beforehand and the government had issued its White Paper on Full Employment before Beveridge's work itself was formally published. Another great factor in postwar social change was the so-called Butler Education Act of 1944 which extended secondary education to all and opened up the higher education sector to large numbers of less-well-off people. Another was the Barlow Royal Commission Report of 1941 which was reprinted in 1943 and which dealt with industrial location and population trends.

On the international scene there was a great proliferation of new institutions which applied either on a worldwide scale or on a regional basis. The major worldwide schemes, which have had a profound effect on European development, were the International Monetary Fund (IMF) and the International Bank for Reconstruction and Development (IBRD), usually called 'the World Bank'. With modifications these have survived to make a major contribution to international economic stability and cooperation. Another body of great long-term importance has been the Organisation for Economic Cooperation and Development (OECD). This was originally the Organisation for European Economic Cooperation

(OEEC). Initially, the defeated powers, Germany and Japan, were excluded but were incorporated once their industrial and political potential was required as a pillar of American anti-communism. West Germany was resurrected into full ally status after NATO was formed as a response to the blockade of Berlin by the USSR. Japan was 'recreated' when its geographical position made it vital as a base for United Nations' operations during the Korean War of 1950–53. Meanwhile, in Eastern Europe the previously independent nations became communist by fair and foul means and were eventually welded into an economic trading block with the formation of Comecon in 1949.

In Western Europe a bewildering variety of organisations was created. Out of some of these eventually emerged the European Economic Community (EEC), the European Community (EC) and the European Union (EU) as it is now generally known.

The New Organisations

Three broad types of organisation were created. The United States and Canada had been deeply involved in the European war and in reconstruction afterwards. It was natural, therefore, that the first type had North American involvement.

The Organisation for European Economic Cooperation

In 1948, the USA sponsored the formation of the OEEC. This organisation made possible the successful implementation of the Marshall Plan. This plan, named after the American Secretary of State, provided immense amounts of financial aid in return for European cooperation in reconstruction. The sum of $17 billion was spent in the four years of the plan's operation from 1948 to 1952. It was this scheme that enabled West Germany, Italy, France and the Benelux countries to modernise their industry, to provide employment, and to create political stability in the democratic mould. The United Kingdom, which benefited only marginally or indirectly from the Marshall Plan, was left largely to its own devices. The United Kingdom, mainly from its own resources, had to reconstruct war-ravaged capital goods industries, its transport system and its housing. As a matter of what can be regarded as misplaced honour, the government committed itself to repaying its debts to the United States, thus adding a further burden to the nation. As a partial consequence of this, and of the problems of reconstruction, a large additional loan had to be obtained from the USA. As that was spent, the pound had to be devalued in 1949. It is from this period that some of the seeds of Britain's poor postwar economic performance relative to other European nations dates. It can be argued that the United Kingdom concentrated on social reforms, on the creation of educational and health systems, on redistribution of wealth, and on social justice at the expense of reconstructing its obsolescent industrial structures. In the long run, there has proved to be little truth in the saying that the spoils of war go to the victor.

The OEEC was formed after an attempt in 1947 by France, the USSR and the United Kingdom to reach an agreement on a European recovery plan failed because of Soviet objections to the impairment of national sovereignty. France and the United Kingdom then invited all European countries except Spain (which was still a fascist dictatorship) to a conference. The list of those who accepted and took part is interesting in the light of later developments. They were Austria, Belgium, Denmark, Ireland, Greece, Iceland, Italy, Luxembourg, the Netherlands, Norway, Portugal, Sweden, Switzerland and Turkey. (Czechoslovakia initially accepted but withdrew into the Soviet bloc.) These 14 countries, plus the United Kingdom and France, signed a convention in 1948. The zones of Germany occupied by the British, the French and the Americans were also signatories, as was the Anglo-American zone of Trieste.

The initial requirement for the OEEC was to solve the problem of Europe's enormous trade deficit with the USA, to promote maximum cooperation among the 16 nations, to establish internal financial stability and to maximise production. In order to achieve this a Council, a Secretariat, an executive committee and several *ad hoc* committees were established. There was a very great incentive to make the system work because American aid under the Marshall Plan (European Recovery Programme) was contingent upon intra-European cooperation. It is generally agreed that the OEEC was very successful, so much so that an American administrator of Marshall Aid, Hoffman, called on the nations of the organisation to create a Western Union, a permanent free trading area of 270 million people when the European Recovery Programme ended. This was slow to materialise because the countries of Europe diverged for a time into different economic groupings, the EEC and EFTA (European Free Trade Association) but the European Economic Area (EEA) agreed in 1991 merged them together. It started on 1 January 1994 and was almost the fulfilment of Hoffman's idea.

In 1961, the OEEC was transformed by a change of membership and by new objectives. It was renamed the Organisation for Economic Cooperation and Development (OECD). Its membership broadened to include the USA, Canada, Finland, Spain, West Germany, Japan and several other countries. In 1994 membership reached 25 when Mexico joined. The organisation has a Council on which each country is represented, and a secretary-general with a permanent staff. Its fundamental purpose is 'to achieve the highest sustainable economic growth and employment and a rising standard of living in member countries, whilst maintaining financial stability, and thus contribute to the development of the world economy'. The intention was to achieve this by freeing international trade and movements of capital. New ground was broken by the additional aim of coordinating economic aid to developing countries. The organisation is consultative and its decisions are not binding on its members.

The North Atlantic Treaty Organisation

NATO too was sponsored by the USA. It was formed in 1949 to create a counterweight to the military strength of the USSR and its allies. In the first phase NATO was dominated by the USA which provided huge financial and military assistance. West Germany's membership in 1955 began a new phase and the balance of power within NATO shifted more towards Europe. The period until 1967 saw the adoption of nuclear policies and the relative relegation of conventional arms into second place. This was partly a response to manpower problems but was also due to the economic and political cost of any attempt to possess both full-scale conventional and nuclear forces. In the late 1960s France withdrew to the sidelines of NATO but has recently taken a more active part. Other countries such as Spain and Greece have reviewed their positions in relation to American bases and there have been major squabbles about the sharing of costs on an equitable basis. A trend developed for the

USA to negotiate directly with the USSR over the heads of her NATO allies and subsequently with Russia and the Commonwealth of Independent States.

In terms of our subject, the European Union, NATO is of importance in several ways. First, its existence should prevent any future European war because the military commands of the nations, their equipment and logistics are so interdependent. Secondly, the accumulated expenditure, capital investment and annual expenditure on arms and defence-related research are so enormous that they have a profound effect on industrial and scientific development, location of industry, communications and employment. Although the standardisation of equipment still leaves a lot to be desired, NATO purchasing exerts a great influence. A successful order for NATO equipment enables economies of scale to be achieved in manufacture and reduces costs and prices in the international market. Thirdly, the existence of NATO, with its transatlantic component of the USA and Canada and its non-European Union membership of Norway and Turkey, can be regarded as a major obstacle to the permanent, closer political unity of Europe. Its presence makes a common foreign policy harder to achieve, especially because of different national attitudes to nuclear weapons. It also creates difficulties with Russia because of the desire of some central European nations to join NATO. Some would disagree and assert that NATO should make political unity easier because it has created a mechanism for systematic cooperation and consultation.

The whole purpose of NATO, and its future, has been under very close scrutiny since the negotiation of the 1987 Treaty on Intermediate Range Nuclear Forces (INF Treaty), and the Strategic Arms Reduction Talks (START Treaty) which began in 1988, continued with interruptions, and resumed in April 1991. It has been called even more into question by the progress of the talks on Conventional Forces in Europe in 1990–91 after the Paris summit agreement in November 1990, and subsequent troop withdrawals. The détente between the USSR and NATO, the end of the cold war, the breakup of the Warsaw Pact in 1990, and the reunification of Germany in 1990, have all put pressure on the Union to develop both a common foreign policy and a new, common, defence policy. NATO appears to have little purpose now there is no longer a Warsaw Pact and there is a powerful body of opinion in the Union which wants to have a common defence policy to replace NATO. The European Stability Pact of March 1995 reinforces this view. The United Kingdom has been extremely reluctant to see any diminution in the role of NATO but the Gulf crisis, in 1990–91, accelerated the trend towards a new *Union* foreign and defence policy. The details emerged from the Maastricht meeting of the European Council in December 1991. Some countries have seen the revival of the Western European Union as the way forward and the new Franco-German, Spanish and Belgian army corps of 50 000 men announced in May 1992 is under the control of the WEU. In June 1992 it was decided that NATO would be prepared to operate outside its members' borders in a peace keeping role, as is shown by the use of air power in Bosnia and of ground forces in 1995–6 in support of the Dayton Agreement.

The Brussels Pact and Western European Union

At the end of 1947 a Four Power Conference on the future of Germany failed to reach agreement. The division of Germany became inevitable. In early 1948 therefore, the British Foreign Secretary, Ernest Bevin, put forward the idea of a 'Western Union'. The Russian *coup d'état* in Czechoslovakia, overthrowing the democratic government, hastened the signing of the Treaty of Brussels, in March 1948, between the United Kingdom, France, Belgium, the Netherlands and Luxembourg. These countries agreed to support each other militarily and to cooperate in economic matters. They set up a permanent consultative council in London. In 1949, they set up the Council of Europe which has a ministerial committee that meets in private, and a consultative body that meets in public. Under the Treaty of Brussels a defence establishment was set up at Fontainebleau under the command of Field Marshal Montgomery. He became very frustrated whilst in that job because of the vacillation of the politicians and the rigid nationalist aspirations of the French. He felt that little was achieved in terms of effective military organisation. The formation of NATO in 1949 overshadowed this aspect of the Brussels Pact.

In May 1955, the Brussels Treaty was extended to include West Germany and Italy and create the Western European Union. (Portugal has since joined.) This modification of the treaty took the form of a 50-year Western European Unity Treaty and the formation of the Western European Union. This resulted from an idea, born in 1948 at The Hague Conference, to form a supranational European army. The plan was conceived by the French Prime Minister René Pleven and later put forward to the Council of Europe in 1951 by Robert Schuman, the French Foreign Minister. It was intended to make German rearmament acceptable. It would also make progress towards a federal Europe easier. This idea of a European Defence Community was supported by the USA but opinion in France, Italy and Scandinavia was very divided. A preliminary treaty was concluded but gradually East–West tension decreased. De Gaulle was strongly opposed to the plan because he favoured a confederation of sovereign European states with France in the ascendancy. He wanted Europe to be independent of American dominance. The plan for a European Defence Community failed because the United Kingdom would not cooperate as a result of its commitment to the defence of its remaining empire. There was no further discussion on the political union of Europe until 1961. The British government under Churchill and Eden refused to sacrifice British independence to a European integration of forces. The French Assembly rejected the European Defence Community in 1954 and the United Kingdom proposed a compromise in the form of a high level of cooperation between the national armies. This was to be controlled by the Council of the Brussels Treaty. As a result the Western European Unity Treaty was signed and the Western European Union established. It was under this treaty that West Germany agreed not to attempt any changes to its borders by force, and not to make nuclear, chemical or biological weapons. It also agreed not to make large naval vessels, long-range bombers or long-range missiles.

In practice, as has already been said, the major military cooperation in Europe is currently through NATO rather than through the Western European Union, but the balance is gradually changing. Although the cooperation on defence matters has been largely carried out by NATO the WEU has, since 1984, become a vehicle for establishing a stronger European voice in the defence of Europe as against American influence. France, which became a peripheral member of NATO under President de Gaulle, has instigated a revival of the WEU. This has been significant as the USA and USSR took increasingly to direct negotiations with each other on armaments, as in the Geneva Treaty of 1988 and the Conventional

Forces in Europe agreements of 1990–91. In October 1991 the USA announced large-scale, unilateral reductions in its nuclear arsenal, especially of short-range tactical weapons, after only a peremptory discussion with other NATO members. The failure of the anti-Gorbachev coup in the USSR in September 1991, and the break-up of the Soviet federal union followed by its partial replacement by the CIS, gave greater emphasis to the Conference on Security and Cooperation in Europe (CSCE) as a peacemaking body. This body has now been reconstituted as the Organisation for Security and Cooperation in Europe (OSCE). The Yugoslavia crisis which began in 1991, the Russian military suppression of the independence movement in Chechenia in 1994–95 and the Turkish incursion into Northern Iraq in March 1995 to defeat Kurdish separatists, all put the Union and the OSCE to the test.

The Brussels Treaty signed in March 1948 setting up the Western European Union was for 50 years, and the issues raised by its renewal have become very important as 1998 approaches. The role of NATO is being seriously questioned because its functions will overlap those of an improved WEU. The discussions at Maastricht in 1991 were a prelude to what has become a major clash of opinion between the NATO supporters and those of the WEU. See Chapter 12 for details.

The Council of Europe

The second type of organisation aimed to attract as many members as possible. European nations differ greatly in the degree to which they are able or willing to sacrifice or subordinate their sovereignty to international or supranational bodies. Sweden and Switzerland have a long history of neutrality. Austria has neutrality forced upon it by the treaty re-establishing it as an independent state. It has also come to value neutrality. Others, such as France and the United Kingdom, are very reluctant to cede sovereignty. There is, therefore, a place for an organisation which enables states to belong without commitment to ideas of political union, federal or confederate. The Council of Europe is just such an organisation. It was established in May 1949 by ten nations (United Kingdom, France, Benelux, Italy, Ireland, Denmark, Norway and Sweden). The number had increased to 25 in 1994 by the addition of Austria, Germany, Cyprus, Switzerland, Portugal, Spain, Greece, Turkey,

Iceland, Malta, Liechtenstein, San Marino, Finland, Hungary and Poland and to 38 in October 1995. Russia was admitted in January 1996 as the 39th member. The Council of Europe is an important means through which nations cooperate. Superficially, its constitution looks unpromising; its decisions are made by a Committee of Ministers and they must be unanimous. In practice, therefore, each nation can operate a veto. There is a consultative body called a Parliamentary Assembly, which cannot pass legislation but simply makes recommendations to the Committee of Ministers. After they have agreed a proposal it still has to be ratified by the parliaments of each nation. Despite this inauspicious arrangement the Council of Europe has produced many agreements in legal, social, cultural and economic spheres. Most noteworthy is the European Convention for the Protection of Human Rights and Fundamental Freedoms which was adopted in 1950. This convention set up the European Court of Human Rights and the European Commission for Human Rights.

The Economic Organisations

The third type of organisation was economic. The daily operation of the Organisation for European Economic Cooperation after 1948 in putting the European Recovery Programme (Marshall Plan) into effect forced the nations into economic and financial cooperation. As the Marshall Plan was scheduled to end in 1952 there was pressure to create a permanent economic organisation. It is from this area that the European Community came into being. The Community is technically and legally three organisations operating together. These are the European Coal and Steel Community (ECSC), the European Atomic Energy Community (Euratom) and the European (Economic) Community (EEC or EC).

When these three bodies and their development are studied it is apparent that they have created a unique structure. They have not adopted either of the two major suggestions for a unified Europe that have been put forward over the years – that is the federal and the confederate solutions. A federal system is one where states form a political unity while remaining independent as to their internal affairs. This sounds a simple concept but the main problem, and area of future dispute, is the degree of decision-making given to the central government. The central government always manages defence and foreign policy but there remain 'grey' areas of disputed jurisdiction which emerge over time. The written constitution of such federal states usually includes a statement about 'residual' powers and who is to possess them. This is frequently the central government. Two classic cases are nuclear energy and air transport regulation in the USA. The founding fathers of the American constitution could not predict either. Such conflicts make the existence of an arbitrating body essential, as in the US Supreme Court. None of the suggestions for a federal state of Europe has made progress despite the relative success of the federal system in Germany, the USA, Canada and Australia. One of the most interesting discussions during the 1996 Intergovernmental conference reviewing the Treaty on Union will be whether there should be a stronger structure for a more federal approach, that is a European Union foreign policy and defence policy.

Until June 1991, the word 'federal' had not appeared in discussion of the Community's future. It then appeared in the preamble to a draft treaty for political union presented to the Luxembourg meeting of the European Council where mention was made of a 'federal goal'. The word was again used in a replacement version of the treaty which was presented to Community foreign ministers in October 1991. The United Kingdom, which places a different interpretation on the word 'federal' from that used by the other members, objected strongly and the argument affected the timetable for the draft treaty on political union presented to the European Council at Maastricht in December 1991. The basic argument, however, was about the change in the powers and functions of the European Parliament and the Commission, and the adoption of common foreign and defence policies. In the preamble to the final Treaty on Union the words were replaced by 'ever closer Union among the peoples of Europe' but no one really thought that the intention had changed.

A confederation is an alliance or league of states who retain their independence and who make decisions by consultation. Although central administration and decision-making bodies have to be set up, the emphasis is on the sovereignty of the separate states. Confederacies tend to be weak and relapse into separatism and acrimony in times of stress. Some of the European organisations already discussed are essentially confederal in nature.

The unique structure of the Community lies in the fact that the 15 members have adopted what is generally called 'integration' as a policy. They have ceded parts of their national sovereignty to the Union and given it some sovereign powers which it can exercise. These powers, in certain circumstances, have the force of national law. The objective is to create a permanent and indissoluble organisation and political entity. It should be remembered that a major motive in the steps towards European unity was the removal of any future possibility of the re-emergence of an expansionist, militarily strong, Germany. The way to prevent this was to bind Germany inextricably into an economic web and into a mutual defence organisation. The USSR, whilst not wholly in favour of a rich, economically powerful West Germany, was happier that no independent West German military power could be envisaged. It is ironic that Germany, whose constitution forbade the use of its armed forces abroad except as part of a NATO defence force, was criticised for not sending forces to the Gulf in 1990. There has been a modification of her constitution to enable, under strictly control-led circumstances, contributions to be made to European Union forces when they are sent to places such as Yugoslavia as part of United Nations peace-keeping forces.

The first economic institution – the European Coal and Steel Community

The ECSC was formed by a treaty signed, in April 1951, by Belgium, France, Germany, Italy, Luxembourg and the Nether-lands. It came into force in July 1952. It originated in a plan put forward in May 1950 by Robert Schuman, the French foreign minister. He and Jean Monnet proposed that French and German coal and steel production should be put under a joint authority in an organisation which other countries could join. The ECSC Treaty is another 50-year agreement and discussions began in the early 1990s on how to replace it, if at all. Some see this plan as stemming from a typically Churchillian proposal at Zurich in 1946 when he called for a United States of Europe in order to create Franco-German cooperation. Needless to say, he did not see the United Kingdom as a member of such a United States because of Britain's imperial, world status, but merely as a sort of benevolent promoter.

After the formation of the ECSC there followed a period of political manoeuvring to ensure that a rearmed Germany could be contained. German rearmament had become essential for political and manpower reasons after the Berlin blockade by the USSR in 1948–49. NATO had been formed and the Warsaw pact signed. The so-called Iron Curtain dividing East and West had fully descended and the 'Cold War' had begun in earnest. As mentioned above, one attempt to solve Europe's defence problems was the European Defence Community (treaty 1951) which would have created a supranational European defence force. Britain refused to join in and the French Assembly rejected the plan in 1954. As a result a new way forward had to be found. This took the form of an initiative by the ECSC foreign ministers in 1955. Their experience of working through ECSC indicated that a united Europe could be created. They met at a conference at Messina and set up a committee under Paul Spaak, the Belgian foreign minister to study possibilities for further integration. The committee reported in 1956. A series of negotiations followed and two treaties were signed at Rome on 25 March 1957. These established the European Economic Community (EEC) and the European Atomic Community (Euratom). They took effect on 1 January 1958.

The British responded by a proposal to set up a European Free Trade Association (which became known as EFTA). This had the great benefit of involving no loss of national sovereignty and was, therefore, more attractive to those members of both the Conservative Party who were in government and of the Labour Party in opposition, who were strongly antagonistic towards any transfer of parliamentary powers to a European body.

We have seen the long, involved and uncertain progress of ideas into real organisations from the early 1920s to 1956. To understand the process fully we need to try to see it from the point of view of a continental European trying to prevent yet another devastating power struggle from following two world wars. This gives a completely different perspective from that of the Briton who tends only to see loss of sovereignty, Brussels bureaucracy, budget problems and some peculiar consequences of the Common Agricultural Policy when looking at the European Union. In terms of its political objective of securing peace and cooperation between France and Germany the Community and Union have been an outstanding success. The problem for the future will be to apply and review the Treaty on Union from 1993 onwards in such a manner as to sustain this cooperation in the context of a reunited Germany, an enlarged Union and a new situation in Central and Eastern Europe.

Date Chart

1923–29 Pan-European movement within the League of Nations. It proposed a federal state of Europe. It failed with the onset of the depression.

1948–52 European Recovery Plan (Marshall Plan) This pumped American money into the reconstruction of Europe.

1948 The Organisation for European Economic Cooperation was formed to make the Marshall Plan effective. Sixteen countries joined initially: Austria, Belgium, Denmark, Ireland, France, Greece, Iceland, Italy, Luxembourg, Netherlands, Norway, Portugal, Sweden, Switzerland, Turkey and the UK. It also included the zones of Germany occupied by Britain, France and the USA. In 1961 it was renamed the Organisation for Economic Cooperation and Development and has extended to include the USA, Canada, Finland, Spain, Germany, Japan, Australia, New Zealand and Mexico (June 1995).

1949 The North Atlantic Treaty Organisation (NATO) was instituted in April by 12 nations: USA, UK, Luxembourg, Canada, France, Netherlands, Belgium, Norway, Italy, Denmark, Portugal and Iceland. (West) Germany joined in 1955.

1948 Brussels Treaty signed in March by UK, France, Belgium, Netherlands and Luxembourg to create military and economic cooperation. It led to:

1949 The Council of Europe (May 1949). This originally consisted of ten nations, UK, France, Belgium, Netherlands, Luxembourg, Ireland, Italy, Denmark, Norway and Sweden. (In early 1996 it had 39 members.) It, in turn, led to:

1950 The European Convention for the Protection of Human Rights and Fundamental Freedoms which led to the setting up of the Court of Human Rights and the Commission for Human Rights.

1951   European Defence Community Treaty. This failed to set up a supranational European army.

1955   Western European Union set up in May by UK, France, Belgium, Netherlands and Luxembourg, the signatories of the Brussels Treaty of 1948, plus West Germany and Italy. In 1995 it had a wider membership of 27 including observers and associates. It was a compromise suggested by the UK after the 1951 European Defence Community Treaty failed in 1954.

1951   The European Coal and Steel Community Treaty was signed in April by Belgium, Netherlands, Luxembourg, France, Italy and West Germany. It came into force in July 1952.

1957   The Treaties of Rome were signed on 25 March by the 'Six', Belgium, France, West Germany, Netherlands, Luxembourg and Italy creating Euratom and the European Economic Community. They came into force on 1 January 1958.

1972   Accession of Denmark, Ireland and the United Kingdom. Signed 2 January 1972. Came into force 1 January 1973.

1979   Accession of Greece. Signed 28 May 1979. Came into force 1 January 1981.

1985   Accession of Portugal and Spain. Signed 12 June 1985. Came into force 1 January 1986.

1986   The Single Act, signed 17 and 28 February 1986. Came into force 1 July 1987. Established the Single Market from 1 January 1993.

1990   The newly unified Germany was incorporated as a single market state in the Community on 3 October 1990. On 1 July 1990 monetary union between the two states of Germany was begun. Full political reunion took place on 3 October 1990.

1991   European Economic Area, EC plus EFTA minus Switzerland and Liechtenstein, formed. Signed October 1991. Came into force 1 January 1994. Liechtenstein joined EEA in 1995.

1991   Maastricht agreement on Treaty on Union signed. The Treaty was initialled in February 1992 and after delays in ratification by national parliaments during 1992, came into force 1 November 1993.

1995   Accession of Austria, Finland and Sweden. Agreed March 1994. Came into force 1 January 1995. (Norway's referendum rejected membership.)

Development and Change

3

The Six

The Six set themselves economic and political targets. People in the United Kingdom and elsewhere viewed these at first with scepticism and then with trepidation as they were achieved or surpassed. Some of the targets had a time-scale attached. The first major objective, without which the others could not be achieved, was to form a customs union. There was a wide diversity of customs tariffs on imports into and between the six countries. They tended to be low into Germany and the Benelux countries and high into Italy and France. The Six aimed at abolishing these differences within 12 years from 1958. They wanted all duties on the movement of goods within the Community abolished. They would then set up a common customs tariff (a CCT) on goods entering the Six from abroad. They achieved this ahead of schedule. In 1968, customs duties within the six states were abolished. They then established a common external tariff on all goods entering the Community from non-member states. As the stages towards the successful accomplishment of this target were completed, those outside the Community became more keenly aware that they would eventually be forced into a very uncompetitive position in their major European markets because their goods would have to overcome the CCT. Meanwhile, the European producers would have the benefits of the greater economies of scale derived from their larger home markets. These would give them lower average costs of production within Europe and in world markets. The benefits obtained from similar reductions in tariffs between EFTA countries were not enough to compensate for this disadvantage.

What are the Economics of the European Union as a Customs Union?

The European Union is a classic example of a customs union. The members agree to remove customs or tariff barriers between them and to impose a common external tariff on imports from non-member countries. This external tariff can be used as a protectionist hurdle by being set at a level that places the imports at a cost disadvantage. It can be made more favourable to friendly nations. Such an action has tended to provoke retaliation and bilateral or preferential trading agreements. The General Agreement on Tariffs and Trade (GATT), renamed The World Trade Organisation (WTO) in 1995, was set up to reverse the 1930s' trend which had seen the world sink into a desperate round of protection and 'beggar my neighbour' policies. The Community has been an important participant in GATT and in the regular 'rounds' of discussions that try to improve its application and effectiveness. Three major rounds, the Kennedy, Tokyo and Uruguay rounds, and some minor rounds, have been completed. The Uruguay round was resumed in 1992 after lengthy delays in 1990 and 1991 and finally agreed in 1994. Parts of it came into force in 1995 and the remainder will be gradually implemented according to an agreed timetable.

Despite its members being signatories of the GATT agreements, and despite the participation of the European Community as a single entity in the successive rounds, the Community has frequently come into conflict with other nations about its trading policy. The Community gradually removed its less-acceptable practices in relation to the Third World in a series of negotiations ending in the 1975 Lomé Convention. The convention is regularly updated and the Fourth Agreement will run from March 1990 to 2000. Discussions have already begun on proposals to modify this agreement and to prepare for the Fifth. The conventions are mainly concerned with aid but also relate to trade. Some critics think that there is a cosmetic element in the conventions to cover up the real harm that they allege stems from European Union trading policies, especially the subsidising of exports from the Fifteen. The Lomé Convention is also criticised for perpetuating dependency on the European markets.

One of the most constructive and promising developments from the Lomé Conventions is a fund called Stabex. This is used to stabilise the earnings of the 70 African, Caribbean and Pacific (ACP) countries in the agreement. It applies to exports of 48 agricultural commodities. Stabex is an insurance fund financed largely from the European Development Fund and augmented by payments from the ACP countries when their export earnings exceed certain levels. This principle has also been extended to mining products with a fund called Sysmin.

Whilst Developing World opposition to the European Union has become muted there has been growing criticism from the United States. Japan too has voiced its concern. The United States has traditionally been a fairly protectionist country, some say excessively so. The nature of the United States Congress means that each Senator and Representative must fight for his own state or district and its industries. As a result the United States has a formidable set of quota and tariff barriers together with a maze of administrative and health regulations. They all tend to restrict imports. In recent years, therefore, it has been inevitable that major clashes should have occurred between the United States and the Union. The main areas of dispute have been steel products, agricultural goods and textiles. Other products have been drawn in to the fray as part of retaliatory measures. It is usually the United States that is alleging 'unfair' competition. From its point of view the European Union has protected its own markets and sometimes subsidised exports. Most of these disputes are eventually resolved peacefully although a dispute about steel has rumbled on for years.

The main theoretical objection to customs unions such as the European Union is expressed in the so-called Law of Comparative Cost Advantage. This theory concludes that free trade maximises the use of the world's resources and that any interference, such as tariffs or quotas, with the free movement of goods and services reduces mankind's economic satisfaction. It states that a country will tend to specialise in, and export, those goods in which it has the greatest comparative cost advantage in production, or, in which it has the least comparative cost disadvantage. It should be emphasised that trade benefits both the most and the least favoured nation if their comparative costs of production differ. This applies even if one country is superior, in cost terms, at producing everything. These comparative costs and the terms of trade can explain which goods a country exports and which it imports. Most economics textbooks contain a numerical example to illustrate the principle of comparative cost advantage. The theory is a specific application of Adam Smith's demonstration of the gains to be had from the division of labour and specialisation. The theory tends to rely too heavily on the idea of the factors of production, land, labour and capital, being more mobile within each country than they actually are. It also tends to gloss over problems related to transport costs, economies of scale and different currencies. The simple versions conveniently overlook the growing role of powerful multinational corporations in world trade. Having said that, it is still generally accepted that free trade is an ideal that should be aspired to by all nations. The reader who would like a very detailed theoretical analysis of the economics of the Community as a customs union is advised to read *The Economics of Europe* by Edward Nevin (Macmillan, 1990, especially Part II.

The European Union's external tariffs, although very low, are a clear breach of the ideal of free trade and so are the various methods used by individual members to restrict imports. Unfortunately, it is always possible for nations to ignore the economic imperative of the theory of comparative cost advantage and to argue in favour of protectionism for strategic reasons. They also sometimes claim that foreign countries are 'dumping' goods on them. This is a complex field but means that the seller is selling at a price below the average cost of production. This was certainly done with some of the old Soviet bloc products. It is also alleged that it is done for gains in short-term market share with some Japanese products. Needless to say, it has been alleged by the USA that the European Community 'dumped' agricultural products and some types of steel. The World Trade Organisation (previously GATT) is intended to help prevent and stop dumping.

Have the Hopes been Met?

The statistical problems of determining the economic effects on growth and trade from the creation of the Community are enormous, if not unsurmountable, because of the large number of economic variables involved. It also requires the comparison of what has happened, assuming that that can be agreed or measured, with what might have happened if the European Community and Union had not been formed. There is an additional problem that the operation of the Union has involved large shifts, or redistribution of funds among the members. Some of these have been intended and are, therefore, presumably desirable. The conventional measures of economic welfare do not take much account of the non-monetary welfare obtained by, say, the German people from assisting the economic growth of Greece, Portugal or the other relatively poorer members.

If we examine the case of the United Kingdom there is no doubt that those who believed the optimists who predicted enormous gains from trade from joining the Union, have been sadly disappointed. The accession of the United Kingdom, Denmark and Ireland in 1973 coincided with the onset of the international recession so the effects of joining are difficult to isolate. The major gains have apparently been to continental firms who have exploited the United Kingdom market. This is not too surprising since they were already obtaining some of the benefits of a larger market. It could be argued also that British industry and commerce was too complacent, too sheltered and too much in the grip of slack management and over-powerful trade unions. Moreover, few could have predicted the powerful expansion of the Japanese into British, European and world markets. They, of course, achieved this success through very thorough planning, marketing skills and a very close partnership between government, civil service, business leaders and trade unions.

Gradually, the United Kingdom has begun to exploit and benefit from the larger European market. Lessons have been learned, firms have become more efficient and competitive. Many large British firms are developing into market leaders in Europe and are assuming a more multinational aspect. It was stated that the removal of barriers to trade by 1992 would present a great challenge to businesses. This was a statement of the obvious. What was less accepted was that it also represented an enormous challenge to government to ensure that the right infrastructure was in place in time. This required first-class transport and communications systems. There is little evidence that this need was recognised and there are signs that British industry is not able to benefit fully from the greater freedom of the single market and its potential economies of scale. More and more British industry and commerce, for example confectionery, motor vehicles, banking, water and electricity, is coming under the control of foreign companies which may confer short-term benefits but also create long-term insecurity. The United Kingdom may end up as a peripheral backwater economically unless the means of moving goods cheaply, quickly and competitively are provided. The other members of the Union see this as a role for government. They have been proved right in the past. Three of the initial fourteen Trans European Networks (TENS) schemes will be in the United Kingdom, the Channel Tunnel rail link, the West Coast mainline railway modernisation, and a cross-country road from east to west. All of these, it can be argued, should have been begun some years ago.

Experience reinforces the view that the United Kingdom government has realised too late and will probably react with inadequate resources. Its response in the discussions on the Union Treaty at Maastricht in December 1991 seemed restricted to the principle of keeping the United Kingdom as a low-wage economy with poor employment conditions, in order to compete with the Pacific rim countries. The stated motives for its opting out of the Social Chapter evoked echoes of Victorian debates on restricting child labour or on providing cheap bread in order to keep factory workers' wages down. At every opportunity it has reinforced this opinion at meetings of the Council and in the United Kingdom parliament. The lesson that well-paid workers with good working conditions and job security have higher overall productivity than those paid wages close to social security benefit levels and working unrestricted hours in poor conditions seems to have been ignored.

The benefits of membership of the European Union to the United Kingdom need to be seen against the enormous potential advantages conferred by the possession of North Sea oil and gas. There has been some analysis discussing the vexed question of what happened to the North Sea oil revenues. It appears that they have been used to finance the high levels of unemployment in the United Kingdom in the 1980s and early 1990s. An alternative view is that they have been partly invested abroad to provide interest, profits and dividends. They could have been used to create an infrastructure suitable for the single European market.

Other members of the Union have benefited in varying ways and to differing degrees from their membership and the passage of time has sometimes changed initial benefits into disadvantages. Countries such as Ireland, Greece, Portugal and Spain have gained financially from their membership but have had to pay a cost in terms of social adjustment and upheaval. There have also been transfers from sector to sector with the agricultural sector gaining at the expense of others despite the redressing effects of the regional and social funds. The main financial net contributors to the Union, Germany, France and Britain, have gained in terms of the greater political and social stability of Europe and from its increased 'cohesion'. Donne's statement that 'no man is an island unto himself' is frequently quoted but remains true nonetheless, especially in the context of the rich Northern states benefiting from the improved standards of living of the poorer Southern states.

Economies of Scale – the Great Sales Pitch?

The concept of economies of scale needs to be understood if the motivation for creating the Community, and for the United Kingdom's desire to join, are to be appreciated. 'Economies of scale' was a phrase very much in vogue in the 1960s and was used to justify many mergers, take-overs and nationalisation schemes. The proponents of such schemes conveniently forgot that there are *diseconomies* of scale, particularly in management, and that a high level of demand needs to exist to enable large plants to produce at their most efficient or lowest cost per unit. For example, a steel plant designed to produce 3 million tonnes of steel per year only has cost advantages derived from large-scale output if it is actually producing its designed output. If it is producing only 1 million tonnes as a result of depressed demand, it may have average costs per tonne which are higher than a smaller plant which *is* producing at *its* designed optimum. Large plants have larger capital costs in terms of interest charges and depreciation. These need to be spread over a greater volume of output. 'Economies of scale' is still a popular phrase despite a great deal of evidence to indicate that 'medium'-sized firms are frequently more efficient and profitable than 'large' firms.

An economy of large-scale production simply means that the average cost of production per unit of output falls as the level of output produced by additional inputs of all factors of production together is increased. The costs may fall because of technical factors derived from the size of plant and equipment. For example, a 200 000-tonne oil tanker does not cost twice as much to build and operate as two 100 000-tonne tankers. A larger internal market, such as the Six, or the present Fifteen, obviously increases the potential for obtaining technical economies of scale. There is, however, a risk of diseconomies arising from having inflexible levels of output. This occurred with steel production where too many extremely large plants were built at a time when the demand was dropping. This happened because of recession and the growth of demand for substitutes for steel. These substitutes are mainly plastics and aluminium alloys, or, in the case of office machinery or cash registers, electronic chips.

The other two main types of economy of scale which were most relevant to those viewing the early development of the EEC were those normally called 'commercial' economies and 'marketing' economies. Commercial economies refer to those reductions in costs derived from being able to buy raw materials and components in bulk at cheaper prices per unit. These apply most obviously in the types of large-scale retailing pioneered by Tesco, Sainsbury and Marks and Spencer and the equivalents such as Aldi, LeClerc and Intermarché in other countries. They also apply to large-scale manufacturers of domestic consumer durable goods such as cars and white goods. 'Marketing economies', which have been used to justify all sorts of mergers between firms producing unconnected products, derive from reductions in costs per unit in the selling, distribution and advertising of products and services. Certain volumes of sales are usually necessary before national advertising, particularly on television, is worthwhile. These economies partly explain the trend towards 'product ranges', company 'logos', company own-brands and international firms, or multinationals. Economists and entrepreneurs saw endless scope for these types of economies in scale within the Six, particularly as the growth of incomes and demand was very high.

The pursuit of economies of scale went hand in hand with attempts to spread the risks of enterprise. This partly explains the growth of conglomerates and diversifying mergers since 1970 although the late 1980s and early 1990s saw a contrary trend towards the break-up of some conglomerates and the shedding of subsidiary companies in an attempt to concentrate on the 'core' business. The Union's competition and monopoly control policies have had little impact on these trends.

There are other types of economies of scale in the usual classifications. In one of these, 'financial economies', many people in the United Kingdom felt that they had a great deal to teach the Europeans. This sense of superiority, which has turned out to be largely unfounded, was based upon the different historical experience of the United Kingdom and most European countries in the financial crash of 1931 and the great depression generally. It was also based upon the then dominant international role of the City of London in world financial and capital markets, and sterling in the 'sterling area'. This dominance in the 1950s (except over New York) has disappeared in some spheres as the relative isolation of markets has vanished with the advent of advanced telecommunications. It has also succumbed to the effects of stronger economic growth in Japan and West Germany. Moreover, the supposed superiority of the United Kingdom banking system over the continental system is now regarded as a source of relative weakness. This weakness is reflected in recent mergers and take-overs; for example the Midland bank, once the United Kingdom's largest, has been absorbed by the Hong Kong and Shanghai Bank, and Baring Brothers, the oldest Merchant Bank, was bought by the Dutch bank ING after it went into receivership following its disastrous performance on the far-eastern derivatives markets in 1995. In the 1930s continental banks suffered very badly because they were directly concerned with the ownership of shares in large, and small, companies. Their fortunes were entwined and, as the depression bit deeply, the companies collapsed and brought down the banks. The recession in Japan in the period from 1992 has been partly caused by a similar linkage. In the United Kingdom, the system of branch banking and the avoidance of direct investment in company equities enabled United Kingdom banks to survive. They preferred purchases of government stock (gilt-edged investment) and secured loans to industry, to the purchase of stock in companies. This tradition has persisted and some people regard it as a major cause of the alleged failure of the City of London to provide risk capital to British entrepreneurs. The continental system encourages a longer-term view of the return on capital than the British which tends towards an extremely short-run view. There is also a different attitude to dividends. United Kingdom firms are reluctant to cut dividends when profits fall because of pressure from financial institutions and because it makes them more vulnerable to takeover bids. They often use reserves to maintain dividends instead of using them for new investment to prepare for the end of the recession.

It was, therefore, the 'holy grail' of economies of scale which acted as a major lure to British business and politicians in the early 1960s as they saw the Six successfully building their customs unions and achieving faster economic growth than the United Kingdom.

The economic case for the United Kingdom joining the EEC was strongly based on the idea that British Industry could compete effectively against continental firms in the larger market, especially with the backing of a large overseas market as well. It was also thought, though not as frequently expressed, that the new competition would give British industry a much needed jolt and force it to adopt a more cost-conscious and consumer-oriented approach. (There were grave doubts about the effects on United Kingdom agriculture. These will be discussed in Chapter 5.) The economic case for entry seemed strong although some prescient folk realised that the United Kingdom might suffer in its internal markets from fierce competition from some already more efficient continental producers. These doubters' fears were borne out in the 1970s, 1980s and 1990s in the case, for example, of motor vehicle manufacture. By early 1995 the largest (in terms of annual output) British-owned car producer was Reliant which made a fibreglass-bodied three-wheeler. Some long-sighted folk worried that the United Kingdom might become a mere periphery of an industrial and commercial economic core centred between France and Germany and spilling over into Belgium and Holland. Improvements in road transport, containerisation, specialised vehicles, refrigerated lorries and higher average speeds and loads, favour the drift to location in larger markets. 'Larger' here means in terms of numbers of people and in terms of average incomes per head.

The economic case for joining was gradually accepted, although many thought a similar case could be made, in the case of Britain, for staying with the European Free Trade Association (EFTA) and the Commonwealth and the North Atlantic link. There was, however, a major change in British political attitudes in the 1950s and 1960s arising from the decline of the empire with the granting of independence to colonies. An understanding of this background is useful if the later events leading to the Single European Act in 1986 and to the Union Treaty of 1992 are to be understood.

Changing Political Attitudes in the United Kingdom

The emphasis of victory over Germany and Japan in 1945 after six weary years of war disguised for a time the reality of the United Kingdom's position in global politics. Politicians of all complexions were slow to grasp the new conditions of world dominance by the USA and USSR. For a time all efforts were concentrated on the reconstruction of a distorted and investment-starved industrial structure from war production to peaceful applications. Demobilisation and redistribution of labour were at the forefront of everyone's minds. Rationing intensified despite the peace, and a fuel shortage persisted. Power cuts were an accepted winter occurrence until the early 1960s as demand outstripped supply. Efforts were made by all the colonial powers, including the United Kingdom, to restore their prewar colonial possessions. From these efforts, which were only temporarily successful, stemmed the Vietnam War and the Algerian conflicts as the French colonial yoke was resisted. Britain, for its part, faced a succession of colonial struggles, all of which ended in independence for the colony. To many British people, however, the full knowledge of the 'end of empire' only came with the debacle of the Suez Canal in 1956. This humiliation in late 1956 was a watershed in British political thinking. The Prime Minister Anthony Eden resigned, ostensibly through ill health, and was succeeded in January 1957 by Harold Macmillan.

A Slow Change in the United Kingdom's Political Orientation

A conflict developed in the late 1950s and early 1960s between those who saw Britain's future in the European context and those who saw it in an international, outward-looking role rooted in the Commonwealth and transatlantic special relationship. Some saw the European Economic Community as a narrow, self-seeking, inward-looking customs union. The issue caused splits within the parties. The anti-Common Market faction tended to attract supporters from the left and the right of British politics. They were concerned with parliamentary sovereignty, with the alleged bureaucracy of the Community and with the effects on food prices and agriculture. The impact on the poorer members of the Commonwealth and on New Zealand, which relied heavily on the United Kingdom market for its lamb sales, caused great concern. The issue of the Commonwealth Sugar Agreement loomed large, as did the future of the Commonwealth Preference system which favoured imports from, and exports to, ex-colonies. Their arguments of that time would sound very familiar to those who have listened to British 'Eurosceptics' in the early 1990s; it is like a gramophone record stuck in its groove.

The pro-common Market factions extolled the economies of scale available in a larger market. They welcomed what they thought would be a breath of competitive fresh air throughout British industry. They were forerunners of the Thatcherite vision of a free market, except of course that a more detailed study revealed the Community to be a strongly regulated market with a weak anti-monopoly policy and a powerful interventionist philosophy.

As the United Kingdom shifted its role away from colonialism, France, Belgium and Holland were also involved in disengagement from their colonial past. General de Gaulle returned to power in France in 1958, in the wake of the political chaos caused by the Algerian War. He replaced the Fourth Republic with a new constitution. Against powerful and violent opposition he settled the North African crisis. An independent Algerian state was recognised in 1962. In 1960, Belgium withdrew from the Congo. This led to a long-drawn-out, and bloody, civil war together with foreign intervention, before the new nations were firmly established. The Netherlands withdrew from most of their overseas possessions in the period 1949–54. France subsequently withdrew from the southern Saharan and West African states, although she has retained a powerful political and military presence in some of the countries. The rise to power of General de Gaulle, with his strongly nationalistic attitudes, was of great significance in delaying the United Kingdom's entry into the Economic Community.

De Gaulle cultivated personal aloofness and obviously believed that 'familiarity breeds contempt'. He carried this personal attitude over into his political life in attempting to restore French pride and self-esteem by an aggressively independent stance. He created a separate French nuclear strike force and withdrew from operational participation in NATO. De Gaulle wanted a restoration of the Gold standard for settlement of international debts. He even issued silver coins, most of which quickly disappeared from circulation. In addition he was suspicious of Anglo-American relations and treated the United Kingdom's avowed aspiration to be 'European' with scepticism. There was much reference to 'perfidious Albion'.

In October 1961, the United Kingdom made its first formal application to join the EEC. Negotiations took place which ended in January 1963 when de Gaulle exercised his personal veto, on behalf of France, against Britain's application for membership. His remarks about the United Kingdom not being truly European were a reflection of his intense anger at the Nassau Agreement of December 1962 between Macmillan and President Kennedy. This agreement was for the USA to supply missiles for British nuclear submarines, that is the Polaris system. Ironically Macmillan had been forced into the Nassau Agreement by the failure of a proposed independent British nuclear weapons delivery system. The French veto was a severe blow to Macmillan and it also blocked the applications of Denmark, Norway and Ireland.

Macmillan resigned because of ill health in October 1963 and was succeeded by his Foreign Secretary, the Earl of Home, who renounced his peerage in order to become an MP. Home was a foreign affairs expert and was, self-confessedly, not an economist. His government was narrowly defeated by Labour, under Harold Wilson, in October 1964. Wilson called another election in March 1966 and received a greatly enlarged majority. The whole course of his government was dominated by balance-of-payments problems and the necessity of maintaining the pound at its fixed level. The reader might well ask how this differed from the problems of the early 1990s arising from membership of the Exchange Rate Mechanism with its relatively fixed rates against the German mark and other European currencies. Economic growth was slow and attempts at national planning quickly foundered. Envious eyes were cast on the successful French system of indicative planning and at the higher rates of growth and lower inflation rates of the EEC. Thus despite strong ideological objections from the left wing of the Labour Party, Wilson applied for the United Kingdom to join the

Community in 1967. This second application of the United Kingdom, together with those of Denmark, Norway and Ireland, was again rejected by de Gaulle in 1967. The way was blocked until de Gaulle resigned his office in April 1969 after badly misjudging the mood of the French people over a referendum to modify the constitution.

EFTA

There was a nine-month gap between the signing of the Treaties of Rome in March 1957 and their coming into force on 1 January 1958. The United Kingdom used this period to try to establish a different type of organisation, a European Free Trade Association among the seventeen members of the OEEC. Such a market would be free from tariffs and trade barriers between members but would allow each country to set its own trade conditions with non-members. This would combine the benefits of a partial customs union with the advantage of no loss of sovereignty to the member. It was a 'partial' customs union because it did not have a common external tariff. The system appealed to countries which favoured political neutrality and to the United Kingdom which had obligations to its Commonwealth friends. It did not, however, satisfy the basic desire of the six signatories of the Rome treaties because they wanted deeper political involvement and commitment, with a view to obviating any future European war. France was strongly opposed to the British initiative and ended discussions in November 1958. When EFTA was formed by the Stockholm Convention of January 1960 its membership was the United Kingdom, Austria, Denmark, Norway, Portugal, Sweden and Switzerland. Iceland became a full member in March 1970. Finland became an associate member in June 1961 and a full member in 1985. EFTA became operational in May 1960. Over the years its membership has fluctuated as countries joined and/or left to join the EEC instead. The 1996 membership is Iceland, Norway, Switzerland and Liechtenstein. Close working agreements between the Community and EFTA were developed from 1972 in the form of Free Trade Agreements (FTAs). These required revision as the completion of the single European market, aimed at January 1993, drew closer. The result of the revision was the agreement between the European Community and EFTA in October 1991 to create the European

Economic Area (EEA) which came into force on 1 January 1994 and is discussed below.

Britain quickly realised that EFTA would not satisfy its economic and political needs in a changing world. Its markets were not large enough for sufficient economies of scale to be derived, compared with the EEC markets. More importantly, it did not provide sufficient opportunity for the United Kingdom to exercise its political weight. The United Kingdom was in danger of becoming a politically isolated off-shore island near the continent of Europe. It is ironic that, at the negotiations at Maastricht in 1991 leading to the Union Treaty, the policies of opting out of the Social Chapter and the monetary union sections of the treaty created the risk of producing exactly the isolation which was once feared and avoided. An alternative future was as an undeclared state of the American Union, dependent on the USA economically and politically. The so-called 'special relationship' between the United Kingdom and the United States had never been one of equals but no one wanted it to degenerate into an overtly master–vassal relationship. By 1995, after disagreements over Bosnia and Northern Ireland, it was obvious that the special relationship was being buried as an appendix in the history books and that President Clinton's foreign policy was concentrating on relations with the European Union as a whole and Germany in particular rather than with the United Kingdom.

EFTA is very different in operation from the European Community. It is run by weekly meetings of officials and meetings of ministers two or three times a year. There are no powers devolved by each country on a central organisation so there is nothing supranational about it. It has been successful in abolishing almost all import duties on industrial goods between members and has generally harmonised its external tariffs with those of the EC. It was expected that the departure of the United Kingdom on joining the EC would see the end of EFTA but that did not happen. It was, however, struck a serious blow when Austria, Finland and Sweden left in January 1995 to join the European Union.

The United Kingdom's Successful Application

Soon after the fall of de Gaulle in April 1969, his successor, President Pompidou, made it clear that his government would not object in principle to the entry of Britain and the other applicants provided that enlargement would strengthen rather than weaken the Community. In December 1969, a summit was held at The Hague. This agreed to major alterations in the way that the Community was to be financed and developed; it also agreed to prepare for negotiations on its enlargement. In May 1970, the Labour government announced that it would restart negotiations as soon as possible. There was a change of government in June 1970 and the Conservative government under Mr Heath began negotiations at the end of June. The continuity of policy irrespective of governing party is shown clearly by the fact that the negotiations were on the lines prepared by the Labour government. Within a year the negotiations were complete except on the issue of fisheries.

There was no United Kingdom referendum on entry to the EEC. In the 1960s and early 1970s the only referendums held were on whether Welsh public houses should open on the Sabbath! Although there was eventually a referendum in June 1975 called by the Labour government on whether the United Kingdom should *remain* in the Community, the original entry was by decision of the House of Commons. In May 1967 the Labour government had announced its decision to apply for membership. There was a three-day debate which ended in a vote in favour of the application of 488 to 62. This majority of 426 is one of the largest ever majorities of the House of Commons in peacetime. This fact has tended to be obscured over the years as more and more politicians have found it expedient to side with the critics of the development of the Community. Those who objected at the time did so on grounds of fear for national or parliamentary sovereignty, on fears for the Commonwealth relationship, or on sectional interest grounds related to agriculture or fishing. They were drawn from both extremes of the political spectrum. Some of the opponents of membership at that time are still making the same speeches in 1995 against the Union in general and the Maastricht Treaty in particular.

When it was decided to reapply for membership in 1970 a new White Paper, *Britain and the European Communities: An Economic Assessment* (Cmnd 4289), was published in February 1970. This updated the figures of likely costs and benefits of membership, concluding that the economic balance was a fine one and that in the short term there would be some economic disadvantages. The range of figures given for possible balance-of-payments changes, agricultural expenditure changes and alterations in capital movements was very wide. The statisticians had to make many assumptions about such variables as growth rates, patterns of trade and agricultural prices. In general, the conclusion was that it was the long-term economic advantages and, even more, the political advantages, which would prove decisive. In the background was the knowledge that it was impossible to calculate the full economic consequences of *not* entering the European Community: these consequences were in terms of being both excluded from and being in competition with an increasingly integrated European economy, on our doorsteps, and several times the size and probably faster growing than our own. It was also impossible to quantify the so-called 'dynamic' effects resulting from membership of a much larger and faster-growing market. Figures which had a powerful persuasive effect were comparative growth statistics which were presented in a more readily understood form in a nationally distributed booklet, *Britain and Europe*, which explained the government's White Paper *The United Kingdom and the European Communities* (Cmnd 4715).

The Entry Terms

The terms negotiated for entry on almost all major points were published in a White Paper in July 1971. In October 1971, the House of Commons voted by 356 to 244 in favour of joining the EEC on these terms. In January 1972, the Treaty of Accession was signed and the resulting European Communities Act received the royal assent on October 1972, after a fairly stormy passage through Parliament.

The agreement fixed a transitional period of five years from the start of Britain's membership on 1 January 1973 to 31 December 1977. In that period all tariffs between Britain and the Six were to be abolished in five equal stages, so that within three years of entry there would be virtually free access to the European market for British exporters.

Agriculture required very detailed terms involving a gradual increase in market prices so that direct subsidy payment to farmers (in the form of deficiency payments) could be phased out. The government kept the power to help groups such as hill farmers and to retain the marketing boards. It was anticipated that agricultural output would increase by about 8 per cent over the transitional five years as home production was substituted for imports. A special agreement was made so that New Zealand could continue to have access to the British market for at least 75 per cent of its current exports of butter and cheese to Europe beyond the end of the transitional period. Similarly, the United Kingdom retained its obligations under the Commonwealth Sugar Agreement to buy agreed quantities of sugar from existing sources until 1974 and to protect the relationship thereafter. This was to quell well-substantiated fears that Caribbean cane-producing countries would suffer if the United Kingdom were forced to buy European beet sugar.

The question of budget contributions was resolved by fixing the British part of the total budget as a gradually rising percentage from 8.64 per cent in 1973 to 18.92 per cent in 1977.

There were additional agreements on the free movement of labour, regional development, the Coal and Steel Community, and Euratom. In most cases the United Kingdom accepted existing practices without reservation, although Northern Ireland was excluded from free movement of labour for five years. Commonwealth countries in Africa, the Indian Ocean, the Pacific and the Caribbean were offered 'association' with the EEC in order to protect access for their exports to the Community. Australia and Canada were not thought to require any special arrangements.

Renegotiation and the Referendum

A significant number of important persons and groups within the Labour Party were against the United Kingdom's membership of the EEC. This opposition went so far as to prevent any Labour Party representatives going to the European Parliament (until July 1975). As a result of this pressure the party manifesto at the February 1974 general election promised that the electorate should have the opportunity of deciding on whether Britain should stay as a member or not. The new Labour government under Wilson, therefore, began talks in April 1974 for renegotiation of the terms of membership. These were concluded in March 1975 and Parliament endorsed the terms of the agreement on a free vote by 396 votes to 170 in early April.

This was a rather confusing period politically and indicates the extent to which the European Community concept split the parties.

Mrs Thatcher became Leader of the Opposition in February 1975 after the fall of Mr Heath who was the great champion of membership and who, according to his critics, was willing to accept any terms, however harsh, for entry. The Prime Minister, Mr Wilson, was having trouble within his party and had to accept the idea of giving his Cabinet colleagues a 'licence to differ' instead of insisting on the traditional doctrine of collective responsibility. As a result, on the free vote in the House of Commons, the 396 votes in favour of remaining in the EEC consisted of 249 Conservatives, 135 Labour and 12 Liberals. The 170 votes against were 144 Labour, 7 Conservative, 11 Scottish Nationalist, 6 Ulster Unionist and 2 Plaid Cymru. No fewer than seven Labour Cabinet ministers voted against together with 30 other ministers.

The Labour Party responded to this Commons vote by calling a special Labour Party Conference at the end of April. This approved a recommendation from the National Executive Committee that Britain should leave the EEC. The party was not happy with the renegotiated terms: the voting was 3 724 000 to 1 986 000. A few days earlier, the TUC had adopted a document opposing the United Kingdom's continued membership, although individual unions were left free to express different opinions.

The solution for the government was to lie in the promised referendum. This took place on 5 June 1975. Voters had to vote 'yes' or 'no' to the question 'Do you think that the United Kingdom should stay in the European Community (the Common Market)?' The overall result was a 64.5 per cent vote of 'yes' but there were significant regional differences as can be seen in Table 3.1.

TABLE 3.1
The Referendum of June 1975

	% Turnout	*% 'Yes'*
England	64.6	68.7
Wales	66.7	64.8
Scotland	61.7	58.4
Northern Ireland	47.4	52.1
United Kingdom	64.5	67.2

Only the Shetland Isles (56.3% 'No') and the Western Isles (70.5% 'No') voted against

TABLE 3.2
The Basis for the United Kingdom's Grievance: United Kingdom's
Contributions and Receipts from the Community Budget (£ millions)

	Gross contributions	Receipts	Net contributions
1973	181	79	102
1974	181	150	31
1975	342	398	−56
1976	463	296	167
1977	737	368	368
1978	1348	544	804
1979	1606	659	947
1980	1767	1061	710
1981	2174	1777	997
1982	2863	2257	606
1983*	3120	2473	647

*Estimates

SOURCE *The Government Expenditure Plans, 1977–78 to 1982–83*, Cmnd 7439 (London: HMSO, 1984), quoted in Butler, D. E., *British Political Facts, 1980–85*, 6th edn (London: Macmillan, 1986)

The resounding and unequivocal 'yes' vote cleared the air and national energies could now be devoted to making Britain's membership work to the nation's greatest benefit. Despite this, membership of the Community was often made a scapegoat for problems which were already deeply ingrained in Britain's industrial and social structures. The early years of transitional membership coincided with rapidly rising unemployment, swift decline of manufacturing industry, poor industrial relations, international inflation and recession, and uncertainty in politics. Inevitably, the Common Market was thought by some to exacerbate these problems. The Labour Party, for some years, promised withdrawal from the Community if it were re-elected to government. In 1983, however, it modified this stance and made withdrawal 'an option' rather than a certainty if it should be returned to power. The Conservative Party, for its part, concentrated upon altering the budgetary imbalance and on pursuing an aggressively self-interested national policy. General de Gaulle might very well have admired Mrs Thatcher's approach although there often seemed to be a major discrepancy between what was agreed between the members and what the British public was told had been achieved. In December 1979, Mrs Thatcher, at the Dublin summit meeting asked for 'Britain's money back'. There was a short-term palliative agreement in 1980 but it was not until the Fontainebleau agreement in June 1984 that there was a full settlement of the United Kingdom's grievance (see Chapter 4). The figures in Table 3.2 support the validity of the sense of injustice. Figures for recent years are given in Chapter 4.

The Enlargement of the Community

The accession of the United Kingdom, Denmark and Ireland was agreed in January 1972 and took effect on 1 January 1973. The next addition to the Community occurred when Greece acceded in May 1979 with effect from 1 January 1981. There was then a five-year gap involving complex negotiations before Spain and Portugal acceded in June 1985 and began active membership on 1 January 1986. In all three cases one of the factors taken into account by the existing members was the welcome return of the applicant to full democratic forms of government after periods of authoritarian rule. The terms of entry included special provisions for the transition periods as their economies adjusted to the full force of competition from the established members. Topics of particular concern were agriculture, fishing quotas, vegetables, fruit, and wine production.

The accession of these three countries marked a profound change in the nature of the Community although the full effects have not yet been absorbed. Until then, with the exception of Southern Italy, the Community had been essentially a Northern European institution of a predominantly industrial character, albeit with a large agricultural sector in certain countries. Its average income per head and standards of living had been high. Well-established democratic forms of government were accompanied by good standards of social provision and effective bureaucracies and financial systems. The three newcomers presented problems of redistribution of income through the budget from North to South, of absorption of higher and more expensive standards of social care and employment conditions, and of low-wage competition. Remarkable progress has been made in overcoming these problems since 1981, although there is much still to be achieved before an acceptable level of 'cohesion' is achieved. The Treaty of Union agreed at Maastricht in 1991 was made possible, in part, by the acceptance by the richer Northern members of the need to set up a 'cohesion' fund to finance the raising of standards in the poorer Southern members and in Ireland. In other words, they had to receive promises of more money from regional and social funds, as well as from the new cohesion funds required to achieve monetary union, before they would agree to the new treaty on economic and monetary union and to progress on political union. The EFTA countries similarly had to contribute cohesion funds as part of the price of forming the European Economic Area.

The experience of absorbing the three new members was influential when countries such as Sweden, Austria, Finland and Norway applied to join the Union. It also helped to deter the Union from accepting the idea that there should be a 'big bang' increase in membership with all the EFTA members and countries such as Hungary, the Czech Republic, Slovakia, Poland and Yugoslavia (before its civil war) joining at once.

The Treaty of Rome says that an application to join the Union from any *European* country must be considered by the Council of Ministers after it has asked the advice of the Commission. There must then be a unanimous vote for the application to succeed and it has been this need for unanimity that has prevented Turkey, which applied for membership in 1987, from joining. Turkey's request presented the Community with a problem in that its average income per head is well below that of the poorest members' least prosperous areas, and it gave rise to an embarrassing debate as to whether Turkey was '*European*'. Another problem is that Turkey's population was 59 million in 1992 which would make it second to Germany's 81 million in the enlarged Union, and it is projected to rise to 84 million in 2020, above Germany's projected 82 million. Turkey's application was effectively vetoed by Greece which has a long-standing dispute with Turkey over the invasion and partition of Cyprus. As a result decision on the application has been postponed into the indefinite future, presumably until the resolution of the dispute. In the meantime Turkey's associate status granted in 1962 has been reaffirmed and improved, in 1980, to make its trade with the Community easier. The implementation of a further agreement in 1995 was delayed. An additional complication in the issue has been Turkey's membership of NATO, its cooperation with the United Nations over the Gulf crisis in the war against Iraq and, more recently in early 1995, its military incursion into Northern Iraq to suppress Kurdish separatists. The two former added weight to its claim for membership but the latter created anxiety about Turkey's attitude to human rights. The main bone of contention, Cyprus, is also intent on joining and was granted entry in 1987 to what will become a full customs union with the Union by the end of the century. Its acceptance as a member depends on the settlement of the dispute between Turkey and Greece. Malta, which was granted an association agreement in 1976 has also applied for membership. It has been agreed to negotiate the accession of Cyprus and Malta after the 1996 Intergovernmental Conference.

The European Economic Area

In January 1989 Jacques Delors, President of the Commission, initiated discussions between the European Community and the European Free Trade Association (EFTA) with a view to greater integration. His motive was mainly to provide an alternative to full membership applications to the Community by the seven members of EFTA. He also aimed at creating a pause whilst the process of deepening and strengthening the institutions of the EC was completed. The formal negotiations began in June 1990 and sufficient progress was made for the optimists to expect an agreement to be initialled in June 1991, but the final problems were not resolved until 22 October 1991. The agreement, and the EFTA–EC Treaty resulting from it, had to be ratified by national parliaments and the European Parliament. A referendum in Switzerland rejected membership and this initially kept Liechtenstein out as well. The EEA was intended to come into force in January 1993, at the same time as the single market, but it was delayed until January 1994. The agreement will be reviewed every two years.

The EEA consisted of the 12 European Community countries and the seven EFTA members, Austria, Finland, Iceland, Liechtenstein, Norway, Sweden and Switzerland. (It is now, in 1995, the 15 European Union members and the four EFTA countries). The EFTA nations accepted about 12 000 pages of Community legislation which is known as the *acquis communautaire*. They also accept any new Community laws that are relevant and are consulted in their formulation, although they do not have voting rights or a veto. The EEA is not a customs union like the European Union because there are still controls, though not taxes, at EU borders for goods coming from the EFTA countries.

The EEA is a tariff-free zone for industrial goods and for some processed agricultural products. Non-tariff and technical barriers to trade will be removed along the same lines as in the Single Market legislation. The common agricultural policy does not apply to the EFTA countries and they will continue with their own individual policies in respect of trade quotas or tariffs on non-EEA countries' goods. The two groups must agree on a system for classifying which goods are to be regarded as originating within the EEA, a task which is not as easy as it might appear at first glance if experience with the long-drawn-out row over Japanese cars assembled in the United Kingdom is anything to go by. Special arrangements persist for fish, food, energy and coal and steel.

The Common Fisheries Policy does not apply to the EFTA countries although the agreement includes improved access for Icelandic cod and haddock into the Community together with a general reduction of 70 per cent in the levy on EFTA fish products entering the Union. Norway will allow Spain, Portugal and Ireland, who have been excluded from Norwegian waters, to fish 6000 tonnes of cod from its waters, and will double the present quota allowed to United Kingdom fishermen. Foreign investment in the Norwegian and Icelandic fishing industries will not be allowed, an arrangement that will not be popular in the United Kingdom industry where some UK quotas have been expropriated by Spanish boats being registered in the United Kingdom. The 1988 Merchant Shipping Act that was intended to restrain this practice was declared illegal under Community law by the European Court in July 1991.

One of the most important effects of the agreement results from the inclusion of services in the free trade category. Beforehand, the agreements between EFTA and the Community covered only goods, and the service sectors were highly protected. Under the new arrangements any national of the EEA countries will be able to provide financial, commercial or professional services throughout the 19 countries. Many of the restrictions on capital flows will also disappear but some controls will remain on investment in real estate and some direct investment in the EFTA countries.

Flanking policies

The creation of the EEA has extended the use of Eurojargon. A 'flanking' policy is one which *accompanies* other policies. In the case of the EEA the flanking policies are a strengthening of cooperation in the areas of the environment, information services, social policy, consumer protection, education, training and youth, research and technological development, small and medium-sized enterprises, tourism, the audio-visual sector and statistics. There are indications from the negotiations leading up to the creation of the EEA that the EFTA countries want a stronger approach in some of these areas, particularly the environment. They want to go beyond what is stated in the Treaty of Rome and aim for sustainable development. They also want the principle of precautionary action to prevent damage to the environment to be embodied into policies and actions as they are developed. These concerns on the part of Sweden, Finland and Austria can be expressed more strongly as full members of the Union.

Although the EEA commenced on 1 January 1994, some of the flanking measures have been delayed. For example, the EFTA members have not participated fully in the education, training and youth programmes until 1995 because the Union wanted a transition period to occur. The area of social policy is very complex but the EFTA countries are committed to incorporating Union laws into their rules in areas such as health and safety at work, workers' rights and labour law, and the equal treatment of men and women, and action for the elderly. The cooperation is intended to extend what is called the 'social dialogue' between management and workers. Some areas are explicitly excluded. These include health, including nutrition, and programmes dealing with Aids and cancer. The EFTA states have had a declaration included in the treaty stating their wish to contribute actively to the social dimension of the EEA as embodied in the Community Charter of Fundamental Social Rights for Workers. The United Kingdom, which alone refused to sign this Charter in 1990, and also opted out of the Social Chapter at the Maastricht decisions on the new Treaty on Union in 1991, became even more isolated after the EEA became effective. This isolation is even more apparent since Austria, Finland and Sweden became full members of the European Union.

Flanking policies are accompanied by what are called 'horizontal' policies, which means the broadening of cooperation into new areas such as company law and statistics. Both flanking and horizontal policies come under what is called 'mixed competence', that is the main responsibility remains with the individual member state and not with the institutions of the Union. The principle of subsidiarity also applies, that is an action should only be undertaken at Union level if it cannot be done better at national level.

The cost of the agreement

Entry to the benefits of an enormous free trade area is not free and the EFTA countries paid a high price for the agreement. The main price is through their acceptance of the proposal that they should establish and manage a fund to help the development of some of the less-favoured regions within some countries of the European Union; that is, Northern Ireland, Greece, Ireland, Spain and Portugal. This is a version of the so called 'cohesion' fund established by the richer members of the Community at Maastricht in 1991 to persuade its poorer members to accept monetary union and other aspects of the Treaty on Union. Although this is usually called the EEA Cohesion Fund its official title is 'The EEA Financial Mechanism'. The money will be channelled through the European Investment Bank (EIB). In the case of the EEA they will put 500 million ECU into the fund for grants over five years, and make another 1.5 billion ECU available as soft loans over five years.

Another cost will be that of resolving the problem of road transport over the Swiss and Austrian Alps. The Swiss, although not members of the EEA are still in EFTA and have close relations with the European Union. They have very severe restrictions on lorries in order to protect their environment and way of life. A referendum has been held that will eventually ban the transit of foreign heavy-goods vehicles through the country except on special trains, some of which operate already. Greece, which relies very heavily on road links, used its bargaining power to force an agreement which will maintain its competitive position. The solution will also benefit Switzerland and Austria in the long run and is extremely impressive in its far-sightedness and vision. The Swiss are going to invest about 24 billion Swiss francs in building two tunnels under the Gotthard and Loetschberg passes, and

Austria will build a new tunnel under the Brenner pass. These rail tunnels will take lorries through the Alps and keep them off the roads, and will enable Switzerland to keep its 28-tonne limit on lorries and Austria to keep its severe anti-pollution laws.

On the Union side there is likely to be a growing demand from the fishing industries of some countries for subsidies to protect them from decline as a result of increased competition from the EFTA states. It will be very hard to separate the effects of the creation of the EEA from those of the recent changes on the Common Fishing Policy which are aimed at conserving stocks.

Implications of the creation of the EEA

The statistics speak for themselves to some extent. The nineteen members of EFTA and the EU include some of the richest in the world, and have a population of 380 million. They are responsible for over 40 per cent of world trade.

The institutions of the EEA

'The EEA Council', comprises ministers from all the members and a representative from the European Commission. Its job is to provide a political oversight to the EEA, and not to legislate. Under the EEA Council, a Joint Committee of officials meets roughly monthly to take care of the practical running of the agreement. The Joint Committee is able to make decisions by consensus and has the important role of settling disputes. The Treaty proposed to create an independent EEA Court of Justice from five judges of the European Court of Justice and three judges from EFTA. Its decisions were to be binding. In addition EFTA would set up a body to police the agreement on its own side and the European Commission would exercise the surveillance role in the Community.

The EEA Treaty had to be vetted by the European Court of Justice and, in December 1991, the whole timetable for its adoption was put in jeopardy by the Court's ruling that the proposed EEA Court of Justice and its system of judicial supervision were incompatible with the Treaty of Rome. The ruling meant that parts of the EEA Treaty had to be renegotiated. This, together with problems caused by Switzerland's referendum that rejected membership of the EEA, caused the starting date to be postponed by a year until

1 January 1994. Liechtenstein intended to join the EEA but first had to renegotiate trade agreements with Switzerland. In mid-1995 the shift of the three members from EFTA to the European Union led to a shedding of labour by the EFTA administration. The institutional structure of the EEA is shown in Figure 3.1 and some basic statistics are given in Figure 3.2.

Europe Agreements

'Europe Agreements' have become the usual mechanism for preparation for full membership of the European Union. It was once thought that membership of EFTA and then of the EEA would be the normal channel to full membership but this process has appeared too slow to appeal to Central European countries. It was thought that EFTA would be of value as a 'half-way house' for the countries of Central and Eastern Europe in the adaptation of their economies to the free market model on the route to full membership of the European Union. Jacques Delors referred to a 30-nation 'Greater Europe'. There has been a divisive debate about whether to deepen the Community before widening it. The 1996 Intergovernmental Conference will discuss the problems of coping with a greatly extended membership. Membership of EFTA prior to a full membership of the European Union might have proved a useful compromise route, but in 1994 the Secretary General of EFTA acknowledged that the idea was not popular among Central and Eastern European politicians because they thought that membership of EFTA would delay rather than hasten their full membership of the Union.

Europe agreements began with Poland, Hungary and Czechoslovakia (now the Czech Republic and Slovakia) in December 1991. The Poland and Hungary agreements came into force in February 1994. Further agreements have been negotiated with Bulgaria and Romania and these became effective in February 1995 together with those of the Czech Republic and Slovakia. In June 1995 Europe Agreements were signed with the Baltic States, Estonia, Latvia and Lithuania. Negotiations with Slovenia were under way. The Baltic States' agreements broke new ground by including provisions to prevent illegal immigration, drug trafficking and the illegal trade in industrial waste.

FIGURE 3.1

The Institutional Structure of the EEA

The legal framework of the EEA is based on the so-called 'two pillar' solution, which to some extent means that the two sides are each responsible for the application of the Agreement in their member countries. This has resulted in the creation of two new EFTA institutions, the EFTA Surveillance Authority and the EFTA Court. The need to administer the Agreement has also resulted in the creation of a new committee on the EFTA side (the Standing Committee) and in a new role for the existing EFTA Secretariat.

The EFTA Secretariat
is responsible for servicing the EFTA Standing Committee, as well as the EEA Joint Committee and the EEA Council in rotation with the European Union. As such the Secretariat is involved in the development of new acquis. It also services the two advisory bodies set up by the Agreement. The Secretariat employs about 80 persons at its headquarters in Geneva and a similar number in Brussels.

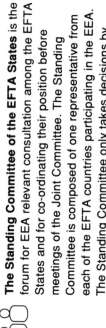

The Standing Committee of the EFTA States is the forum for EEA relevant consultation among the EFTA States and for co-ordinating their position before meetings of the Joint Committee. The Standing Committee is composed of one representative from each of the EFTA countries participating in the EEA. The Standing Committee only takes decisions by consensus, with the exception of certain limited areas where majority voting may apply. It supervises the work of five sub-committees.

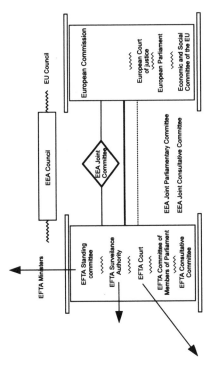

The EFTA Surveillance Authority

is responsible for ensuring that the EFTA countries fulfil their obligations under the EEA. As such, it has certain powers comparable to those of the European Commission, especially in such fields as competition, state aid and public procurement. It has the power to investigate infringements of EEA rules and to administer fines accordingly. The Surveillance Authority is governed by an independent board, or college, made up of five members, one from each participating EFTA State. The Surveillance Authority is based in Brussels.

The EFTA Court

is responsible for cases concerning the surveillance procedure and appeals concerning decisions of the Surveillance Authority in competition matters. The Court may also settle disputes between EFTA States. It may also be asked to hand down advisory rulings on EEA matters by a national EFTA court. The Court is made up of 5 judges, one from each participating EFTA country. The Court is based in Geneva and employs about 30 persons.

SOURCE *EFTA Bulletin*, January 1994

FIGURE 3.2

Basic Statistics of the EEA

The European Economic Area	
Total area	3 662 200 km^{2}**
Population	372 million**
Average number of persons per household	2.6*
Life expectancy at birth	men: 72.9 / women: 79.2*
Foreign residents	15.3 million*
Working population	160.6 million*
GDP	7501 (billion US$)**
Annual exports per inhabitant	3878 (US$)**
Net disposable income	15 141 (EC PPS/inhab.)*
Number of cars	128.9 million*

* 1990 / ** 1992 [PPS = purchasing power in ECU based on EU price indices]

The economic basis of the EEA   **EFTA–EU trade**

EFTA and the EC are each other's largest trading partners and this provides some of the economic rationale for the Agreement.

The European Economic Area 1990	
Percentage of total EFTA exports to the EU	57.9
Percentage of total EFTA imports from the EU	60.8
Percentage of total EU exports to EFTA	10.3
Percentage of total EU imports from EFTA	9.6

If taken as a whole, the EEA countries send over half of their exports to other EEA countries.

Percentage of exports to other EEA countries, 1992

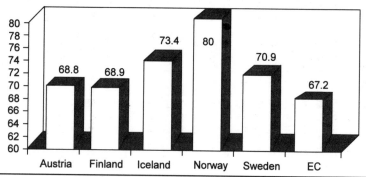

Europe Agreements are bilateral agreements between the individual state and the European Union. There are, therefore, differences between them but they all have the same aim, full membership of the Union. The agreements require a transition to market economies and to liberal democracy. In addition they aim at a raising of the average income per head to the levels of those of the poorer members of the Union. In the process the industrial and agricultural structures of the country are to be brought more into line with those of the Union so that any future integration will be less disruptive. The agreements are backed by various forms of assistance, financial, technical and statistical. The extent of financial help to Central and Eastern Europe as a whole has been criticised as inadequate and over concentrated in Hungary and the Czech and Slovak republics. The use of bilateral agreements which have so far restricted free trade in agricultural and some industrial products has had adverse effects. Trade has not grown as much as was expected and most growth has been to the benefit of the Union. Moreover, and perhaps more importantly in the long run, Central Europe is becoming more fragmented economically and such fragmentation may seriously delay integration. There is a strong case to be made for a more collective approach to integration in Central and Eastern Europe.

Partnership and Cooperation Agreements

Partnership and Cooperation Agreements (PCAs) are a device for managing the relations between the new states formed from the breakup of the Soviet Union and the European Union. The most important was signed at the Corfu summit in June 1994 with the Russian Federation. This will lead to negotiations on free trade agreements and possibly, according to Boris Yeltsin, President of Russia, to eventual Russian membership of the Union. The trade related parts of this agreement came into force in February 1996. Other PCAs were signed in 1994 with Ukraine, Kazakhstan and Moldova and, in January 1996, with Georgia, Armenia and Azerbaijan. PCAs are usually for ten-year periods. In June and July 1994, free trade agreements were signed with Estonia, Latvia and Lithuania which envisaged a free trade zone for industrial products within four years.

The European Union has several programmes that help CEE countries financially. The most important is called PHARE which, in the five years to the end of 1994, provided ECU 4.3 billion. By the end of 1994 PHARE had contributed ECU 1 billion to environmental programmes. The Commission's programme for 1995–99 is for a further ECU 7 billion. Another programme is called TACIS which in 1994 contributed ECU 300 million to improving nuclear safety and technical know-how. Between them they provide financial and technical help for a wide range of schemes such as women's rights in Russia, the environmental movement in Georgia, human-rights education in Albania and the prevention of conflict in Russia and Ukraine. Over 100 projects were helped before the end of 1994.

The states of Central and Eastern Europe are emerging at very different rates from their relative economic backwardness. Their progress has depended on their political, ethnic and social stability, their economic resources and the policies adopted. The transition has proved easier for states such as the Czech Republic with its relatively short period of communist centralised control than for the Russian Federation. Having said that, however, Latvia applied to join the Union in October 1995 and Estonia applied in November 1995. Estonia is in the favorable position of having a balanced national budget and a currency tied to the German mark. It is reasonable to expect some of the states of Central Europe to become full members of the Union within the foreseeable future but the economic disparities with most of the breakaway states of the Soviet Union are too great to expect anything other than a very long delay in their membership. The so-called Visegrad countries, Hungary, Poland, the Czech Republic and Slovakia, formed the Central European Free Trade Association (CEFTA) in December 1992. It came into force in March 1993 and Slovenia was admitted at the end of 1995. There is a queue of countries waiting to join CEFTA; Romania, Bulgaria, Latvia, Lithuania and Estonia are all prospective members. The ex-Soviet Union countries other than the Baltic States might prefer to establish a different form of union among themselves. The applications of the Central European states for full membership of the Union will not be considered until after the 1996 Intergovernmental Conference.

Governing the Union **4**

This chapter will be better understood if the details of the main channels of decision-making in the European Union, as outlined in Chapter 1 under the heading 'Decision-making in the European Union' are consulted. Figure 4.1 summarises these relationships.

Figure 4.1 can only give a broad impression of where decisions are actually made. Ministers are advised by their civil servants. As a result, departmental policy refined over time is frequently more powerful than an individual minister who may have only a short stay in office. The officials of the Commission are also career civil servants who have a profound long-term effect on Commission policy. The Commissioners since 1995 serve for five years and some have served more than one term. They may, however, switch portfolios because these are reshuffled every five years (every four years until 1995). A very important role in decision-making is played by a committee called COREPER, the Committee of Permanent Representatives, which comprises officials of the member states with the rank of Ambassadors to the Union and their advisors and is the vital link between member governments and the Union. What may be said definitively is that no decision can be finally reached without the agreement of the Council of Ministers, and how they reach that decision and whether they are sometimes a 'rubber stamp' depends on their personalities, the detail of the proposals and political factors. In some instances the Council has devolved powers on to the Commission for the execution of policy and this devolution may, in practice, involve the formulation of the detail of the policy.

FIGURE 4.1
The Community's Decision-Making Process

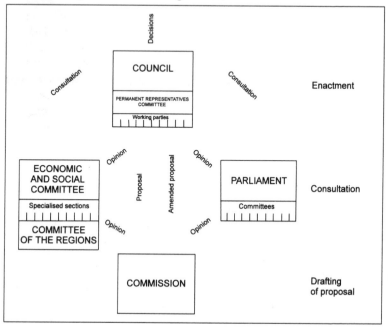

SOURCE   Modified from *The ABC of Community Law*, Klaus–Dieter Borchardt European Documentation (Luxembourg: Office for Official Publications of the European Communities, 1994)

How are Laws Made?

There are three methods of passing legislation that creates instruments (laws) of general application such as directives and regulations:

1. The proposal procedure;
2. The cooperation procedure introduced by the Single European Act;
3. The codecision procedure introduced by the Treaty on Union.

The *proposal procedure* is used where the other two do not apply. It consists of three stages, formulation, consultation and enactment. The Commission, under its *right of initiative*, prepares a draft, usually after consulting experts from the member states. The draft is a very detailed, complete text and goes before the whole Commission for approval. Once approved it is a 'Commission proposal'. The next step is for the Council to study it. At this point the Council may need to consult other Union bodies. This consultation may be compulsory in the case of the European Parliament when it is a politically important matter. Any failure to consult would be a breach of the Treaties. Even where consultation is not compulsory the Commission invariably asks Parliament's opinion in an 'optional consultation'. Parliament produces a formal written opinion which may contain amendments to the proposal but the Commission is not legally obliged to take account of opinions or amendments from the Parliament.

The Commission may also be compelled by the Treaties to consult the Economic and Social Committee or the Committee of the Regions established in 1994 after the Treaty on Union. It also chooses to consult the former Committee on many other occasions but not invariably. The Commission is not bound by an opinion expressed by the Committees.

At the enactment stage, when all the consultations are over, the proposal is again put before the Council and may be amended in line with some of the opinions and amendments expressed, but before it reaches the Council the proposal will have received a thorough reexamination by specialised working parties and by COREPER. It is COREPER that finalises agreements on detail and technicalities. The Council then adopts the proposal and the final text is published in all 11 official languages of the Union.

The *cooperation procedure* is similar to the proposal procedure but gives the European Parliament a much stronger role. It is also quicker. The main areas of application are matters applying to the internal market (since the Single European Act of 1986), to social policy, to economic and social cohesion and to research and development. The method is quicker mainly because the qualified majority voting system can be applied except where taxation and the free movement of workers and their rights and interests are concerned. In these cases decisions must be unanimous.

FIGURE 4.2
The Institutional Cooperation Procedure

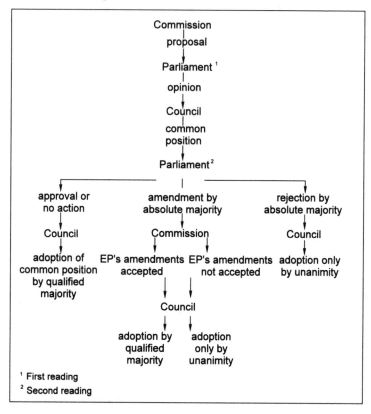

Commission
proposal

Parliament [1]

opinion

Council

common
position

Parliament [2]

approval or
no action

Council

adoption of
common position
by qualified
majority

amendment by
absolute majority

Commission

EP's amendments
accepted

EP's amendments
not accepted

rejection by
absolute majority

Council

adoption only
by unanimity

Council

adoption by
qualified
majority

adoption
only by
unanimity

[1] First reading
[2] Second reading

SOURCE *The ABC of Community Law*, Klaus–Dieter Borchardt European Documentation (Luxembourg: Office for Official Publications of the European Communities, 1994)

The cooperation procedure is shown in Figure 4.2. The essential difference from the proposal procedure is that the original Commission proposal is sent to the Parliament as well as to the Council. After Parliament's first reading, the Council reaches a common position that goes to Parliament for a second reading. Parliament has three months to reach one of four decisions: (a) accept the common position; (b) do nothing which is the same as accepting;

(c) reject it, thus placing a need for unanimity on the Council; or (d) propose amendments. This latter is its usual action and provokes a different response from the Council as shown in the bottom centre of Figure 4.2. The Council retains a veto in this procedure in the form of a blocking tactic whereby it simply fails to make any decision on Parliament's amendments or on an amended Commission proposal. There has however, been general satisfaction with the working of the cooperation procedure.

The *codecision procedure* is shown in Figure 4.3. It is worth spending time studying the diagram and following a proposal through the various possible different branches. Codecision represents a small but significant increase in the powers and authority of the European Parliament as a result of the Treaty on Union. Those who wanted the so-called democratic deficit of the European Community removed or drastically reduced by the Maastricht Treaty have not been satisfied by the new codecision procedure, but others regard it as a step forward. It will be reviewed as part of the 1996 Intergovernmental Conference. The system places the Parliament on a equal footing with the Council in limited but important areas. These are free movement of workers; freedom of establishment; freedom to provide services; education and vocational training; recognition of diplomas; youth, culture and health; consumer protection; research and development; some environmental programmes; and the harmonisation of legislation to establish and operate the single market.

One important provision of the codecision procedure is the Conciliation Committee that helps to reach compromises. It comprises equal proportions of members of the Council and Parliament. The conciliation would normally be expected to produce an agreement but the Parliament has an effective veto if, at its third reading, it rejects the proposal by an absolute majority of its members. It is this section of the Treaty on Union that most effectively increased the power of the European Parliament.

How are Legislative Measures Implemented?

Usually, the Council gives the Commission the power to issue the type of measure that implements its instrument. There are a few

FIGURE 4.3

The Codecision Procedure

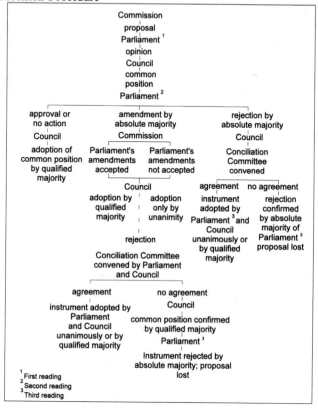

SOURCE   *The ABC of Community Law*, Klaus–Dieter Borchardt European Documentation (Luxembourg: Office for Official Publications of the European Communities, 1994)

special cases where the Council keeps the power of implementation for itself. If the Commission is given the task, it is not allowed to alter the Council's instrument by amending or adding to it. Sometimes such changes are desirable and there are three committee procedures for doing so. These are called the Advisory Committee, the Management Committee and the Legislative Committee procedures. The first applies mainly to instruments to achieve the single market, and the second has applied to agricultural matters since

1962. The third has applied to other matters since 1968 and leaves the Commission in a relatively weak position if the proposed measure is rejected by the Council.

There is also a system called the *simplified procedure* that applies where there are non-mandatory instruments involved, such as recommendations and opinions to be implemented. There are also a few areas that are specifically within the Commission's powers to which this procedure applies.

Unanimous or Majority Decisions?

The Treaty of Paris which set up the European Coal and Steel Community led to a limited requirement for unanimous decisions by the Council. It was intended that this principle would also eventually apply to the European Economic Community set up by the Treaty of Rome, but in the first two periods of transition from 1958 to 1965 most Council decisions had to be unanimous. It was intended that the third stage beginning in 1966 would extend majority voting but instead a lengthy and sometimes bitter debate began about national self-interest. The outcome was the 'Luxembourg compromise' that recognised that the six members disagreed over the application of majority voting. For the next 20 years, until the Single European Act, majority voting was restricted to administrative and budgetary affairs. New members tended to demand unanimity to protect their vital interests, a term that was never precisely defined. In the late 1970s the Community was almost paralysed by disputes over the Common Agricultural Policy and the United Kingdom contribution to the budget. The insistence on unanimity in the Council effectively gave each member a veto.

The European Parliament put pressure on the member governments and majority voting returned as a result of the Single European Act which was signed in 1986 and came into force in July 1987. The Act included provision for a qualified majority decision in the Council of Ministers. The QMV, as the qualified majority vote is called, applies to measures which have as their object the establishment and functioning of the internal market and prevents delays imposed by a single reluctant member. The qualified majority system was extended by the Treaty on Union at Maastricht, especially to economic and monetary union matters, but QMV does not apply to every area of European Union decision-making; the Council must remain unanimous when dealing with revenue, taxation and social policy. Majority voting does apply to transport, the environment and other matters related to the establishment of the internal market. The details of the qualified majority system in the Council of Ministers are shown in Table 4.1.

TABLE 4.1
Qualified Majority Voting

	Pre-1995	*After 1995*
Germany	10	10
France	10	10
Italy	10	10
UK	10	10
Spain	8	8
Belgium	5	5
Greece	5	5
Netherlands	5	5
Portugal	5	5
Austria	–	4
Sweden	–	4
Denmark	3	3
Ireland	3	3
Finland	–	3
Luxembourg	2	2
Total	76	87
Qualified majority	54	62

The use of majority voting in the Council has become common and the national veto allowed in the Luxembourg compromise is rarely used, although the United Kingdom used it in 1994 to prevent M. Dehaene, Prime Minister of Belgium, from succeeding M. Delors as President of the European Commission. Having said that, there has been no use, for the first year and a half, of majority voting in the areas covered by intergovernmental cooperation in the Treaty on Union, that is security and foreign policy. This absence is seen by the Commission as a weakness in its 1995 report on the functioning of the Treaty. Since 1987 there have been detailed rules on voting procedures in the Council. The introduction of QMV has had an observable effect on the nature of discussions. The weighted voting powers enable a single important state to be outvoted but enable two large states together with smaller ones to prevent policies being implemented against their wills. The system prevented total obstructionism by one state but encouraged dealing between nations to modify or promote policies.

The success of the qualified majority system of voting in the Council of Ministers gave rise to support for its extension to other decision-making areas, and the draft treaties on European Political Union drawn up by Luxembourg in June 1991, and by the Netherlands in September 1991, contained provision for such an extension. This, combined with the proposals to reinforce the powers of the European Parliament, gave rise to a bitter dispute leading up to the meeting at Maastricht in December 1991 to agree the new Treaty on Union. The United Kingdom indicated that it would use its veto to prevent any extension of majority voting into foreign affairs or defence matters. The two draft treaties differed in the extent to which they would increase the powers of the European Parliament and the areas of application of majority voting. The Netherlands version, which was rejected in favour of a reconsideration of the Luxembourg proposal, was firmer in its intention to strengthen the democratic element of the Community, especially the Parliament. The discussions for the Inter-governmental Conference in 1996 have again raised the issue of the national veto. The President of the Commission, M. Santer, has indicated that he would like to see the end of the national veto. The United Kingdom Prime Minister, Mr Major, with his eye on the 'Eurosceptical' wing of his party, has reaffirmed his determination to retain a national veto. M. Santer was considering not just the United Kingdom's recent obstructionist phase in European Union affairs but also the role of Greece in delaying agreements with Turkey. The failure to use qualified majorities in areas covered by intergovernmental cooperation on security and foreign policy and the consequent failure to create coherent and effective policies is another reason for ending the national veto.

One of the odder incidents in the relationship between the United Kingdom and the European Union occurred in March 1994 when the UK tried to retain the level of the blocking minority at 23 votes when the QMV system was modified to cope with the accession of new members. The practice had always been to retain the level at 30 per cent of the total number of votes but the United Kingdom, with some brief support from Spain, thought that raising the figure from 23 would be detrimental to large countries. The United Kingdom was forced to accept the proposed rise but obtained a small concession that there would be a 'reasonable delay' to give the Commission a chance to reach a solution if a minority opposition vote was between 23 and 26 votes. This is sometimes referred to after the Greek location of the decision as the Ioannina compromise. (At the time it was expected that Norway would join and she would have had three votes and the blocking minority would have been 27.) The United Kingdom's position was regarded as very peculiar, especially as the number of votes is not related to population. If it were, Germany with a population of almost 80 million and 10 votes would have had a very good case for an increase, especially as Luxembourg, with 400 000 people, has two votes. The episode reflected badly on the United Kingdom's reputation in Europe but serves to illustrate the importance of the debate within the United Kingdom, and the Conservative party in particular, on the issue of sovereignty.

In 1995 yet another new phrase entered the language, 'super qualified majority voting'. Some people would like this to be adopted by the 1996 IGC and it would be applied in the Common Foreign and Security Policy field and mean that a country that disagrees with a proposal and is defeated by a QMV need not carry out the decision. No doubt some would like it applied everywhere.

What is the Problem of National Sovereignty?

Each nation, because it is an internationally recognised separate entity, has institutions which constitutionally have the power to make decisions on its behalf. This power of decision-making may be called sovereignty. Most nations have written constitutions and it is clearly laid out in them which bodies make laws and which court can vet those laws constitutionally. All nations at some time have chosen to subjugate this power of decision-making to some form of international agreement such as the Universal Declaration of Human Rights, or the European Convention on Human Rights, or the Geneva Convention on behaviour in war. Theoretically they retain the right to withdraw their agreement thus retaining their national sovereignty. In practice, however, such a withdrawal would be politically unthinkable in normal circumstances. This does not, of course, prevent some regimes ignoring or flagrantly flouting human rights. Yet they all, eventually, are subject to the international law to which they have subscribed.

In some forms of agreements some states have gone much further in surrendering the power of decision-making to other bodies. The best examples lie with the various federal governments that exist, as in the United States of America, the Federal Republic of Germany, Belgium, Australia, the pre-1991 Union of Soviet Socialist Republics or the current Russian Federation. In the American federal system the individual states voluntarily surrendered certain decision-making powers to the federal government consisting of President and Congress. The more important of these powers were the making of foreign policy, national defence, the currency and the regulation of interstate commerce. Note that the states gave the right. It is not a system where the federal government has all power and deigns to delegate some to the states. Some people persist in putting forward the view that the future for the European Union lies with a federal system especially with the various proposed enlargements. The attitude of the German government and the German Christian Democratic Party in discussions during 1995 on the review of the Treaty on Union appears to support a movement towards a federal structure. The French government under its new President Chirac may also be moving towards this position although that would be a major shift in French policy. The suggestion of a federal structure for the government of the Union arouses great antagonism in the United Kingdom.

The draft Treaty on Political Union produced at the Luxembourg summit in June 1991 referred for the first time in a Community document to the Community having 'a federal goal'. This phrase was repeated in The Netherlands version in September 1991 despite the great furore that the wording had caused in the United Kingdom. The row revealed a basic difference in the interpretation of the word 'federal' between the British government and political commentators and those on the continent. The British tend to see federalism in terms of a centralised power taking authority and decision-making away from the individual nations. They see the British cabinet and parliament as being neutered. Continentals see federalism as a different concept with much less sacrifice of local powers. This is partly because some of them, such as Spain with its system of autonomous regions, are more accustomed to devolving extensive powers to regions than is the United Kingdom with its centralised unitary state. They emphasise the principle of 'subsidiarity' which entails decisions being taken as close as possible to the point of application of a policy, that is at local level where relevant and at European Union central level where appropriate. The words 'federal goal' were removed from the Treaty on Union and replaced by a phrase that has basically the same meaning, 'the process of creating an ever closer Union among the peoples of Europe'. The Treaty also incorporated statements on the importance of subsidiarity.

There is a deep inconsistency in the approach of the United Kingdom government because it has systematically centralised powers since 1979 (a case could be made for earlier dates), and has steadfastly refused to delegate authority to regional bodies in Wales, Scotland or England. A strong campaign has been waged since 1993 against devolution for Wales and Scotland and the importance of the Union of the United Kingdom has been stressed. On the contrary, the United Kingdom government removed a whole tier of local authority, the Metropolitan Counties and Greater London Council, and reduced democratic participation in bodies such as Health Authorities. There has been a trend towards establishing non-elected and non-representative quangos. It has even removed most of the financial independence that local authorities once enjoyed. It has also established direct rule from Whitehall of Northern Ireland. It is on firmer ground when it argues that a federal structure would probably make it harder for the Union to absorb the other nations who are queuing up to join.

There seemed to be relatively little support among European governments for federalism except as a long-term objective expressed as a general aim in the preamble to the Treaty on Union, but it is significant that some of them were willing to resist strongly any attempt by the United Kingdom to have the reference removed, although that may have been a negotiating ploy. Germany in particular has been keen to reduce the 'democratic deficit' in the Union and strengthen the European Parliament and extend majority voting in the Council of Ministers. Many would say that there is no real need to quarrel over the word 'federal' because the European Union has been developed in a unique way to render federation unnecessary.

Most of the members of the Union have suffered from foreign occupation, whether from Napoleon or from Prussia and Hitler's Germany. Most have experienced the need for coalition governments and compromise in decision-making. Some are small states which have always existed under the shadow of their larger, more powerful neighbours. Too much dwelling on theoretical ideals of sovereignty is, to them, a waste of time. The original six members took the pragmatic line that led to the signing of the European Coal and Steel Community (ECSC) Treaty and the Treaties of Rome. In these they set up institutions which made decisions affecting wide areas of their national lives, especially in the economic sphere. They set up the Court of Justice to judge the constitutionality of decisions made by member states, the European Commission, Parliament and Council of Ministers. This 'surrender of sovereignty' was made with open eyes and in frank recognition that the sacrifice of some degree of independence was essential if the great ideal of a Europe without strife and poverty was to be achieved. Opinion in the United Kingdom was not influenced by the same historical factors and was less pragmatic. 'Sovereignty' is still an important issue in some areas of British political debate.

The United Kingdom has no written constitution although certain laws and documents are part of its constitution. There is a great contrast in the United Kingdom between the 'formal' parts of the constitution, Queen and Privy Council for example, and the 'effective' parts, namely the Prime Minister and Cabinet. The role of the United Kingdom Parliament is very debatable nowadays. It has become increasingly 'formal' as its willingness to check the executive has waned and as the ability of the government to control through the whip system has increased. Yet, in the final analysis, Parliament, or the 'Crown in Parliament' to be pedantic, is sovereign. A Parliament can, in theory, undo any act of any of its predecessors. No Parliament can bind its successors. In practical politics, however, things are different. The United Kingdom government and Parliament are irrevocably committed to those international conventions which are compatible with what all Britons are alleged to hold dear – freedoms of expression, property, religion and so forth. They accept international law and generally follow United Nations edicts. The room for genuine independence or sovereignty had been increasingly constrained over the centuries. All this did not prevent a major outcry about 'loss of sovereignty' if the United Kingdom signed the Treaty of Rome and joined the European Community. This outcry was repeated, in minor vein, when the Single European Act was passed in 1986. The Treaty on Union produced more protests some of which had a faint echo in other countries such as Denmark. It seems to be very difficult for some groups of British politicians and journalists to accept the idea that the United Kingdom can, and has, voluntarily given powers of decision to European institutions in which it may have only one-fifteenth of a say. The United Kingdom Parliament is then relegated to a rubber-stamping function and, moreover, has failed to create sufficiently good vetting and criticising committees to monitor European legislation so that it might have a more positive role.

The United Kingdom government has, for the sake of an easy life in getting its measures through Parliament, connived at this emasculation of the British legislature. Yet, in the hypocritical way of governments, leading United Kingdom politicians have not hesitated to wave the stick of 'threats to British or parliamentary sovereignty' when their policies are frustrated on the European mainland. There has been a tendency to resort to sovereignty as an excuse for stalling or obstructionism when the other members of the Community have agreed on a policy. Patriotism is said to be 'the last refuge of a scoundrel'. It also could be said that sovereignty is the penultimate refuge.

It is possible to defend the British government's approach in pushing the Single European Act through Parliament yet, later, arguing on the grounds of sovereignty and national interest against the logical outcomes of the Act. The defence is on the grounds of expediency. The government was fully aware of the extent to which it was surrendering sovereignty to the Council of Ministers, the Commission and the European Parliament but it knew that public opinion could easily be whipped up against such a surrender. It therefore played down this aspect and concentrated on the positive economic benefits of harmonisation and the removal of barriers. Once the necessary legislation was passed, it has found it expedient to calm public fears about specific measures by quoting the national interest and sovereignty in its arguments with its European partners. It has done this over sensitive proposals about border controls, VAT, harmonisation, joining the third stage of the EMS, and the Social Chapter. Increasingly, however, in a multitude of day-to-day decisions the issue of sovereignty is becoming irrelevant. The legislation has been agreed to, the power delegated and the individual nation's veto is largely a thing of the past although the United Kingdom Foreign Secretary told the Conservative party Conference in October 1991 that he would apply a veto if his government considered that the sovereignty of the United Kingdom parliament was at stake. This determination was confirmed by the Prime Minister, Mr Major, in mid-1995 when referring to his government's line in the approach to the 1996 Intergovernmental Conference. The United Kingdom government's continued re-emphasis of the need for subsidiarity is based on the desire to maintain its sovereignty.

Will Sovereignty be an Issue in the Future?

The issue of sovereignty will never go away completely because groups of people and nations will always come to feel at some time that they could do better if they made all their decisions for themselves. There is, for example, a Basque separatist movement, a Walloon independence movement and similar aspirations in Cornwall, Wales, Scotland and the Italian Alps. It is easy to dismiss these trends as the stirrings of adolescent independence. They represent attitudes which arise in any arrangement that has dominant partners. It is inevitable, therefore, that as the effects of the creation of a genuine single European market are understood that two major strands of opinion are developing. The first has come to dominate and is incorporated in the Treaty on Union. It is a generalised federal approach but without federal structures.

The first says 'haven't things worked out well, and look what can be achieved by close cooperation and common objectives – let's try to achieve even closer political harmony in an eventually more federal structure'. Small nations feel safer, more protected and more influential. They want a common currency, a single central bank, a Union police force and perhaps a Union defence and foreign policy.

The second strand of opinion says 'look at the negative effects, the growth of regional disparities, look how badly we have done and see how the big nations dominate decision-making at our expense. Let's go our own way'. The Treaty of Rome is rather exceptional in that it does not provide any means by which a signatory can leave the Union. It appears to be an irrevocable decision. Despite this Greenland chose, after a referendum, to separate itself from Denmark in this context and to negotiate a separate associate status. The European Union is not likely to wish to restrain a member who wants to leave.

Such polarisation of opinion is, of course, somewhat exaggerated and a great deal will depend on how the Union's institutions perform over the next few years, particularly the Parliament. In the United Kingdom the issue of sovereignty is a perpetual preoccupation of the 'Eurosceptics' of all parties. Populists, demagogues and constitutional theorists have all begun to raise the question in the preparations for the 1996 Intergovernmental Conference. We should always bear in mind the seemingly endless ability of groups in society to splinter into smaller groups. Events in the Balkans are a constant reminder of this.

Will the European Parliament be Adequate in the Future?

The European Parliament became more effective after its powers were extended slightly under the Single European Act of 1986 and, more particularly, since its indirect election system was replaced by direct universal suffrage in 1979. Many British MEPs (Members of the European Parliament) take the rather parochial view that it was the advent of the British with their long parliamentary tradition that changed the nature of the European Parliament.

The Parliament has 626 members elected by proportional representation, except in Great Britain where the election is still by the traditional first-past-the-post method. Northern Ireland uses the Single Transferable Vote system of proportional representation to elect its MEPs. In October 1991 the European Parliament voted in favour of all elections of its members being held by proportional representation but this has yet to be confirmed by the Council. Many MEPs, except from the United Kingdom, do not have a specific constituency to which they are directly accountable. This reduces their work burden and their direct contact with the people. The Parliament divides into groups by political tendency rather than by nationality. MEPs are increasingly subjected to the approaches of pressure groups of different types despite the fact that their powers are very restricted.

The European Parliament's powers are very much less than those of national Parliaments, so much so that Ritt Bjerregaard, the Danish nominee as Commissioner for the Environment, rather tactlessly told a press conference that 'The European Parliament is no real Parliament'. Its main job is to oversee and approve the work of the Commission. It can vote the Commission out of office with a two-thirds majority but the relationship between Parliament and Commission is such as to make this event extremely unlikely. Since the Treaty on Union it has to approve the Commission and did so in January 1995 after interviewing the proposed members. Parliament has relatively little control over the budget although it must give its approval and can propose certain increases. It has rejected two budgets but mainly as a short-lived protest. It cannot itself create new sources of revenue. The Budget is divided into compulsory expenditure, mainly agricultural, and non-compulsory. The Parliament is able to propose alterations to the non-compulsory items within limits set by the Treaty on Union. Since 1979 the Parliament has become more effective in criticising the Commission and Council of Ministers through its questions and committee system. It has been helped in the area of the budget by the fifteen-member Court of Auditors which supervises the implementation of the budget.

The above is necessarily a brief analysis of the European Parliament's power but more details are given in Chapter 11, especially with regard to the Treaty on Union. MEPs tend to give a rosier picture of their effectiveness and that of the Parliament. Some critics would be much more damning and allege that the Parliament is a self-important talking shop with the minimum of influence over decision-making. Its quaint movements between Strasbourg, Brussels and Luxembourg do not help its efficiency, although this may eventually be ended and the Parliament may settle in Brussels where a new and very expensive 'hemicycle' building has been provided.

The European Parliament has gradually tried to increase its role and influence. There is plenty of evidence since 1986 to show this trend. Proposals to increase its powers were at the centre of the arguments over the Treaty on Union in 1991. The Parliament's review of the working of the Maastricht Treaty and its proposals for the 1996 Intergovernmental Conference show that it is seeking an equal status with the Council of Ministers in some areas. If the United Kingdom introduces proportional representation in

European elections, as it should eventually do, then there may be an injection of more 'democratic' blood into the Parliament. As the single market extends and intensifies, the electorate of Europe and pressure groups will increasingly look to the European Parliament rather than to national Parliaments. Each national bureaucracy will also increasingly work through European channels. Most important pressure groups already have representatives in Brussels. Over time the European Parliament will be seen to be more important and will certainly want more powers. Some countries, such as Germany, are willing to grant these extra powers in order to reduce the 'democratic deficit'. It may prove to be the best defence of democracy for the British people whose own Parliament has become decayed and ineffectual.

Is the Union Bureaucratic?

The word 'bureaucratic' is often used as a term of abuse by critics of an institution or system. It is frequently used with reference to the European Union and in particular the Commission. Articles which dwell on the 'bureaucratic' nature of the Union usually include a picture of the building in Brussels which houses the headquarters of the Commission. Articles on a similar theme about the United States frequently include a photograph of the Pentagon.

The word 'bureaucratic' has two main meanings when used critically. The first is that the number of employees engaged in administrative tasks is excessive in relation to the size of the whole organisation or to the task in hand. (A classic case is the British Navy which now has more Admirals than large surface ships.) The implication is that many will be engaged in pointless and repetitive clerical tasks which hold up the implementation of policy. The Union definitely does not suffer from this kind of bureaucracy. It employs only about 23 000 employees, 15 000 in the Commission, 3500 in the Parliament, 2200 in the Council, 700 in the Court of Justice, 500 in the Economic and Social Committee, and 400 in the Court of Auditors. Of those employed by the Commission an estimated 2700 are language staff. The administrative cost of the Union, including the Commission is only about 4.6 per cent of the budget of which the Commission takes up 3.3 per cent, the Council 0.41 per cent and Parliament 0.81 per cent. These figures may, of course, be regarded as simply the tip of the iceberg. The individual member states employ many others on European Union-related work and the implementation of its policies. They are, however, counted as national civil servants and not as European Union employees.

The other meaning given to the word 'bureaucratic' is more nebulous and implies a ponderous, labyrinthine decision-making process with a complex hierarchy that causes decision-making to be delayed. It is obvious that the Union, comprising 15 nations, might lend itself to this type of bureaucracy because proposals and decisions have to be constantly referred back and forth between the individual states and the Union institutions. There is no real evidence, though, that the European Union is more bureaucratic than it need be. It can be argued that it is highly efficient and effective in its decision-making processes, even allowing for the inevitable time delay required for compromises. There are specific time scales for the consultation and legislative processes in Figures 4.2 and 4.3. Its achievements in meeting deadlines in the drafting and passing of directives for the arrival of the single European market by 1992 were impressive, achieving most of the 282 measures well on schedule. There were some major areas of dispute such as merger policy, banking regulation and border controls that delayed matters but compromises were nearly always achieved, in most cases without sacrificing the spirit of the single market. Such delays as did occur, and are still occurring, arose from the tardiness of national governments in incorporating the measures into national law. In the sense of the word 'bureaucratic', as discussed in this paragraph, it may be said that the European Union is nowhere near as bureaucratic as the United States or the defunct Soviet Union.

In the context of the 'bureaucratic' criticism some people hope that the creation of the single European market will remove a great deal of administrative work. This happened with the use of a single document for commercial vehicles crossing internal frontiers of the Community, and even that requirement was discontinued in 1993. The abolition in many sectors of such controls as those on capital movements and the harmonisation of regulations should both help reduce bureaucracy. There is a fear, though, that a new structure of rules, regulations and controls will actually establish a tighter and, eventually, more extensive bureaucracy. Since 1993 the Commission has been systematically reviewing European Union legislation to codify, simplify or reduce it. Mrs Thatcher, the Bruges Group, and their successors in the Eurosceptic wing of the Conservative party expressed this fear especially in the context of social policy and tax harmonisation. Their view of an extension of free market forces is at variance with the common European and Community view of a benevolent guiding hand or direct interventionist role for the state.

There is one area where the Union suffers from the delays endemic in the unanimity requirement, and that is under the second pillar of the Maastricht Treaty, the Common Foreign and Security Policy. There has been an obvious failure to react quickly and effectively in Bosnia and Croatia in 1993–95. This is a failure of intergovernmental cooperation rather than a failure resulting from bureaucracy and, in any case, obviously irritates the Commission if one judges by its submission to the Reflection Group for the 1996 IGC.

A Budget Problem – Where to Get the Money

Community budget problems changed in nature over the years. The most persistent, until 1988, was that revenues never matched the levels of expenditure required to meet all the desirable objectives. The Union budget is fundamentally different from national budgets in that it is not an instrument of economic policy using deficits or surpluses to achieve economic objectives. (There is, of course, a fashion in the United States and in sections of some European political parties, for a balanced budget objective for governments. This is almost certainly one of those damaging delusions that strike economists and politicians every so often. Unfortunately it is mainly the ordinary citizen who suffers as a result.) As expenditure under the agricultural programmes got out of control, especially on the price guarantee side, there were less resources available for regional, social and technological programmes. The budget became the cause of annual conflicts between the Commission and the European Parliament and between nations at the Council of Ministers. All sorts of expedients and varieties of creative accountancy were adopted as temporary palliatives. When, eventually, the issue of controlling agricultural payments was successfully met in 1987–88, there was more scope for sensible budgetary policies. Unfortunately the relief was short lived because the agricultural surpluses returned and further reforms of the CAP were necessary in 1992. By 1995 agricultural surpluses and finances were under control. Unfortunately, turmoil on foreign exchange markets in 1994 and 1995 caused the rapid depreciation of some currencies such as the pound sterling and Italian lira. The effect was to create new problems for the budget because agricultural prices are denominated in ECU and the so-called 'agrimonetary' payments escalated (see Chapter 5).

There was a welcome increase in revenues for the Community from January 1986. Between 1970 and 1983 members paid up to 1 per cent of their VAT revenues to the Community. A decision was made in 1984 to increase the VAT revenues payable to the Union by each member up to the equivalent of a 1.4 per cent rate of a uniform basis of assessment. This decision, implemented in January 1986, has provided much needed extra revenue and there has been some pressure to increase the percentage further. In 1988 an upper limit or cap was placed on each member's VAT contribution. This cap was based on a limit on the uniform rate for VAT financing at 55 per cent of its GNP. From 1995 the cap has been lowered to 50 per cent as part of a policy to help poorer members. Since VAT receipts constitute about 55 per cent of the Community's income they yield the greatest return if the rate of contribution is increased.

The Community's revenues also began to take a healthier turn after the Brussels agreement in February 1988 on what is usually called the Delors I proposal. The national leaders agreed to have additional national contributions to the revenues based on relative national wealth (GNP). They allowed the Community to collect up to 1.2 per cent of European Union GNP. This very welcome increase in potential revenue, together with the rise in VAT contributions, permitted a rise of up to 30 per cent in the revenues over time, compared with the 1987 budget. It was agreed in 1992, in discussions on the Delors II package of proposals, that the percentage of GNP would rise gradually from 1995 onwards to reach 1.27 per cent in 1999. The 1995 figure was 1.21 per cent. After 1995 consideration will be given to the introduction of a European Union Tax but no details are yet available. An intense debate can be expected.

In its early days, between 1957 and 1970, the Community's revenue was based on contributions from the six members paid in accordance with an agreed scale based on shares of Gross National Product and other criteria. As was always intended by the Treaty of Rome, the Community shifted its revenue base once the Common Customs Tariff (CCT) was introduced in mid 1968. After the 1970 Hague summit the Community developed a system of revenue from 'its own resources' – that is it was guaranteed money from specific sources. At this time the United Kingdom, Ireland and Denmark were in the process of joining so the changes took place over some years. These sources were: customs duties, agricultural levies, sugar levies and a percentage of the VAT receipts.

The change-over to 'own resources' financing was slow in several respects; it was only speedy in relation to sugar levies. These charges on the production and storage of sugar were transferred to the Community in 1971. They were extended to isoglucose in 1977. The money is used to finance support in the markets for sugar. In the case of customs revenue the complete transfer of all revenues to the Community was not achieved until 1975. Even then customs duties on coal and steel were not handed over to the Community.

Revenue from customs duties has been of decreasing relative importance because of the series of international GATT talks which have reduced tariffs – that is, the Kennedy round (1962–67), the Tokyo round (1980–86) and, progressively from 1995, from the Uruguay round (1986–94). Various other agreements have also cut customs revenues – the Lomé agreement, for example, and the agreement with the EFTA countries, and bilateral agreements with Mediterranean and Central European countries. The general rise in imports and their prices has not compensated for this general decline in tariff levels. If, as the single market develops, the Union successfully replaces imports with home produced products then it can expect a further reduction in its revenues from tariffs. The member states keep 10 per cent of the revenue from customs duties and agricultural levies in order to meet administration and collection costs.

The transfer of agricultural levies also took place over the years 1971–75. These levies were placed upon imported agricultural products to bring their prices to above the level of the Community products' prices. They are being phased out from June 1995. The revenue from them depended on price movements and exchange rates. The United Kingdom, being a relatively large importer of food products, contributed disproportionately to agricultural levies. They have not been a very good source of revenue because they tended to fluctuate unpredictably. The revenue from them has been used to help support intervention buying within the Union but it has been nowhere near sufficient for this purpose. Intervention buying is also being phased out under the reforms of the CAP and being replaced by income support measures. Table 4.2 illustrates the problem as it was in 1985 with the dominance of agricultural payments and absence of revenues based on GNP.

TABLE 4.2
The Dominance of Agricultural Payments: The Community Budget, 1985 (percentage)

Receipts	*%*	*Expenditure*	*%*
VAT	55.5	Agriculture and fisheries	72.9
Customs duties	29.6	Regional policy	5.9
Non-repayable advances	5.9	Social policy	5.7
Agricultural levies	4.0	Development cooperation	3.9
Sugar and isoglucose levies	3.8	Research, energy, transport	2.6
Miscellaneous	1.2	Administrative costs	4.6
		Miscellaneous	4.4

Total payment appropriations + 28 000 million ECU

It was decided in 1970 to make VAT the main source of the Community's own revenue, but it was not until the budget of 1980 that every member paid its full VAT payments. Proceedings before the Court of Justice were required to make Ireland, Italy, Luxembourg and Germany comply in 1979 with the sixth VAT Directive of May 1977. The members agreed to give the Community up to 1 per cent of a uniform basis of assessment of value added tax. This limit was raised to 1.4 per cent in January 1986 after the Fontainebleau summit resolved the United Kingdom's contribution problem. There was pressure to raise the figure further but the United Kingdom and Germany were reluctant because they thought that the limit imposed more budgetary discipline on the Community, particularly on the agricultural budget.

VAT was chosen as a source of revenue because the sixth VAT Directive of May 1977 harmonised the turnover (or VAT) systems. The tax is paid by all Union citizens and its revenue closely reflects the economic capacity of each member state. This may be regarded as an equitable system and is, to a degree, progressive because high revenue from VAT reflects high levels of consumption which, in turn, reflects high disposable incomes. Spain would dispute this statement because it raises a higher percentage of its tax revenues from indirect taxes than most members. The amount paid is based on a uniform basis of assessment defined as 'the sum of all taxable supplies of goods and services to the final consumer in the Community'. This means that it does not depend on the VAT rates which continue to differ quite widely among member states. As mentioned above, the uniform rate of assessment for VAT-based financing was capped at 55 per cent of GNP from 1988 to 1995, and at 50 per cent from 1995.

TABLE 4.3
VAT Rates Current When it was Decided to Apply a Standard Rate of a Minimum of 15% from 1 January 1993 (per cent)

Country	Reduced rate	Standard rate	Higher rate
Belgium	1 and 6	17 and 19	25 and 33
Denmark	—	22	—
Germany	7	14	—
Greece	4 and 8	18	36
Spain	6	12	33
France	2.1, 5.5, 13	18.6	22
Ireland*	2.3, 10, 12.5	21	—
Italy	4, 9	19	38
Luxembourg	3, 6	15	—
Netherlands	6	17	30
Portugal*	8	17	30
UK*	—	17.5	—

*Ireland, Portugal and the United Kingdom had a significant extent of zero rating. The VAT system and the approximation of rates will be reviewed in 1997

SOURCE   European File, *Approximation of Taxes. Why?* (Luxembourg: Office for Official Publications of the European Communities, 1991)

As part of the progress towards the creation of the single European market in 1992 an attempt was made to harmonise VAT rates. The word 'harmonise' caused a great deal of political difficulty because it implied coercion and the new politically correct word is 'approximate'. In 1991 an agreement was reached which represented a compromise to overcome short-term conflicts between the members. It was decided to have a 15 per cent minimum standard rate of VAT by 1 January 1993 for a transitional period up to the end of 1996 (see Table 4.3). There will also be minimum excise duty rates on fuel, tobacco and alcohol. Member states have the option of applying one or two reduced rates, not lower than 5 per cent. Existing rates and zero rating can be kept for a transitional period. The higher rates on hi-fi, videos, perfumes and cars were abolished in January 1993. The Commission will propose fundamental reforms of the Union's VAT system in 1996.

If the market becomes a genuine single unit, market forces are likely to produce a close approximation of rates over time. Otherwise there will be considerable distortions of the market with tax considerations influencing the location of production. There are still many details to sort out in the context of indirect tax harmonisation over the next few years. The United Kingdom government has been opposed to full harmonisation of rates of VAT because it would have to impose the tax on goods at present exempt, notably food and children's clothing. It did, however, quietly extend VAT in 1988 and 1989 to some areas hitherto excluded, such as opticians's services and parts of the construction industry. In 1990 it raised the standard rate of VAT in the United Kingdom to 17.5 per cent as part of its policy of shifting the tax burden from income on to expenditure. In 1994 VAT was extended to domestic fuel in what was intended to be a two-stage imposition, 8 per cent followed by a further 9.5 per cent in 1995, but parliamentary opposition caused the second stage to be withdrawn and other tax increases substituted. The French too are opposed to full harmonisation because they would have to lower many of their rates and find alternative sources of revenue. In mid-1995 France raised one of its VAT rates.

How are the Budget and Exchange Rate Fluctuations Reconciled?

It was essential to devise a system for payments between members and the Community to take account of changes in foreign exchange rates. Before 1977 budgets were drawn up and implemented in terms of 'units of account' (u.a.). Each u.a. was equivalent to a fine ounce of gold – this was the content of the US dollar between 1934 and 1972. In other words the exchange rate in relation to the US dollar was the basis of calculation. Between 1978 and 1980 the European Unit of Account (EUA) was used instead and was based on a 'basket' of currencies. Since 1980 the budget has been drawn up and executed in terms of the ECU (European Currency Unit). This is described and explained fully in Chapter 7. The ECU is based upon a 'basket' of currencies in which individual currencies are weighted according to objective measures such as a country's share of the Union's Gross Domestic Product, and share of European Union trade. This weighting has hitherto been reviewed every five years but the advent of Stage 2 of Economic and Monetary Union has ended this practice. From 1979–80 the ECU was used for all legal and financial purposes and in the budget from January 1981.

The value of the ECU is worked out on a daily basis for each country's currency in relation to the currency's standing on the exchange markets. The Union budget is drawn up each year using the ECU rates for 1 February of the previous year. For example, the 1995 budget was drawn up on the ECU rate prevailing on 1 February 1994. The application of the ECU to the CAP is discussed in Chapter 5 under the heading 'agrimonetary compensation mechanism'.

Additional Community Budget information is shown in Tables 4.4–4.8 and in Figure 4.4.

TABLE 4.4

United Kingdom Contributions to and Public Sector Receipts from the Community Budget (£ millions)

	1992	*1993*	*1994*	*1995*
Gross Contributions				
Agricultural and sugar levies	205	199	201	210
Customs duties	1559	1754	1796	1903
VAT own resources (before abatement)	4357	4966	4189	4635
Fourth resource payments	934	1609	2340	1753
VAT and fourth resource adjustments	−317	−543	−1337	292
United Kingdom abatement of VAT	−1881	−2539	−1726	−1474
Total Contributions	4857	5446	5463	7319

Public Sector Receipts				
EAGGF Guarantee	1646	2153	2246	2757
Stock depreciation	96	0	0	0
EAGGF Guidance	71	104	52	71
European Regional Development Fund	556	425	608	654
European Social Fund	437	589	321	668
Other receipts	22	20	25	22
Total Receipts	2827	3291	3252	4172
Net Contribution	2030	2155	2211	3147

NOTES
1. For all years sterling figures reflect payments made during the year, not payments in respect of particular budgets
2. The figures for contributions of agricultural and sugar levies and customs duties in 1995 are based on UK projections of our sterling payments to be made during the year
3. The figures for 1995 are forecasts, those for earlier years outturn
4. Because of rounding the column totals do not necessarily equal the sum of the individual items

SOURCE *European Community Finances*, HM Treasury, Cm 2824 (London: HMSO, 1995)

TABLE 4.5
Expenditure on the Community Budget: Commitments by Type of Expenditure (£ million)

	Commitments			
	1992	*1993*	*1994*	*1995*
1. Agricultural Guarantee	**22 962**	**27 052**	**26 917**	**29 851**
2. Structural Operations	**13 891**	**17 555**	**17 932**	**20 723**
Agricultural Guidance	1986	2367	2910	2956
Regional Development Fund	5093	6397	6987	8338
Social Fund	3651	4372	4996	5072
Cohesion Fund	0	1218	1434	1694
Other Structural Operations	3160	3200	1605	2664
3. Internal policies	**3158**	**3183**	**3369**	**3980**
Other agricultural operations	133	159	159	164
Other regional operations	60	25	24	40

Table 4.5 *Continued*

| | Commitments | | | |
	1992	*1993*	*1994*	*1995*
Social and education policies	379	427	498	575
Energy and Environment policies	233	242	183	172
Industry and internal market	206	334	444	574
Research and Development	2033	1986	2029	2337
Other internal	115	10	32	118
4. External policies	**2898**	**3336**	**3333**	**3842**
Food aid	588	447	662	667
Aid to Eastern Europe/FSU	1066	1167	1132	1246
Other Development Aid	1086	1563	1305	1462
Other external	158	159	235	468
5. Administration	**2257**	**2618**	**2813**	**3155**
Commission	1490	1756	1879	2039
Parliament	426	487	515	664
Council	217	234	249	242
Court of Justice	60	70	81	91
Court of Auditors	26	30	33	42
Economic and Social Committee/Committee of the Regions	38	44	54	79
6. Reserves and repayments	**644**	**0**	**1183**	**2120**
Monetary reserve	0	0	774	394
Emergency reserve	0	0	164	254
Loan Guarantee reserve	0	0	246	254
Repayments	644	0	0	1218
Total	**45 808**	**53 743**	**55 547**	**63 670**

NOTES
1. Because of rounding the column totals do not necessarily equal the sum of the individual items
2. Unallocated amounts for enlargement included under 'other' expenditure in categories 2, 3 and 4

SOURCE   *European Community Finances*, HM Treasury, Cm 2824 (London: HMSO, 1995)

TABLE 4.6
Members' Contributions to Community Budget Revenues 1995 (£ millions)

Country	Agricultural and sugar levies	Customs duties	VAT contributions	4th resource payments	Totals
Belgium	93	659	963	539	2254
Denmark	32	184	551	341	1108
Germany	313	2819	9626	4791	17 549
Greece	26	120	471	229	846
Spain	130	405	2135	1124	3793
France	274	1294	6017	3098	10 683
Ireland	11	278	252	111	652
Italy	208	732	3676	2344	6961
Luxembourg	0	12	84	37	133
Netherlands	101	1054	1535	769	3458
Portugal	80	107	477	210	873
UK	205	1913	3106	2379	7602
Austria	22	232	900	461	1615
Finland	16	134	431	234	816
Sweden	35	242	750	455	1483
Totals	1546	10 187	30 973	17 121	59 827

Figures are rounded

SOURCE *European Community Finance*, HM Treasury, Cm 2824 (London: HMSO, 1995)

TABLE 4.7
Contributions to, and Receipts from, the European Community Budget,*
1993 (£ billion)

	Contributions	Receipts[+]
Germany#	14.9	5.6
France	9.0	8.2
Italy	8.0	6.8
United Kingdom	5.9	3.5
Spain	4.0	6.5
Netherlands	3.1	2.1
Belgium	1.9	1.9
Denmark	0.9	1.2
Greece	0.8	4.0

Table 4.7 *Continued*

	Contributions	*Receipts*[+]
Portugal	0.7	2.6
Ireland	0.5	2.3
Luxembourg	0.2	0.3

* From The Court of Auditors Report, 1993

+ Excludes £4.9 billion which is mainly development aid and administrative expenditure for the other institutions. The receipts are Community payments to both private and public sectors in member states

As constituted since 3 October 1990

SOURCE: *Social Trends 95*, 1995 Edition (London: HMSO, 1995).

TABLE 4.8
Financial Perspective for the Enlarged Community

	1995 Prices (£ million)				
	1995	*1996*	*1997*	*1998*	*1999*
Commitment appropriations					
1. Common Agricultural Policy	29 865	31 126	31 694	32 275	32 872
2. Structural operations	20 723	21 810	23 121	24 529	25 939
3. Internal policies	3983	4119	4289	4468	4639
4. External action	3853	4063	4304	4616	4990
5. Administrative expenditure	3166	3235	3331	3381	3431
6. Reserves	902	897	897	897	897
7. Compensation	1218	552	167	78	0
Total commitment appropriations	63 710	65 802	67 802	70 245	72 769
Payment appropriations	60 786	62 375	64 720	66 960	69 270

SOURCE *European Community Finances*, HM Treasury, Cm 2824 (London: HMSO, 1995)

Another Budget Problem – the Winners and Losers

Some countries are net gainers and some are net losers from the financial transactions of the European Union. The gainers tend to keep quiet and hope that their luck continues. They are usually the poorer members such as Greece and Ireland although Italy has frequently been a substantial winner. Portugal has become a net beneficiary. The net contributors or 'losers' have been Germany, the United Kingdom and, usually, France. The Netherlands contributes most per head of population. Germany and France, on the one hand, have usually accepted the 'losses' as a reasonable payment to maintain peace and stability in Europe and as a means of helping economic development in less-favoured regions. The United Kingdom, on the other hand, made loud, continuous and aggressive complaints about its net contributions. In Mrs Thatcher's words 'we want our money back'. Indeed, the problem of the United Kingdom's contributions persisted so long that it threatened to become the bore of the century.

Fortunately for us the matter was largely resolved following the Fontainebleau summit in June 1984. The leaders agreed that expenditure policy is at the heart of any method of controlling budgetary imbalances. This agreement led to subsequent controls on agricultural spending. They also agreed to a system of abatement or correction for excessive budgetary burdens with a specific formula for the United Kingdom. These corrections are deducted from the United Kingdom's share of VAT payments in the year following that for which the correction is made. The repayment, rebate, or correction obviously places a burden on the other members – the cost being shared among them according to their normal VAT share – but it is adjusted to allow Germany's share to move to two-thirds of its VAT share. In other words, Germany bears a disproportionate part of the burden of the United Kingdom's rebates despite the fact that it is the largest net contributor (loser) to the Union.

It became apparent very soon after the United Kingdom's accession to the Community that there was likely to be a growing problem of excess budgetary contributions. Denmark, in contrast, was a major net beneficiary. The United Kingdom wanted a closer relationship between payments and receipts. Its wishes were partly granted when the terms of entry were renegotiated. In 1975 the European Council agreed on a corrective mechanism which was to apply for an experimental period of seven years until 1983. This financial mechanism was inadequate since the net debit was not removed and the growth in the size of the United Kingdom's net deficit balance continued. By 1979 the situation was extremely bad.

FIGURE 4.4
Developments in Community Spending

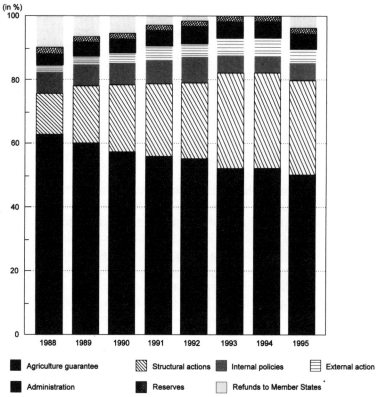

*Includes transitional refunds to Portugal and Spain in 1988–1992 and budgetary compensation to Austria, Finland and Sweden in 1995

SOURCE *European Community Finances*, HM Treasury, Cm 2824 (London: HMSO, 1995)

In 1980 it was agreed to reduce the net United Kingdom contribution for 1980 and 1981 from an aggregate of 3924 million ECU to 1339 million ECU. This reduction of 2585 million ECU was financed by the other members, partly by direct payments to the United Kingdom Treasury and partly by generous extra payments from the Regional Fund. This did not satisfy Mrs Thatcher who wanted a long-term solution and a control on expenditure. There followed several years of wrangling and almost every summit was soured by this until the 1984 Fontainbleau summit, as previously mentioned. There are regular attempts within the Conservative party to resurrect the question of the United Kingdom's budgetary contributions but there seems to be a marked reluctance for the government to pursue the matter at the European level, probably for fear of German reaction.

Fraud

The European media seem to have discovered, in November 1994, that fraud existed in the European Union. Newspapers were full of lurid reports of £6 billion being fraudulently misappropriated, in an unspecified time period. The spark that set off this frenzy was the Annual Report of the Court of Auditors in November 1994 which criticised the lack of action to remedy faults found over the previous ten years. The Commission felt unjustly accused and thought that not enough account had been taken of more recent efforts to prevent fraud. It was also pointed out that national governments are responsible for administering more than 80 per cent of the Union's spending so that if fraud takes place it is probably their fault. The Commission accused the press of distortions and incorrect statements and said that since 1989 it had disbursed £30 billion in regional, structural funds and only four cases of fraud had been detected by national governments and three by the Commission. The press tended to reply along the lines that this simply showed that where there was no smoke there must be a hidden fire, that is undiscovered corruption.

The Commission had pursued an anti-fraud campaign in 1994 and has started another programme in 1995. In 1992 it set up a database to record fraud with, inevitably, an acronym title, IRENE, which stands for irregularities, enquiries, exploitation. It appears from the Auditors Report that, in 1994, there were 4264 cases of irregularity and fraud discovered, a two-thirds increase over 1993. Was the existence of IRENE responsible for the rise? The amount involved was ECU 1.033 billion or 1.2 per cent of the budget total. About half the detected fraud is in the agricultural sector, especially in the export of cereals and their storage, and in the payments for olive oil and the export of beef. Fraud is also significant for imports of highly-taxed products such as cigarettes and sugar. The Commission has set up a special anti-fraud unit to detect fraud and recover funds. The Union and national governments are setting up special task forces with the same purpose. Informers and 'whistleblowers' are to be rewarded and a free phone service established for them to use. IRENE may be joined by another information network called SID. No doubt they will breed and produce some offspring. Table 4.9 shows some statistics of reported irregularities from member states. The United Kingdom does not emerge too well, unless one assumes it is extra diligent in reporting cases. Only Germany with 36 per cent of the notified cases exceeds the British 22 per cent. The Italians seem to make up in value what they lack in numbers of notified cases; they also recovered only 1 per cent of the value against the United Kingdom's 2 per cent.

TABLE 4.9
Fraud

Communications of Member States on Irregularities, Traditional Own Resources
period: 1991–1994 (1+2 quarter)

	Cases			Amount in ECU		
	notified	closed	open	notified	recovered	to be recovered
Belgium	328	203	125	49 205 846	7 267 239	41 938 607
Denmark	86	41	45	6 848 827	2 799 554	4 049 273
Germany	1548	115	1433	171 442 258	7 715 408	163 726 850
Greece	66	0	66	3 223 998	0	3 223 998
Spain	192	15	177	14 051 855	1 025 938	13 025 917
France	544	9	535	53 500 248	5 093 467	48 406 781
Ireland	32	13	19	8 001 875	1 183 211	6 818 664
Italy	408	41	367	92 474 916	654 257	91 820 659
Luxembourg	2	1	1	85 220	45 417	39 803
The Netherlands	44	1	43	9 513 448	122 232	9 391 216
Portugal	84	39	45	2 969 940	579 444	2 390 496
United Kingdom	961	224	737	92 167 252	1 844 104	90 323 148
Total	4295	702	3593	503 485 683	28 330 271	475 155 412

SOURCE　*European Commission Background Report* B/05/95, May 1995

The issue of fraud is very important because any widespread perception that the European Union is riddled by fraud and corruption is bound to detract from its political popularity and have an impact on its effectiveness. Allegations of fraud have already become a stick with which anti-European groups beat the Union. Some national governments are also unwilling to accept responsibility for their share of maladministration and are happy to let the Commission take the blame. The Commission is attempting, over the next few years, to achieve greater harmonisation of members' criminal laws in respect of fraud. The attempt is bound to cause friction and, if successful, a greater degree of regulation.

Is the Community a Tower of Babel?

The European Union of Fifteen has 11 official languages – Danish, Dutch, English, Finnish, French, German, Greek, Italian, Portuguese, Spanish and Swedish. This presents a significant financial burden (about £30 million a year in 1991), and a personnel problem. The European Parliament and the European Court of Justice have their own interpreting services. In 1995 the other three institutions employed over 400 full-time and 1600 freelance interpreters. A summit meeting such as the European Council requires about 100 interpreters. All important meetings, about 50 per day, have to be provided with facilities for translation out of each of 11 languages and into the other ten. In addition all the documents have to be translated into all the official languages. It is estimated that the advent of a new official language created a demand for up to 250 translators. Interpreting into and out of 11 languages gives 110 potential combinations. This number may be reduced by translating at second-hand from a language into which the original language has already been translated. Most of the less-important meetings are conducted in three languages, English, French and German.

There is no chance of the number of official languages being reduced because of political and legal reasons. Formal meetings and documents will, therefore, continue to be available in all 11 languages. If Norway and Turkey ever join it will be even more like the Tower of Babel. The possible addition, in the more distant future, of the various Eastern and Central European languages, such as Polish, Hungarian, Czech, Slovak and so forth, has led to suggestions that new entrants should be asked to forgo their right of translation in some meetings or for some documents. In day-to-day practice, however, the usual working languages of the Union are English and French. The cultural imperialism or encroachment of English is resented and resisted by the French, but it is in such a strong position internationally that it is likely to dominate in the long run. Its use by the Americans, the old British dominions and colonies and its adoption by the Japanese and Russians as their second language makes this inevitable. There has, however, been a recent surge in the popularity of German as a second language in Central and Eastern European countries. It will be interesting to see, over the next 20 years, what effect satellite broadcasting has on language use. Will it help to perpetuate local languages and dialects through local stations or will it extend English over a wider area? If it is the latter, perhaps there will, one day, be a 'Euro-English' along the lines of American, Australian or Caribbean English.

Agriculture – Successes, Failures, Reforms

5

Has the Common Agricultural Policy been Successful?

There is no doubt that the answer to this question is 'yes' *if* the policy is seen in the light of its aims. The critics of the Common Agricultural Policy (CAP) tend to take short-term, oversimplified views. They can see no further than the so-called 'food mountains' and usually feel no need to put forward constructive alternatives to the policies that they wilfully caricature. They condemn the whole policy, in all its complexity, out of hand. What they should be doing is suggesting positive improvements in terms of the CAP's flexibility and ability to respond to changing circumstances.

The CAP was conceived against a history of 80 years of cyclical fluctuations in demand, prices and rural prosperity. Rural poverty in Europe was a mainspring of political and social unrest. The United Kingdom, which tends to take a piously superior attitude to the CAP was spared much of this because of its earlier shift of resources away from the land into industry. Even so, the agricultural depressions of the 1918–39 period were devastating in the United Kingdom. The stereotype of the Jarrow hunger marchers obscures the reality of this rural deprivation.

The CAP was also founded against the immediate backdrop of over ten years of food shortages in Europe. These were particularly severe from 1943 into the early 1950s, with many Europeans dying from malnutrition and its side effects at the end of the war. The foremost aim of the CAP, therefore, was to remove any threat of food shortages. In this the policy has been triumphantly successful.

The other objectives explicitly stated in Article 39 of the Treaty of Rome were: to increase agricultural productivity; to ensure thereby a fair standard of living for the agricultural community; to stabilise markets; and to guarantee reasonable prices for consumers. It is possible to put a strong case that 'reasonable' prices for consumers have not been achieved and that, on average, prices are higher than they would have been in a completely free market. Estimates vary as to the extent of the difference.

In order to guarantee food supplies farmers have to be offered secure markets and a fairly high degree of certainty in price levels. This makes some form of state intervention essential. It is the form that this intervention should take that creates division of opinion. Several types of policy are possible and each type can be tailored to the specific characteristics of a country. The CAP began with six nations and has been adapted as the Community and Union have expanded. It now covers fifteen nations with widely differing climatic conditions, and is bound to be less appropriate to some countries than to others. This is not an argument for abolishing it, rather it is a reason for improving its application by fine-tuning to fit national conditions. There is no doubt whatsoever that free competition without state intervention would have resulted in market chaos in Europe with appalling social and economic consequences. It is flying in the face of all human experience of the last 200 years to advocate free market competition in agriculture, although some people do.

Why would Free Market Competition in Agriculture Cause Chaos?

Supporters of right-wing, free market think tanks may have reached for their garlic and crucifixes on reading the last paragraph and may have invoked the spirits of Adam Smith and Hayek to calm their nerves. The free market philosophy is, however, based on a fundamental misinterpretation of human nature, in much the same way as is communist philosophy. Communists tend to assume a high degree of altruism in human nature and a willingness to sacrifice the individual for the good of the whole. Free marketeers tend to assume that producers will *compete*. They obviously do not if they can avoid it which is why we have cartels, monopolies and restrictive trade practices, and why we have state intervention to reduce their impact. Free competition of the text-book variety, if it could exist, would be fine for the rich, the strong and the favourably endowed. Free marketeers dream of Pareto optimality where no reallocation of resources can make anyone better off without making at least one other person worse off. Some also dream of the 'trickle down' effect when the poor benefit from the existence and expansion of the richer elements in society. In practice the poor and weak in society, the small farmer and the low-income consumer, see the trickle down effect, if it exists, in a different light!

'Chaos' here means successive food gluts and shortages with wide and rapid price fluctuation. It also means cyclical booms and slumps, with concurrent movements in agricultural incomes and employment.

The reasons lie in the nature of agricultural products and their production conditions and in the traditional responses of farmers to changes in markets and prices. These factors, when combined, tend to contradict the simple price theory of elementary economics textbooks, where supply and demand are brought into a neat equilibrium in response to price changes. In agricultural products there is just as likely to be a series of short-run diverging price equilibria, as shown in the 'cobweb theorem' (see Figure 5.1), and no long-run equilibrium.

Farmers' responses are of paramount importance. There are two main behavioural patterns that can be seen. The first is embodied in what has usually been known as the 'pig cycle', or as the 'hog cycle' in American writings. Pigs are chosen to illustrate this idea because of their ability to reproduce quickly and to be fattened for market in a short time, although there is still a time-lag between planning and achieving production. The same principle now applies to 'lamb' although the cycle is longer and ewes usually have only two lambs a year. It can also apply to arable crops if farmers can quickly enter or leave production. Modern production techniques may cause it to apply to eggs and poultry meat production. The cycle is one of buoyant demand in relation to supply pushing up prices of pig products. Farmers see the high prices and apparent profitability. Existing producers quickly expand their output and newcomers begin production. The result, if demand fails to rise sufficiently, is an excess supply which tends to depress market prices. The fall in price forces marginal producers out of business

FIGURE 5.1
'Cobweb' Effects

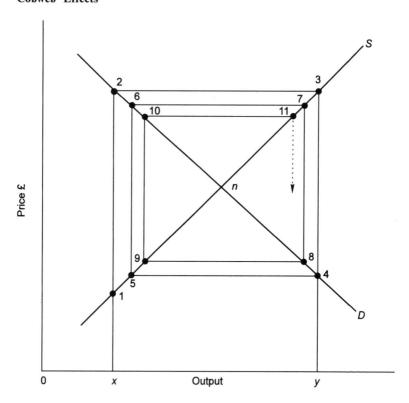

D shows the relationship between the quantity produced in a production period and the price that needs to be charged in order to sell that amount. *S* shows the relationship between the price in one production period and the quantity that will be produced in the succeeding production period.

If output in period *A* is 0*X*, the price will be at level 2. The price 2 will cause output in production period *B* to be 0*Y* (point 3) and the price will be at level 4 (where the demand is). Output in production period *C* will be at level 5 and price at level 6; and so on. Given the relative slopes of these two curves there will be an equilibrium at *n*. If, however, the curves have a different slope, as in Figure 5.2, this is not the case. Price may diverge further and further from the equilibrium unless the curves shift to a new position.

and reduces profits for the more efficient. The consequent decline in output creates a deficiency of supply in relation to demand. Prices tend to rise and we are back at the starting point. This cycle may take less than two years. Its length, and the range of fluctuation of output and price, depends on a number of imponderables such as international price movements, animal feed prices and the movement of the prices of substitutes. Although there may be a similar cycle in some sorts of manufactured goods it is not as intense, partly because many major markets are dominated by oligopolies.

An interesting comparison might be made with the silicon chip market for mass-produced chips for electronic devices. These markets have displayed a 'pig cycle' aspect in the 1970s and 1980s. In agricultural markets the 'pig cycle' effect, if unchecked, can destabilise markets and create wider fluctuations in demand, supply and price of products and factors such as labour, transport, animal feed, packaging materials and professional services. It should be remembered, however, that as in all spheres of business some clever entrepreneurs make their profits by anticipating the cycle and bucking the trend. One of the benefits of the CAP has been to remove most of the effects of the cycle in those areas where intervention prices have been applied.

Those readers who are familiar with supply and demand analysis will realise that the above explanation fits the so-called 'cobweb' theorem. This shows how some markets are subject to price destabilisation instead of tending towards an equilibrium. In these conditions the price oscillates around the potential equilibrium but does not settle at it. It may diverge more and more from the equilibrium over time. In diagrams this can be drawn to show a 'cobweb' effect although the 'web' is nowhere near as geometrically accurate as that made by the humble spider! See Figures 5.1 and 5.2.

In principle, then, farmers have always tended to enter markets where prices have been high in the recent past and to leave those where prices have been low. This may be a movement of 'marginal' producers only or may be a shift of a significant proportion of producers. Not all farmers have the luxury of choice as to what to produce. Their land conditions, expertise and machinery may all be specific to one type of production. (There has been a great growth in specialist contracting firms for various types of harvesting and

FIGURE 5.2
'Cobweb' Effects

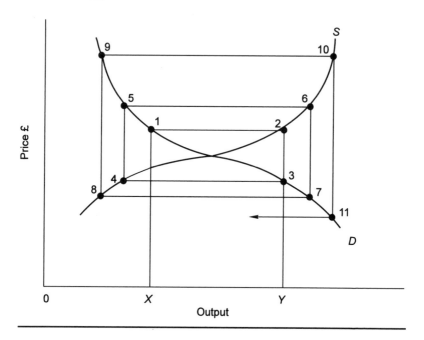

for soil and crop treatments. This cuts the costs for farmers entering a new line of production.) A policy such as the CAP may be used successfully to finance the transfer of land to other uses or to pay farmers to stop producing. The policies adopted need to be flexible and to bear in mind the needs of the individual farmer as well as their effects on aggregate supply.

The second main behavioural pattern of farmers is linked to the first but, to some extent, contradicts it. It consists of farmers, especially those who have a limited range of output options, responding to a fall in their incomes by trying to produce more and to cut their costs. Thus, for example, a typical American Midwest wheat farmer, faced by a falling price of wheat and therefore a falling income, can only compensate by growing more wheat. If all his fellow producers do the same the aggregate supply expands. If demand fails to rise proportionately, excess supply is generated and prices fall even further. This is followed by another fall in net income unless the farmer has managed to cut costs even more. The possible causes of the initial fall in prices and farmers' incomes are many, for example good harvests elsewhere, or falling real incomes of consumers, or a change in tastes and preferences of consumers. Once again, this response of farmers can be forestalled or controlled by the CAP setting target prices for current and future years and by setting output quotas.

These responses of farmers are partly a reflection of the nature of demand for agricultural products, part of which comes from industry and part from domestic consumers. 'Industrial' demand for the products of agriculture has always been important but modern technology has modified this or provided substitutes via modern chemical processes. The main demands, historically, have been for leather, wool, cotton, other fibres such as flax, dyes, alcohol, starch, oils from seeds, timber, products for brewing and, recently, biofuel as a petrol substitute. Related to these uses is the manufactured food processing industry which cans, packages and bottles products after dehydration, freezing, pickling and smoking as a means of preserving the food. Food processing has several effects of great importance to agriculture. Preservation, in itself, can help to smooth out seasonal fluctuations in supply. It can, together with rapid modern transport systems with specialised carriers, make available all sorts of products from all over the world throughout the year, and provides the consumer with substitutes and variety. It also enables surpluses to be extended over time and widely distributed around markets.

Another very important effect is to enable value to be added to what are intrinsically cheap products. This partly explains the great growth since the 1920s of packaged, branded foods. The effect on the market has usually been to create oligopolistic conditions with a few major firms each taking a large share of the market within a given country. They may leave a small proportion of the market to be shared among a larger number of much smaller sellers. These smaller producers survive by producing a specialised product to a narrow section of the market or by giving outstanding personal service or quality. They may enjoy low costs because they are family concerns with fewer overheads. Their continued existence may depend on the larger firms abstaining from trying to take them over because of the threat of investigation under the individual country's, or the European Union's, anti-monopoly laws. Some of the larger firms are multinational and many originate in the USA. There was a distinct trend towards mergers and marketing arrangements among the dominant firms as the December 1992 date for the completion of the single European market approached.

The processing, packaging and branding of food, together with extensive advertising helps to overcome a basic problem of agriculture in higher-income societies. This problem is the existence of a low-income elasticity of demand for some foods and a negative income elasticity for others. Economists give the quaint name of 'inferior goods' to those that have negative income elasticities of demand.

Income elasticity measures the response of the quantity demanded to a change in income. Economists use a formula to measure it:

$$\text{Income elasticity of demand} = \frac{\text{Proportionate change in quantity demanded}}{\text{Proportionate change in income}}$$

Theoretically this can vary between minus infinity and plus infinity. Most products show a modest increase in demand as income rises. This gives an income elasticity between zero and unity. Thus income may rise by, say, 5 per cent and the demand for bacon might rise by 2 per cent giving a measurement of 0.4. Bacon producers could, therefore, expect a slowly expanding demand as society became richer. Many products or services, mainly in the leisure fields, such as sports equipment, restaurant meals or foreign travel show a positive income elasticity above unity. Thus a rise of 5 per cent in income might produce an 8 per cent increase in demand for foreign travel, skis or restaurant meals, giving a measurement of 1.6 per cent. In contrast, there are many foods where a 5 per cent increase in income may be followed by a decrease in demand as people shift their consumption to higher-priced, higher protein content, foods. Hence a rise in income of 5 per cent may be followed by a decline in demand for potatoes, sliced white bread, offal and cheaper cuts of meat. The post-1950s' decline in demand for bread and potatoes can be explained in terms of the negative income elasticity of demand. This has had a profound influence on agriculture in terms of incomes and patterns of production. We are, of course, talking in aggregate rather than individual terms and with reference to Europe, North America and higher-income countries. In most low-income countries an increase in income is reflected fully in increased demand for basic foodstuffs, but even there a greater proportion of income may be spent on widening the variety of foods consumed.

The nature of the income elasticity of demand for food products in Europe has led to shifts in the pattern of production. There is greater emphasis on meat production of all types, on dairy products and on fruit and horticultural products, while there has been a relative decline in demand for basic arable crops except as animal feed. As will be seen below, the implementation of the CAP has accelerated some of these changes and delayed others. The food processing industry is fully aware of the implications of income elasticity and, with an eye on its profits, has concentrated on products which reflect a higher-income elasticity. The relationship between the grower and the food processor has sometimes tended to become one of servant and master. Many farmers have avoided this risk by creating their own cleaning, packaging and branding systems, often in a producers' cooperative.

In terms of conventional price theory the nature of income elasticity of demand for food means that the demand curve is only slowly shifting to the right as incomes and population increase. Indeed, for individual products, the demand curve may be shifting to the left.

Another major problem for farmers, food processors and policy makers is that the demand for most foods is price inelastic although the degree of inelasticity differs enormously between products. Price elasticity is a measure of the responsiveness of demand to a small proportionate change in price. A simple formula for measuring it is:

$$\text{Price elasticity of demand} = \frac{\text{Proportionate change in quantity demanded}}{\text{Proportionate change in price}}$$

If the quantity changes proportionately more than the change in price, then demand is said to be elastic. This usually means that there are close substitutes at existing market prices.

If the quantity changes less than proportionately compared with the price change then the demand is said to be inelastic. This usually indicates a lack of close substitutes or that the product has a very low price in relation to the average income, or that its purchase is habitual. Looked at from a seller's point of view, an elastic demand means that total revenue (price times quantity sold) from sales will decline as price rises and increase as price falls. Alternatively an inelastic demand means that the total revenue from sales will increase as price rises and decrease as price falls. These statements are generalisations because price elasticity will, under normal conditions, vary considerably at different price levels. Thus the consequences of agricultural price changes on farmers' revenues will depend, to some extent, on the original price from which the movement occurs. Frequently, a price fall (assuming no state intervention) is the result of increases in supply rather than of any long-term decrease in demand. This creates a tendency to surpluses whose existence exerts a downward pressure on price. If the demand for the farmers' produce is price inelastic the price reduction does not call forth a commensurately larger demand. This is because we have a physical limitation on our consumption of food. There may, however, be a shift in the pattern of consumption. The overall result of increased output and price inelasticity of demand will, therefore, be a reduction in revenues from sales. This does not necessarily mean that profits fall, because production costs may have fallen faster than revenues. Often, however, farmers' incomes have fallen in years of good harvests and risen in years of bad harvests. These general points about the effects of relative inelasticity of demand and supply on price can be seen in Figure 5.3.

It is a reasonable conclusion then that a free market in farm products will be a rapidly fluctuating market with periodic short-ages and gluts. This fact is illustrated by recent experience in the pig and poultry industries, neither of which receives CAP subsidies or price support. Prices will be unstable and employment will be uncertain and there will be a greater risk of political instability. This is borne out by the history of agriculture in pre-intervention days. The destabilising forces are very strong indeed. They are income and price inelasticity of demand (with qualifications), the nature of the 'pig cycle' and the psychological reactions of farmers to falling incomes. It should be borne in mind also that agriculture is a very large consumer of capital goods in the form of buildings, machinery, raw materials and of items such as energy, fuel and chemicals. Reverses in agricultural prosperity have a severe knock-on effect. In recent periods of rising unemployment, the existence of a healthy farm sector has worked as a very welcome automatic

FIGURE 5.3

Effects of Relative Inelasticity of Demand and Supply on Price

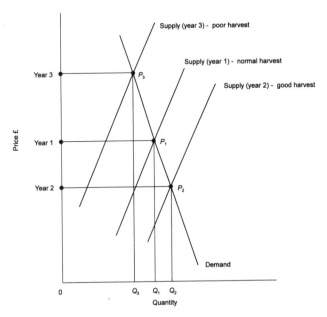

The steep gradient of the curves illustrates the relative inelasticity of supply and demand conditions for this agricultural commodity. Relatively small changes in output produce disproportionately large changes in price.

The figure also illustrates the change in revenue from the sales of this product over the three years. Compare the three rectangles of selling prices multiplied by the quantities $0Q_1$, $0Q_2$, $0Q_3$ in the years 1, 2 and 3.

stabiliser, preventing an even greater variation in employment, incomes, and government revenues and expenditure. There is no doubt that an agricultural price support policy is essential in a modern state. On the whole, in its early years, the CAP proved to be an extremely effective and efficient policy. Latterly its effectiveness was reduced as politicians postponed the difficult, or politically unpopular, decisions required to keep it in line with developing trends. Its great weakness, however, has been its tendency to produce surpluses of some products, which has proved particularly undesirable in a world where famine and malnutrition are endemic.

It is no good telling people that it is simply a problem of distribution – they see it as a moral problem. The evidence is that European Union governments responded to the criticism by trying to eliminate the surpluses, not by redistributing them. The other main criticism of the CAP has been in relation to developing countries. The CAP system of export subsidies has adversely affected their overseas markets and has reduced their sales and incomes. In addition, the external tariff around the Community reduces imports from the developing countries, despite various agreements such as the Lomé agreement, aimed at reducing its impact. The Uruguay round of GATT talks which collapsed in 1990, resumed in 1991 and 1992 and reached agreement in December 1993, focused, among other things, on this aspect of the CAP. From July 1995 the Union began cutting the volume and value of subsidised exports, tariffs and tariff equivalents, in six annual instalments.

Why have the Surpluses Occurred?

It is obvious that some surplus is usually desirable in order to guard against poor harvests or natural disasters, but by 1987 there were unacceptably large quantities of several products in store in the Community. By 1989, several of these excessive surpluses had been eliminated, although some had returned again by 1991. After the 1992 MacSharry reforms of the CAP, most of the excessive surpluses disappeared by 1995 and some stocks fell below the level regarded as prudent. The main products in surplus were grains of various kinds, especially wheat and barley, beef, dairy products such as butter and skimmed milk powder, wine and vegetable oils. These stores of produce were very expensive to maintain and were sometimes disposed of in controversial ways, such as in sales of butter to the USSR at very low prices, or in the cheap distribution of beef and butter to pensioners or institutions. In the United Kingdom the system of distribution via voluntary agencies sometimes led to unseemly scuffles as pensioners and benefit recipients tried to get their share. In financial terms the surpluses were a great drain on resources and imposed an excessive burden on the consumer. The impact varied from country to country. The seemingly bottomless pit of expenditure on agricultu-

FIGURE 5.4

A Simplified Illustration of a 'Buffer Stock' System in Operation

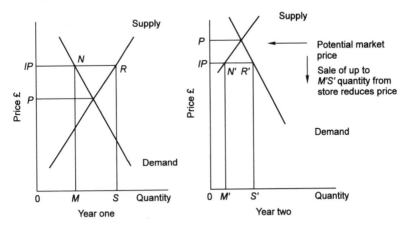

Year one   *Year two*

Year One

Supply exceeds demand at the proposed intervention price (*IP*) so the market price would settle at *P*, which is below the intervention price *IP* guaranteed to the producer by the government, EC, or commodity agreement. The relevant authority buys up enough of the surplus to keep the price up to *IP*. This 'costs' the rectangle *MNRS*, that is the price *IP* times the amount bought, *MS*. Effective demand at the price *IP* is being created by the purchases.

Year Two or some future year

Demand exceeds supply at the intervention price (*IP*), perhaps because of a poor harvest. Thus the free market price (*0P*) without intervention would be above the price guaranteed to the producer, so the authority releases quantities of the product from store. Releasing the quantity *M'S'* would keep the price down to the intervention price. Releasing a smaller quantity would create a price around the target price for the commodity.

NB The CAP intervention system has a target price above the intervention price, which is based on producers' costs. The intervention price is, therefore, a 'floor' price which the producer is certain of getting *if* his product is of the correct quality. Intervention may be restricted to certain quantities.

ral support was the cause of most of the budgetary problems of the Community.

Once the nettle of controlling agricultural price support was grasped, however, the budget problem altered. Indeed, in 1988–89 the Community moved into a budget surplus for the first time. Figure 5.4 shows the principle behind the operation of stock purchases and sales. These are frequently called 'buffer' stocks although some economists argue that true buffer stocks are deliberately accumulated with the intention of selling them during periods of scarcity. Except in the very early days, until 1994–95, European Union intervention stocks were not used to keep prices down in periods of shortage. Table 5.1 shows commodity intervention in action in the United Kingdom for feed wheat and barley in 1993–94 and 1994–95.

TABLE 5.1
Commodity Intervention in the United Kingdom: An Example

'000 tonnes	1993–94			1994–95 forecast			
	*Closing/ opening stock**	*Purchases*	*Sales*	*Closing/ opening stock*	*Purchases*	*Sales*	*Closing stock**
Feed wheat	15	277	—	292	52	279	65
Barley	835	690	246	1286	119	684	720

*The figures, closing/opening stock = opening stock plus purchases = sales, may not always equate because of rounding and stock adjustments as orders from previous years are fulfilled

SOURCE Adapted from *Agriculture in the United Kingdom 1994* (London: HMSO, 1995)

The main cause of the ever-growing surpluses lay in the method of setting prices for products. This method varied between products but usually involved setting a target price which would provide a reasonable return for the farmer in an area where the product was a marginal one – that is, where in some years profits were made and in others losses. The idea was to keep such marginal producers in being by giving them a market price that was certain. In order to achieve something like this target price it was necessary to fix an intervention price which was effectively a floor price, somewhere near, but below, the target price. If the producer could not obtain a price better than the intervention price the product could be sold, if its quality were acceptable, to an intervention board at the intervention price. The board would then store the product and hope to release it onto the market if the market price ever rose above the target price. In theory, therefore, prices would not normally ever fall below the intervention price or rise above the target price for long.

There were, in addition, various rebates or subsidies to exports of some food. There was also an external tariff or levy which, according to a complex sliding scale, 'taxed' imports in order to raise their price, together with transport costs from the ports to the market, to prevailing market levels or above the target price. Since the United Kingdom was a larger importer of food than its fellow members, particularly of American hard wheat, it appeared to contribute excessively to these levies. The general effect of the pricing system was, and is, to place the burden of agricultural support on the consumer in the form of higher prices. This, it may be argued, is not good in terms of the high burden on lower-income groups. There are widely differing estimates of the cost of the policy. The system of import levies and export rebates will be phased out under the Uruguay Round Agreement from 1995 onwards.

The detail of the price support system differs enormously from product to product. These details, and the way in which the regulations are interpreted by the Commission bureaucracy and by national governments, matter a very great deal to the individual producer. Until 1987–88, however, the general effect, in which we are interested, was to encourage marginal farmers to continue in production on a regular basis. This was the intention and helped to maintain prosperity in some regions. The other general effect was to encourage non-marginal farmers to produce more, and for the most efficient to invest large capital sums in expanding output. For many of these farmers the intervention price guaranteed a very healthy profit per unit of output. In pursuit of profit maximisation, they did all the things which now outrage conservationists and created joy among the manufacturers of machinery, chemicals and fertilisers. Banks joined in the fun by lending large quantities of money to farmers. Their lending was safe because of the guaranteed prices of the products. The ownership of land became a desirable investment for institutions such as pensions funds because high agricultural prices enable farmers to pay high rents for leased land. This is Ricardo's theory of rent in operation. To quote the old examination question 'rent is price determined' (see Figure 5.5). Figure 5.5 near here

The quest for higher profits from the expansion of output has been accompanied by technological changes which have also generated extra output. These changes have taken many forms. There have been outstanding improvements in productivity from new

---

FIGURE 5.5
Rent is Price-Determined

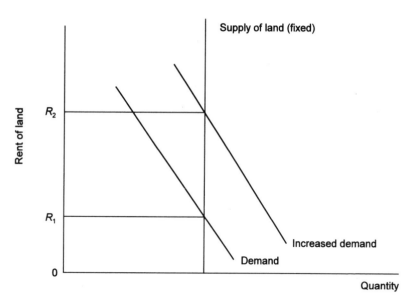

The demand for the product of the land determines the rent paid for the land if it is assumed that land is fixed in supply. If the demand for the product grown on the land, and therefore the product's price, rises then the rent of the land will also rise. The assumption is that the land user can afford to pay more for the land when prices are higher. This assumes that costs remain the same or rise less than the rise in price of the product. It should be remembered that the demand for land is what economists call a 'derived demand'; that is to say, it is derived from the demand for the product of the land whether it be turnips, wheat or office space.

varieties of arable crops, from the introduction of new breeds of animals and from the adoption of better techniques of animal husbandry. There have also been new fertilisers, better pesticides, improved veterinary practices and medicines. All this has been accompanied by larger, quicker, more versatile and more specialised machinery. There have been notable improvements in buildings and plant as well. The costs of applying these new methods and equipment have been a spur to the creation of larger farm holdings.

The central criticism of the CAP before the reforms of 1992 was that the system supported prices and therefore encouraged overproduction rather than supporting the incomes of producers directly. The 1992 agreement has seen a partial shift away from market support towards direct payments to producers. The details of the changes are dealt with later in this chapter.

The EAGGF

The European Agricultural Guidance and Guarantee Fund (EAGGF) is divided into two parts. The Guarantee part creates the market and price structures needed to maintain and raise farmers' incomes. The Guidance section, which has undergone several transformations since it began, is aimed at financing the restructuring of agriculture and helping the less favoured regions. The fund usually provides about 25 per cent of the cost with the remainder coming from the national governments. It has had most impact in France and Germany but is having an increasing, and much criticised, impact in the newer member countries such as Spain, Portugal and Greece. The trend towards larger holdings has been encouraged by this Guidance part of the CAP. It has given financial rewards to hundreds of thousands of small farmers as an encouragement to leave the industry or to alter their production patterns. The land of those giving up farming has usually been swallowed up into larger holdings. The trend to greater output has also been helped by direct subsidies from governments to farmers who wish to drain, plough, build, improve and modernise fields and buildings.

The nature and extent of these improvement grants has altered considerably over the years depending on what the government and Commission have seen as priorities. One of their main uses has been to give direct financial assistance to Less Favoured Areas (LFAs), or special cases such as hill farmers. In 1991 LFAs constituted about 55 per cent of the twelve members' Utilised Agricultural Area (UAA). LFAs are mountain areas, areas threatened by depopulation and areas with specific natural handicaps (see Table 5.2 for details). Since this is an extremely complex field the interested reader should consult *Green Europe 2/93* 'Support for Farms in Mountain, Hill and Less favoured Areas', Office for Official Publications of the European Communities (Luxembourg, 1993, ISSN 1012 2117). In their very nature, however, many of the grants are also available to big 'agri-businesses'. Such grants are partly responsible for the disappearance of traditional meadowland, the ploughing of downland, the grubbing up of hedges, the reclamation of moorland, the drainage of wetlands and the sprouting of industrialised farm buildings. An alternative viewpoint is that they have helped to keep the hill farmer in place, thus maintaining the essential character of what is, in reality, a man-made landscape. They have, it is argued, contributed to the maintenance of the economic and social quality of life in the mountains, hills and border lands.

Other Reasons for Oversupply

Oversupply sometimes originates in the close production relationships of products or in what economists call 'joint-supply'. There is, for example, a direct relationship between an increased demand for dairy products such as butter, cheeses, cream and yoghurt, and the output of skimmed milk and beef. As incomes and population rise there is a greater demand for dairy products; therefore, more milk must be produced. This can be achieved up to a point by feeding cows with better food (adding to costs) and by improved technical efficiency. But it can also be done by keeping more cows which will normally have a calf each year in order to maintain their milking capacity and to produce a valuable 'by-product'. The extra calves are either kept as future milking cows, or for beef, or slaughtered for veal, depending partly on their breeding sire. In practice, of course, a mixture of improved productivity and an increased number of cows is employed. The end result of the attempt to produce more milk for dairy products is the probable output of more beef, although this may not be a problem if the increased population and income also create a greater demand for beef products. It does, however, present problems for farmers who need to feed, house and market the beef cattle because that requires land for growing feed, and, probably, an increased import of animal feed.

TABLE 5.2
Classified Agricultural Areas, 1991

Directive 75/268	*Less-Favoured Areas (LFA) 1991*				*Hectares*	
				Total	*Total*	*%*
	(1)	*(2)*	*(3)*	*LFA (4)*	*(4)*	
Belgium	—	314 400	—	314 400	1 438 000	21.9%
Denmark	—	—	—	—	2 888 000	0.0%
Germany (5)	351 500	5 981 800	201 200	6 534 500	12 196 000	53.6%
New Länder (6)	—	—	—	—	6 562 000	—
Greece	4 978 800	2 007 500	259 500	7 245 800	9 251 000	78.3%
Spain	6 507 800	11 219 000	700 300	18 427 100	27 304 000	67.5%
France	4 475 800	8 804 000	728 700	14 008 500	31 069 000	45.1%
Ireland	—	4 058 000	16 700	4 074 700	5 705 000	71.4%
Italy	5 218 100	3 300 700	217 500	8 736 300	16 826 000	51.9%
Luxembourg	—	123 700	3 100	126 800	128 100	99.0%
Netherland	—	—	48 200	48 200	2 018 000	2.4%
Portugal	854 600	2 274 400	183 100	3 312 100	4 380 000	75.6%
United Kingdom	—	9 894 100	700	9 894 800	18 795 000	52.6%
EUR 12 (5)	22 386 600	47 977 600	2 359 000	72 723 200	131 998 100	55.1%

(1) Mountain areas
(2) Areas threatened by depopulation
(3) Areas with specific handicaps
(4) UAA as defined by EUROSTATS + local plots made available
(5) Before 3 October 1990
(6) A request for classification of about 3 million hectares is being examined

SOURCE *Green Europe 2/93* 'Support for Farms in Mountain, Hill and Less-Favoured Areas' (Luxembourg: Office for Official Publications of the European Communities, 1993)

An alternative policy is the early slaughtering of animals but that tends to reduce their market value and may present problems to the

intervention boards. The argument can have a different line if one
starts from a situation of an increased demand for beef which may
then create excess milk production, depending on how the industry
reacts in using the milk of the cows which bear the calves. One
consequence of the joint supply aspect of milk and beef production
is the dispute over the export from the United Kingdom of calves
to continental countries where they are sometimes processed to
produce veal by methods that are banned in the UK.

Most of the above discussion about the causes of overproduction
has been in the context of traditional northern European products
such as grain, meat and dairy produce. There has also been a major
difficulty with products such as wine, tobacco, olive oil and vegetable oils and some fruit and horticultural output.

How have the Surpluses been Dealt With?

Initially the surpluses were no real worry since they acted as a
traditional buffer stock against future shortages. It was, and remains sensible, to have some surplus. The surplus of output over
consumption of cereals, excluding rice, began in 1980–81. It became
excessive in 1982–83, declined in 1983–84 and became exorbitantly
high in 1984–85 but from then until 1989 it was controlled to
reasonable levels. After 1989 the problem returned. Butter surpluses
of output over consumption began in 1975–76 and reached a peak
in 1983. This coincided with a peak yield for dairy cows and a low
level of consumption as diet conscious and unemployed people
shifted their purchases to non-milk fats. The actual stocks in
intervention stores did not move exactly in line with excess output.
They reached a peak in 1986 but fell temporarily in response to the
introduction of quotas on milk output. The wine 'lake' grew steadily
as output expanded and consumption of ordinary wine declined.
Consumption of wine in Europe fell from an annual average of 50
litres per head in the early 1970s, to below 40 litres in the early
1990s. By 1994, the European Union's surplus of wine was about 35
million hectolitres or about one-fifth of annual output.

The methods of dealing with surpluses up to 1991 varied with the
product but some general attempts were made. There was, for
example, the belief that paying small farmers to give up farming
would reduce the output of some food, especially in France and

West Germany. It did sometimes have this effect but the long-term result was often to increase output, as land which had been inefficiently farmed came into the hands of larger, more efficient farmers. As self-sufficiency has been achieved in some products another general approach has been to encourage the export of food by the use of rebates. These are of great complexity and caused much international disquiet. The USA regarded them as a breach of the General Agreement on Tariffs and Trade. They were a major cause of delays in reaching agreement in the Uruguay Round of GATT talks and their gradual withdrawal had already caused problems in mid-1995. They will probably continue to be a problem for the World Trade Organisation (WTO) that replaced GATT in 1995. Countries such as Australia and New Zealand saw them as creating unfair competition for their products in markets such as Japan. Development economists attacked them for creating unfair competition for indigenous producers in developing countries. They were also, allegedly, a gold-mine for fiddlers, twisters and cheats of all descriptions, or for those who understood and could exploit loopholes in the regulations.

Another method adopted to cut the amounts in intervention stores has been the direct sale, in large quantities, of products such as beef, butter and sugar to the Soviet Union and the Commonwealth of Independent States. The prices obtained for these bulk sales have often been exceptionally low. They are items which are supposed to have been close to the end of their storage life and any revenue is regarded as beneficial, as is the reduced cost of storage. These sales are politically unpopular. Akin to them are 'gifts' of food to famine-stricken countries. The gift of skimmed milk to impoverished people has been criticised on the grounds that it is harmful to young children because it lacks essential nutrients and requires hygienic preparation. This, it is said, is not always emphasised or possible.

One major device for using intervention stocks has been to make them available to institutions at low prices. These include the armed forces, and non-profit-making bodies such as hospitals, residential homes, and higher education establishments. The assumption is that the demand for these products in the normal, high-priced market, is not affected by the offer of low prices for bulk purchase to these bodies. In effect, the intervention board is taking advantage of the differing price elasticities of demand in the two markets – that is, the higher elasticity in the institutional market. This is a form of price discrimination. Similar schemes have been aimed at pensioners in distributing beef and butter. An unusual version of this made cheap butter available to all consumers for a short period in 1987. All these schemes have to be used very carefully in order not to destroy the existing orderly market for the product.

The methods mentioned so far failed to attack the basic problem of overproduction and its causes. There was a marked reluctance to tackle the issue by reducing target and intervention prices because of the political ramifications. It would probably not have cut output very much because of the tendency, explained above, of farmers raising output as prices fall in order to maintain their income levels. The most effective technique, therefore, was to impose quotas on output. A quota is a fixed, legally enforceable limit on the output of a product from each production unit. Quotas were applied to milk in 1984 and they were strengthened in 1986. Despite the enormous political furore and the great hardship imposed in an arbitrary fashion on many farmers, the quotas have been very successful. Indeed, in the United Kingdom in 1994–95 there was a shortage of milk for manufacturers. The subsequent rise in price, aggravated by the abolition of the Milk Marketing Board, forced some smaller cheese makers out of business and stimulated the import of milk. United Kingdom farmers felt particularly ill used by the imposition of quotas, with some justification, because they were the most efficient. Thousands of dairy farmers have gone out of production and the milk quota has become a saleable and transferable financial asset within one country. In 1995 a campaign started to enable quotas to be sold across national boundaries. The quota system, accompanied by 'fines', penalties or levies for over-production, and a gradually imposed price restraint, removed most of the milk product surpluses. There have since been several modifications to the system to make it fairer and less arbitrary and to prevent a return of the surpluses.

The methods used to cut surpluses of grain were also successful initially. They began with a 'coresponsibility levy' on output. This was, in effect, a tax on output and was therefore in direct conflict with the price support principles of the CAP. It was varied and fell most heavily on large-scale producers. The levy was phased out in 1993 after reform of the CAP. Then, in 1988–89, an upper limit, called a 'maximum guaranteed quantity' (MGQ), was placed on the total output quantity on which the intervention prices were payable.

(This was similar to the United Kingdom system that existed before 1972, that limited the financial commitment of the government to a certain preordained volume of output.) Beyond this quantity the producers had no guaranteed price or sale. Moreover, if the MGQ was exceeded intervention prices were cut by three per cent in the following marketing year. The checks on quality were also tightened so that intervention prices became more related to quality. In addition, intervention buying for cereals and oilseeds was and still is restricted to months outside the normal harvest period. This forced producers to look harder for buyers in the market before offering their cereals for intervention buying. Some were in the habit of selling their harvest directly into intervention without bothering to look elsewhere.

Thus, with milk and cereals, the Community managed to get away from the stranglehold of unrestricted price guarantees. It can now limit the guarantee to a predetermined amount and can affect the price received by the farmer by penalties and pre-announced price cuts. The problem of surplus output of oilseeds was tackled by fixing a MGQ which, if exceeded, triggered a reduction in the market support prices and, presumably, a cutback in production in the following year. This system was changed from 1993–94. There is now no guaranteed price but instead there is financial aid per hectare fixed at European Union level, and then regionalised to take account of average historic yields. The aid is adjustable to take account of world oilseed prices.

Several other minor attempts at dissolving surpluses have been made. Some of them have been marginally effective whilst others have been ludicrously expensive to implement. For example, wine growers have been paid to destroy vines. This has been worthwhile. Spain, for example, uprooted 170 000 hectares of sherry and wine vineyards between 1987 and the end of 1994. Schemes which turned excess wine into industrial alcohol and into a petrol substitute for export to the USA and another to turn butter into a condensed cooking fat, were extremely expensive. Yet another scheme feeds surplus skimmed milk products back to cattle. Butterfats can be disposed of at a subsidised price to manufacturers of pastry products and ice cream or to recipients of social assistance. Milk can also be distributed to schoolchildren at a subsidised price.

Eventually, in 1986, the Community adopted a version of a policy that was first adopted in the USA in the 1930s, which consisted of paying farmers to leave land fallow. The European scheme is called 'set-aside' and was more complicated, sophisticated or cumbersome according to your viewpoint. The 1986 scheme was voluntary. In return for a cash payment per year, farmers undertook to remove a percentage of their land from the cultivation of certain arable crops. The policy was accompanied by inducements for what is called 'extensification', broadening the use of land into a greater variety of crops and into non-agricultural uses and adopting lower stocking levels. The environmental lobby had high hopes that set-aside would be a stimulus to reafforestation with broad-leaved trees and to the establishment of new footpaths, bridleways and recreational areas. This has happened to some extent. However, American experience does not give much cause for optimism about the long-term effectiveness of set-aside and in 1995 the US government reduced it to zero. In the United States there were massive improvements in productivity from the land that remained in cultivation, and the result was that overproduction reappeared. In the United Kingdom the risk of this happening was somewhat reduced by the removal of fertiliser subsidies and various land improvement grants.

All these policies, taken together, were initially effective in removing the excessively large intervention stocks, although the take up of set-aside and the degree of extensification were disappointingly low and therefore not a major contributor to the reduction. Consequently, the financial burden of the CAP was lightened and the Community budget was in surplus in 1988–89. The food surpluses began to reappear in 1990 and gave added impetus to the demands for a major reform of the CAP.

Reform Proposals

In early 1991 the Commission published what it called a 'reflection paper' stating its position on fundamental reform of the CAP. This was done against a background of the breakdown, mainly on the issue of the Community's agricultural policies, of the Uruguay Round of GATT talks. There had also been an unwelcome reappearance of large surplus stocks of beef, cereals, butter and skimmed milk in intervention stores. These stocks were well above the levels required for protection against sudden disasters. There was also the very uncomfortable fact that farmers' incomes were falling rapidly whilst record amounts of money were being spent on the CAP. These reflections became known as the MacSharry reforms after the Agricultural Commissioner who introduced them. Table 5.3 gives a statistical background to the reforms.

TABLE 5.3
The Statistical Background to Agricultural Reforms

Total area and utilized agricultural area (in 1000 km^2) 1989–90 and 1993

	B	DK	D	GR	E	F	IRL	I	L	NL	P	UK	EUR 12
1. Total area	31	43	357	132	505	544	69	301	3	42	92	244	2 363
2. UAA 1989/90	13	28	118	37	245	286	44	149	1	20	40	165	1 146
3. UAA 1993	14	30	171	57	264	304	44	172	1	20	45	178	1 300

Trade 1991

	EUR 12	B/L	DK	D	GR	E	F	IRL	I	NL	P	UK
Imports	11.5	9.8	17.1	8.9	12.3	18.3	10.4	8.0	13.8	13.7	26.2	10.6
Exports	8.5	6.7	23.7	4.2	28.3	15.6	11.3	20.2	5.6	20.0	12.3	7.1
Balance of trade in agricultural produce and foodstuffs (ECU billion)	−20.8	−1.4	1.1	−6.5	−0.1	−2.7	0.2	0.6	−5.3	−1.2	−1.1	−4.2

Structure of agricultural holdings (1990)

	EUR 12	B	DK	D	GR	E	F	IRL	I	L	NL	P	UK
Number of holdings (x 1000)	8 168	85	81	665	923	1 593	1014	171	2 664	4	125	599	243
Average UAA (in ha)	−14.0	15.8	34.2	17.7	4.0	15.4	28.2	26.0	5.6	32.1	16.1	6.7	67.9

Agriculture in the economy (%)

	EUR 12	B	DK	D	GR	E	F	IRL	I	L	NL	P	UK
Employment (1991)	6.2	2.7	5.5	3.4	21.6	10.7	5.4	13.8	8.5	3.1	4.5	17.5	2.2

Table 5.3 *Continued*

Gross
value-added

| (1990) | 2.9 | 2.0 | 4.7 | 1.6 | 15.7 | 4.8 | 3.7 | 8.6 | 3.4 | 2.1 | 4.7 | 6.3 | 1.2 |

% Annual rate of change in the agricultural labour force in 'annual work units'

	B	DK	$D(^1)$	GR	E	F	IRL	I	L	NL	P	UK	EUR $12(^1)$
1993/1992	−2.6	−2.6	−7.8	−2.3	−8.7	−5.6	−2.0	−6.9	−2.4	−1.1	−2.4	−0.7	−5.4
1994/1993	−2.6	−2.0	−7.0	−3.1	−2.8	−3.4	−5.0	−0.5	−4.5	−2.6	0.0	−2.1	−2.5

(^{1}) Figures include new German *Länder*

SOURCE *Supplement – Frontier-free Europe*, No. 4–1995 No. 2–1994 (European Commission: Office for Official Publications of the European Communities)

The proposals were aimed at bringing the markets back into balance and controlling surplus production whilst maintaining rural communities and protecting the environment. Their general thrust was to cut guaranteed prices across a wide range of products and to compensate farmers with 'income aid'. The reforms were bitterly debated but eventually agreed with many amendments in June 1992. Many of the changes were first implemented in the 1993–94 marketing year. In the cereals sector, for example, the payment of the aid is per hectare, fixed annually in relation to market prices, and in relation to the size of the holding. Beyond a certain size of holding the payment is dependent upon the farmer withdrawing a proportion of arable land from production. This land can be used for non-food production (human or animal) except that field peas for human consumption can be grown. For example, oil seed for manufacturing purposes can be grown on set-aside. The coresponsibility levies on cereals and milk, which were effectively a sliding-scale tax on producers, have been abolished. In the livestock sector there is also direct income support through a system of premium payments for certain types of producers as in the present hill farming areas. Any farmer who adopts 'extensification' by, for example, reducing the number of animals per hectare, receives compensation. For other products the proposals included a mixture of price controls, direct income support and set-aside and, in the case of milk, reduced output quotas. There is, in addition, direct income support for using environmentally sound methods, together with a long-term set-aside programme aimed at encouraging forestry and protecting the rural environment. A revised programme called a pre-pension scheme, to recompense farmers for early retirement, was incorporated in the plan. Reform of wine, fruit and vegetable markets was not included.

The proposals were modified and adopted by the Commission in mid-1991, but received a very mixed reception ranging from the lukewarm to outright rejection. There were exceptionally tough bargaining sessions before a policy acceptable to all the member states was arrived at. The major obstacle to overcome was that of accepting the idea that large numbers of farmers should be paid considerable sums of money to do nothing. The idea might catch on among other groups! It is a concept that is wrapped up in images of farmers being paid to conserve the rural environment or maintaining the fabric of the countryside, but it is still hard for politicians to sell the idea to urban voters who may justly feel that they are being discriminated against and, to add insult to injury, that they are paying over the odds (that is the world market price) for their food. In order to make the politicians' task easier the proposals were intended to reduce European food prices by about 10 per cent over the years from 1993 to 1997.

The proposals eventually adopted in May 1992 were a modified version of the 1991 scheme. The proposed reforms provoked riots among French farmers but were generally welcomed because they made an agreement on the Uruguay Round of GATT talks more likely. The trauma of the negotiations on agricultural policy led to renewed demands that the quest for a *common* policy be abandoned and for each country to return to having its own national policy. This reversion to an earlier age is probably impossible now that the internal free market without barriers is largely accomplished after 1992, although it may be feasible for small sections of the policy to be hived off to national governments. Examples might be sheep or tobacco, or olives. The entry of Finland and Sweden has created another area of what is effectively national agricultural policy, that is special aid for farmers in Arctic areas. We can be reasonably certain that any common policy that is adopted will be full of compromises to meet individual nations' internal political pressures, that it will need a major overhaul within a few years, and that the necessary decisions for change will be delayed until the last minute or until the breakdown of the system is imminent.

How Successful have the 1992 Reforms been?

The reforms have been successful, according to the Commission in early 1995, in the main areas of cereals, beef, milk and milk produce, and oil seeds. 1993 saw a period of uncertainty, instability and income reductions for farmers, but 1994 produced stabilisation of prices as well as increases in real incomes. Cereal stocks, for example, fell from 33 million to 25 million tonnes during the 1994–95 marketing year. Beef and veal stocks fell from 1.7 million tonnes in 1992 to 40 000 tonnes in February 1995 because of falling production and expanding exports. The beef stocks at the end of 1994 were at an historic low.

The overall effect of the reforms so far has been to keep the agricultural budget within its designated bounds. The 1995 budget of ECU 36.7 billion, including almost ECU 1 billion for the enlargement to fifteen members, was ECU 1 billion less than the guide-line. The budget has been helped to a small extent by measures against fraud. These include the use of satellite sensing of what crops are being grown and comparing the results with what farmers say they are growing and for which they are claiming subsidy. Italy, for example, claimed subsidies for 4.2 million acres of durum wheat but the satellite revealed that only 1.9 million acres had been planted. Southern Europe, especially Greece, appeared to have a large number of phantom olive trees.

The operation of set-aside has revealed many technical and psychological problems. Most farmers do not like being paid for not working and do not like being told what to do with their land, although a few have stopped arable farming and income compensation has become their main source of income. They also object to the paperwork and expense involved in preparing their annual farm plans.

The scheme introduced in 1992 to compensate for a reduction of the price of cereals over three years is as follows:

	ECU per tonne	
	Target price	*Intervention price*
1993–94	130	117
1994–95	120	108
1995–96	110	100

The Threshold Price, on which levies on imports are based, is ECU 45 above the target price. The intervention and threshold prices are subject to seven monthly increases from November to May, that is the period to which intervention buying is limited, in order to keep supply in line with demand.

The amount of compensatory payment is fixed per hectare and is determined on the basis of a regional base area which is defined as 'the average number of hectares within a region sown to arable crops or set-aside (under the old five-year schemes) during 1989, 1990 and 1991'. Each member state determines the base area for each region and that determination can have important practical effects. Members may opt to apply a base-area system for each producer. It is also necessary to calculate yields for these production regions. In effect, the farmer is being paid compensation for the profit on the crops that would have been grown on the set-aside land. The compensatory payment was fixed as follows for cereals:

1993–94	ECU 25 per tonne	multiplied by the cereal yield calculation.
1994–95	ECU 35 per tonne	.. ..
1995–96	ECU 45 per tonne	.. ..

Farmers may choose not to take part in either of the two set-aside schemes. The first is called the 'General Scheme' and, when it first began, involved a compulsory rotational set-aside of 15 per cent of the base area for those producing more than 92 tonnes of cereals. The second scheme is called a 'Simplified Scheme' aimed at the smaller producers of less than 92 tonnes who receive a compensatory payment at the rate applicable for cereals for all areas sown to arable crops. The previously existing five-year set-aside system has been phased out. Areas under permanent pasture, permanent crops or non-food crops at the end of 1991 are not eligible for set-aside. Land that is set aside cannot be used to grow food for humans or animals, except field peas, but it can be used to grow certain crops such as oilseed for manufacturing purposes.

It is difficult to assess the success of the set-aside policy because there have also been shifts in world supply and demand for cereals. There has, however, been such a large reduction in intervention buying and in the stocks in intervention stores that the figure for compulsory set-aside for the year 1994–95 was reduced from 15 to

12 per cent, and flexible set-aside from 18 to 15 per cent. The Commission proposed a reduction from 12 to 10 per cent for rotational set-aside for the 1996–97 harvest year but the Council decided on a 10 per cent level for all set-aside. There are still discussions about a United Kingdom suggestion that land withdrawn from arable production for tree planting and for environmental reasons should count towards a producer's basic set-aside obligation.

It is not possible to attribute the whole of the improvements to the reforms. Other external factors such as increased trade, higher world prices and developing markets in Central and Eastern Europe have contributed to the improvement. The new system of regulation of agricultural markets is exceptionally complex with a variety of methods applied to different products. Even an outline of the system, 'The New Regulation of the Agricultural Markets 1/93' published by the European Commission, is 120 pages long. There are, for example, 42 varieties of raw tobacco grown in the European Union and it costs over ECU 1300 million or about 4 per cent of the agricultural budget to manage the market. The anti-smoking lobby is naturally greatly offended. 'Cereals' consists of common wheat, durum wheat, barley, rye, maize, oats, sorghum, millet, buckwheat and canary seed as well as the results of initial processing such as wheat flour, groats, meal, malt, potato and cereal starch or certain cereal substitutes such as manioc root. Given the complexity of the system, it is not surprising that it sometimes works very well, sometimes very badly and frequently lends itself to market distortions and to fraud.

Agrimonetary Compensation Mechanism

The development of the European Currency Unit (ECU) was important in enabling monetary compensatory amounts (MCAs) to be calculated and adjusted. These were payments introduced in 1971 for agricultural products as they crossed frontiers to compensate for changes in exchange rates or the adjustment in central rates in the days before 1979 when the European Monetary System was introduced. The aim was to stabilise agriculture prices but they never achieved that satisfactorily. In fact they created great opportunities for corruption and immense complexity in agricultural pricing. By 1988 there were 49 separate 'green rates' within 11 currencies. The system was extremely complicated and involved the calculation of a 'green' rate for each currency – hence talk of the 'green pound', or the 'green mark'. The whole system created great problems at the annual discussion of the level of agricultural support prices. There were positive and negative MCAs depending on the movement of currencies. MCAs were a large burden on the Community's budget. The balance between positive and negative MCAs constituted about 10 per cent of the expenditure on price guarantees.

In 1984–85 a new system for MCAs was adopted which aimed at the dismantling and eventual elimination of positive MCAs. Under the new system for compensatory payments the strongest currency with the highest revaluation rate (usually the Germen mark) was used as the basis for calculating the new 'green' rates. The pound sterling was not considered here because it did not participate in the Exchange Rate Mechanism of the European Monetary System until 1990–92. After March 1984 a green central rate was established, replacing the old EMS central rates for calculating MCAs. The creation of a green central rate was usually the equivalent of a 3.4 per cent revaluation of the ECU in the agricultural sector and raised the levies and refunds paid. It was decided that MCAs should be phased out, beginning in July 1987. By the end of 1991 they had almost gone and the process was to be completed by 1993 but it was not.

In 1995 the problem of agrimoney payments as they came to be called, became very serious because of the depreciation of the US dollar and the strength of the Deutschmark. Countries such as the United Kingdom and Italy which had sharply depreciating currencies benefited from the fact that prices under the CAP are denominated in ECUs. UK farmers enjoyed a rapid increase in real incomes as a result.

In February 1995 a new agrimonetary system for the CAP came into force. It ended the old system, called a switchover mechanism, that cushioned producers against currency changes. In 1994 the old system was estimated to have added, over the years, ECU 6 billion to European Union expenditure and raised prices by 20 per cent. The new system took account of a degree of currency fluctuation but did not revalue the green conversion rates used for agricultural prices. It was intended, for example, that a 20 per cent increase in

ECU prices would offset a 20 per cent lowering of the green rates. The reforms applied to price support but not to direct aid for structural changes under the guidance section of the EAGGF. More proposals for change were being discussed in May 1995 because the Commission was concerned that the changes introduced in early 1995 still contained a mini- switchover mechanism and might prove to be too expensive. For example, a 3 per cent revaluation of the green rate in 1995 would cost ECU 1000 million in 1996, and a permanent ECU 750 million a year after 1999.

What of the Future?

Demographic trends do not bode well for European agriculture. The population of the Union is expected to rise by 2 per cent from 1985 to 2005. The populations of the area of the old Federal republic of West Germany and that of Belgium are expected to fall. There may be extra growth in world markets because the world population is predicted to grow by 36 per cent in the same period. Some changes may arise as a result of the creation of the European Economic Area and from the creation of new democracies in Central and Eastern Europe but the effects may simply be to increase the supplies of food available. Embarrassing surpluses may return. One of the main reasons for further reform of the CAP is the likely entry of countries such as Poland that have very large agricultural sectors. It is reasonable to expect, therefore, that within the European Union there will be little expansion of total consumption of staples such as wheat for flour, potatoes and bulk vegetables. Patterns of consumption will continue to change if real incomes rise as anticipated. Allowing for fashions in diet, there will be a continued shift of demand to meat products, dairy products and higher-quality fruit, vegetables and horticultural products. Land use will respond to the need to feed more animals.

   In some areas, there will be a return to mixed farming and a shift away from monoculture. There is also likely to be an extension of afforestation and more land will be dedicated to recreational use of various sorts, including nature conservation areas. Moreover, there will be a continued drain of land into building development for housing and industry. This will be harder to oppose if the required level of food production can be achieved with a smaller area of land in cultivation. Some farmers will apply the benefits of the latest biotechnological developments in plant types, animal breeding and recycling of materials. Production of bio-mass, that is crops such as oilseed and sugar beet, for fuel as a petrol substitute has already begun on an experimental basis, for example in Austria. There is also an effort to encourage a return to wood production and coppicing for environmental, employment and energy reasons.

The Uruguay Round Agreements will have some impact on European Union agriculture. Studies published by the World Bank in April 1995 on the probable effects of the Uruguay Round on agricultural trade indicated that they would be considerably less than predicted because the reductions in tariff levels were based on the high levels prevailing between 1986 and 1988 rather than on the lower levels of 1994. The agreement requires all members to convert their agricultural trade barriers into tariffs which will then be reduced over a number of years. The studies also showed, contrary to many statements, that developing countries would gain more as a percentage of national income than developed countries. The gains from the agricultural agreements were estimated at $48 billion but would have been two and a half times more if the tariff reductions had been based on 1994–95 levels instead of 1986–88.

In the future, there are likely to be two major conflicting trends. On the one hand, there will be pressure to produce standardised, quality-controlled products for a mass market. This will be assisted by established grading and packaging standards which will be extended under the single European market. The continued growth of market share of the large multiple retailers will accelerate this trend. On the other hand, there will be a growing market for high-quality, organically produced food from those who are able to pay the inevitably higher prices. It is in this sphere that the smaller, more localised producer will flourish. There are some signs that even the large multiple retailers are beginning to realise that their customers prefer food that tastes good as well being cosmetically attractive. However, all these predictions will be invalidated if there is a major shift in climatic conditions over the next 20 years and if there is a major change to producing bio-fuel.

Economic Performance – Growth, Employment, Trade

6

Introduction

The measurement of economic performance is notoriously difficult and fraught with controversy. The comparison of the economic performance of two or more countries or trading blocs is even more problematical. European Union statistics are particularly difficult because of the unification of Germany and the frequent additions to membership. Most current statistics are for the 12 pre-1995 members with adjustments being made for the extra three when the 15 are being referred to. When it is eventually agreed what to measure and with what units there may still be disagreement about the relative merits of various aspects of performance. An analogy of the problem may be seen in the task of a motoring correspondent who has to draw up a comparison of a Mini and a high-performance sports car. You can measure, fairly objectively, top speed, acceleration, petrol consumption, luggage room, seats and maintenance costs, but many of these are dependent upon the operating context – urban, rural or motorway. A traffic jam on a motorway reduces them to temporary equality in most respects except the comfort of the seats and the quality of the 'in-car entertainment'. Similarly, two or more economies can be compared objectively but only up to a point. The context of the comparison and the base from which it is made then becomes of paramount importance.

Much of the emphasis of comparison of economic performance is upon rates of growth of various indices or absolute quantity. The implicit assumption is that all growth is good and that higher growth is better. This is, of course, nonsense because the costs of the growth to society may be excessive. It may reduce welfare, increase ill health, raise death rates and exploit developing countries. The growth may also be very unevenly distributed. The present fashion for market-driven economies tends to ignore these facts. Part of the argument about the policies to be implemented to achieve the single market was really about distribution of growth, although the main emphasis has been on overall growth. President Mitterrand of France and Jacques Delors, President of the Commission, were both quoted as not wanting a Europe for bankers only but for workers as well, hence their emphasis, and that of their successors, on the 'Social Charter'.

Having expressed all these doubts it remains necessary to attempt some assessment of relative economic performance. We should, however, bear in mind that we cannot know what might have happened if a particular country had not joined the Union. We should also remember, when making comparisons, that the European Union only partially determines or influences the environment in which it operates. Changes in the international trade cycle, international interest rates and in other countries' economic policies are beyond its control. So too are natural disasters, international conflicts and political upheavals. An added factor is the need to make allowances for foreign exchange rates and their movements.

What Measures of Comparison are Useful?

Almost all international, and for that matter national, comparison starts from the calculation of Gross Domestic Product – that is, from national income statistics. The United Nations has a preferred method for this calculation and one of the best sources of data is the annual Statistical Yearbook. Some nations, including the United Kingdom do not adhere strictly to this method. In Britain's case, for example, it does not put a monetary figure on the value of housewives' services.

This is not the place for a full description of national income accounting but a brief explanation is needed. When measuring the national income the economist is calculating the amount of money income obtained by the nation in the form of wages, salaries and self-employment, profits and rent, in return for producing consumer goods and services, investment goods and government-sector goods and services. By definition, allowing for the niceties of the calculation, national income should equal the value added to the national output. In measuring the national output it is important to avoid 'double counting' of items and to measure only the value added at each stage of production. Also by definition, the national income equals the amount of money spent on the purchase of capital and consumption goods. In this third method of calculation which is called the 'expenditure method', care has to be taken to avoid double or miscounting, especially with respect to indirect taxation and subsidies. There is a 'factor cost adjustment' to take care of this. The statistics can be related to the domestic stage only or can be modified to allow for foreign payments, income and expenditure. The phrase 'national' is then applied to the statistics as in statements such as 'national income = national expenditure = national output'. A final adjustment is made to allow for capital consumption or depreciation because output undertaken simply to replace worn-out equipment is not a net addition to output. This calculation, deducting a figure for capital consumption, turns the figures from 'gross' to 'net'. The figures used for this item of capital consumption are estimates and are among the least reliable of the national income statistics. At the end of all this the economist concludes that national income = national expenditure = net national product (national output).

What then have we got as a basis of comparison? We have a fairly accurate measure of the value of new output in a year, of the income derived from producing it, and of its monetary value in terms of expenditure. If we then wish to compare changes over time we need to make allowances for changes in price levels. This is done by taking a base year and using a price index as a 'deflator'. For example, in order to compare the national income of 1995 with that of 1979 we need to use, say, 1979 price levels for both and convert the 1995 figures by the amount by which an index of general prices has risen over the 16 years. This is called converting money national income into 'real' national income. It simply means that account has been taken of inflation. It is also necessary, sometimes, to take notice of movements in the level of population over time and to calculate money or real national income per head. This is only a rough guide to living standards and it is best to combine it with an analysis of the distribution of income per head, although these figures are among the least reliable of all those available. They are also capable of many different interpretations.

Other useful statistics for international comparison are crude output statistics or changes in them as measured by an index, and levels of possession of standard consumer durable goods such as telephones, video recorders or television sets per head. Interesting results can be obtained from studying how many minutes or hours an average worker must work to be able to buy standard goods or services such as a kilo of butter, a unit of electricity, a small car or a loaf of bread. One light-hearted comparison uses the 'Big Mac' burger as a standard. Other statistics which are valuable for comparative studies are those of working hours, average earnings and productivity. The latest fashion among economists is to construct comparisons of international competitiveness.

These then are some of the basic measurements of comparison. If we take account of all the warnings about their validity and usefulness, how has the European Union fared?

How has the European Union Performed?

The two sets of figures given in Tables 6.1 and 6.2 are a rough measure of how living standards have changed. The first set measures Gross Domestic Product per head. The figures are at current prices and at what are called 'purchasing power standards'. These take account of exchange rates and differences in price levels and are far too complex to explain in this context. Suffice it to say, most economists think they are the best way of coping with changes in foreign exchange rates over time when using statistics. They should be considered in conjunction with the second set which gives figures of Volume Indices of GDP at market prices.

A mass of statistics such as Tables 6.1 and 6.2 is capable of many interpretations or variations of emphasis. The figures for Turkey have been included because it is a potential member. It is clear that Turkey's economic position is well behind that of even the poorer members of the Union such as Portugal, Ireland or Greece, although its recent growth rate has been exceptionally high. Norway has been included because it decided, twice by referendum, not to join the Union. Norway remains part of EFTA and of the European Economic Area. It benefited from oil and gas discoveries at the same time as the United Kingdom but has made much better use of its oil revenues to restructure its economy. The figures in Table 6.3 are at constant prices and, therefore, make allowances for inflation.

TABLE 6.1

Gross Domestic Product at Market Prices per Head (at Current Prices and Purchasing Power Parities, PPS) 1989–93

Country	1989	1990	1991	1992	1993
Europe 12	13 641	14 592*	15 108	15 753	15 835
Belgium	14 092	15 188	16 205	17 299	17 946
Denmark	14 431	15 302	16 465	16 698	17 815
Germany	15 720	17 046*	16 071	17 080	17 147
Greece	8 204	8 433	9 043	9 613	9 998
Spain	10 098	10 936	11 993	12 161	12 330
France	15 191	16 204	17 238	17 676	17 434
Ireland	9 145	10 401	11 292	12 246	12 826
Italy	13 967	14 902	15 916	16 469	16 228
Luxembourg	19 973	21 624	23 250	24 583	25 422
Netherlands	13 717	14 824	15 511	16 057	16 308
Portugal	8 233	8 683	9 705	10 406	10 935
UK	13 908	14 565	14 739	15 448	15 717
Austria	15 382	16 647	17 381	17 102[#]	17 718
Finland	15 597	16 203	15 540	13 754[#]	14 387
Sweden	16 252	17 011	16 881	15 696[#]	15 590[#]
Norway	15 171	16 008	16 801	17 789[#]	18 034
EEA	13 790	14 737*	15 645	16 144[#]	16 193
Turkey	3 022	3 363	3 487	3 727[#]	—
USA	19 300	20 336	20 920	22 133	22 542
Japan	14 767	16 286	17 765	18 752	19 011

*Break in series because of German reunification, 3 October 1990
[#] Estimate

SOURCE for Tables 6.1, 6.2 and 6.3 Eurostat, *Basic Statistics of the Community/Union*, 31st and 32nd edn (Luxembourg: Office for Official Publications of the European Communities, 1994 and 1995)

The growth performance of the European Twelve between 1981 and 1986 was inferior to that of both the United States and Japan. After 1986, the Twelve's annual growth rate between 1987 and 1992 was 2.9 per cent, higher than the USA's but still lower than Japan's 4.2 per cent. The United Kingdom's performance should perhaps be compared with Norway's, in that both were affected by oil revenues from the North Sea. It should also be seen against the rapid deindustrialisation of the early 1980s when British manufacturing industry suffered a devastating decline. It would have been reasonable to expect that the enormous revenues from North Sea oil would have been used to renovate and re-equip British industry. One cannot imagine the Japanese missing such an opportunity. Instead it appears that the advantage, estimated at over £100 billion of extra government revenue in the 1980s, has been used to finance social security for the unemployed or, if you look at it differently, on investment overseas. The long-term opportunity cost of such a policy, or absence of policy, will be immense.

TABLE 6.2
Volume Indices (GDP at Market Prices; 1985 = 100)

Country	1989	1990	1991	1992	1993
Europe 12	113.3	115.8*	121.6	123.0	122.6
Belgium	112.2	115.9	118.5	120.7	118.6
Denmark	105.8	107.3	108.3	109.7	110.9
Germany	109.0	111.7*	133.5	126.1	135.0
Greece	109.9	108.8	112.3	113.3	112.7
Spain	120.1	124.6	127.4	128.2	126.8
France	113.2	115.9	116.6	118.0	116.8
Ireland	121.6	132.1	135.9	142.4	148.4
Italy	113.7	116.1	117.5	118.5	117.6
Luxembourg	128.6	135.4	140.6	131.7	153.7
Netherlands	111.7	116.3	118.9	120.2	120.8
Portugal	123.9	129.2	131.8	132.2	133.9
UK	117.3	117.8	115.5	114.9	117.2
Austria	111.1	115.9	119.3	121.5	121.4
Finland	118.1	118.1	109.8	105.8	103.7
Sweden	110.5	112.0	110.7	108.6	106.3
Norway	106.3	108.1	109.8	113.4	116.2
EEA	113.1	115.6*	120.6	122.1	121.4
Turkey	119.9	131.1	132.3	144.1	150.7
USA	113.1	114.5	114.0	116.8	120.8
Japan	118.8	124.5	129.9	131.3	131.4

*Break in series because of German reunification, 3 October 1990

TABLE 6.3
Annual Rates of Growth of GDP at Market Prices (at Constant Prices, 1987–1992) %

Country	Total	Per head	1994*
Europe 12	2.9	1.7	2.5
Belgium	2.8	2.6	2.3
Denmark	1.1	0.9	4.7
Germany	4.7	1.0	2.8
Greece	1.8	1.2	1.0
Spain	3.7	3.5	1.7
France	2.4	1.9	2.2
Ireland	5.3	5.2	5.0
Italy	2.4	2.2	2.2
Luxembourg	3.9	2.8	2.6
Netherlands	2.7	2.0	2.5
Portugal	3.5	3.6	1.0
UK	1.6	1.2	3.5
Austria	3.5	3.5	2.6
Finland	2.3	3.5	3.5
Sweden	1.0	1.2	2.3
Norway	0.9	−0.2	5.1
Turkey	5.4	3.1	−5.4
USA	2.1	1.1	3.9
Japan	4.2	3.8	1.0

There were significant changes during the period 1986 to 1992, as can be seen from the figures. Events since 1990 such as the world economic recession have affected different countries to varying extents and has caused their relative growth patterns to change. The reader who wishes to keep up to date with these changes is recommended to consult the half-yearly *OECD Economic Outlook*. These reports also contain projections for two years ahead. The OECD information is also available through computer databases.

The causes of economic growth are not always easily identifiable or quantifiable, nor is the relative emphasis to be given to each. It is usually agreed, however, that investment expenditure, the application of new technology, research and development expenditure, improved education and training of the population, and the shift of workers from less-productive to more-productive employment are important determinants of the rate of growth of GDP. In recent years, more emphasis has been placed on the detailed nature of the research and development (R & D) expenditure. Table 6.4 shows the percentage of GDP spent on civilian research and development by member states in 1992. Japan spends a relatively small proportion of its R & D money on defence associated uses; the United Kingdom and the United States spend a relatively high percentage. It will be very interesting to see, over the next few years, what the effects of disarmament agreements will be on the makeup of R & D. The available evidence from the 1980s and 1990s seems to demonstrate conclusively that Japan benefited greatly from her policy and that the United Kingdom suffered from hers.

TABLE 6.4
Total Public Expenditure on Research and Development, 1992 and % of GDP Spent on Civilian R & D

Country	*Total (ECU billion)*	*% on civilian research*
Belgium	1.0	99.8
Denmark	0.8	99.4
Germany	15.4	90.0
Greece	0.1	98.5
Spain	2.3	85.3
France	13.0	65.4
Ireland	0.2	100.0
Italy	7.6	92.9
Netherlands	2.1	96.3
Portugal	0.3	99.6
UK	7.0	57.4
EUR 12	49.8	79.9

SOURCE *Frontier Free Europe* No. 9, 1994 (Luxembourg: Office for Official Publications of the European Communities, 1994)

How do Working Hours Compare?

Another way of looking at comparative economic performance is to analyse the hours worked in each country. This is usually done in conjunction with a study of pay and sometimes an attempt is made to study working conditions. The implication of these studies is that hours worked, and therefore hours of leisure, help us to understand living standards. Statistics of hours worked such as those given in Table 6.5 should be seen against a broader background of levels of unemployment, degrees of job security, the number of part-time jobs, the extent to which people hold more than one job, labour-market flexibility and the extent of social provisions such as pensions, sickness benefit and maternity leave.

TABLE 6.5
Changes in the Usual Working Week, 1983 to 1992, hours worked

Country	1983	1992
Belgium	38.6	38.2
Italy	39.2	38.5
Denmark	40.6	38.8
Netherlands	41.0	39.4
Luxembourg	40.0	39.7
France	39.7	39.7
Germany	40.9	39.7
Ireland	40.2	40.4
Spain	n.a.	40.6
Greece	41.0	40.8
Portugal	n.a.	41.3
United Kingdom	42.3	43.4
EU average		40.3

NOTE the figures do not distinguish between men and women but, in 1992, United Kingdom men worked an average of 45.1 hours per week and women 40.2

SOURCE Eurostat *Community Labour Force Survey*, January 1995 (Luxembourg: Office for Official Publications of the European Communities, 1995)

The figures in Table 6.5 were published by Eurostat in January 1995 and relate to a comparison between 1983 and 1992. The usual working week refers to all hours normally worked, including over-time whether paid or unpaid. It does not include meal breaks or time spent travelling to work. The lengthening of average hours worked in the United Kingdom was roughly the equivalent of one million extra jobs if the working week had fallen at the same rate as the members' average. In 1995 the French government was planning to cut their national average working hours as part of a job-creation programme but to do so might have the effect of raising production costs.

What have been the Longer-Term Trends?

Over the 35 years from 1960 the GDP per head in Europe more than doubled. In contrast, that in Japan rose by over five times whilst in the United States, it grew by about 70 per cent. If we look at it on a per capita basis, in 1992, measured in Purchasing Power Standards, Japan's GDP per head was 20 per cent greater than that of the Twelve and the USA's 42 per cent greater. If we use a straightforward money comparison, in ECU, Japan's GDP per head was 70 per cent higher than that of the Twelve and the USA's 37 per cent higher.

If we use the actual level of GDP rather than a per capita comparison, the European Union's (15) GDP in 1993 was 64 per cent greater than Japan's and 10 per cent greater than the USA's. Germany contributes almost 28 per cent of Europe's total GDP, twice as much as the United Kingdom. Europe has caught up and overtaken the USA in the absolute size of its GDP, as the following figures show. In 1989, the United States' GDP, in thousand million ECU, was 4658, the Community of Twelve's was 4407, and Japan's 2559. By 1993 the figures were: the USA 5300; the European Union (15) 5900; the European (12) 5500; Japan 3600. When average figures are given, they hide wide regional disparities within the individual nations. The broad national differences can be seen in the tables of GDP per head. The alleged North–South divide in the United Kingdom, which, if it existed, disappeared from 1990–93 only to return in 1994, is one obvious example of the regional variations in income, employment and other variables used to measure the quality of life. *Eurostat* produce very detailed figures of regional incomes based on GDP at market prices and on PPS. These permit detailed analysis and comparison and enable maps to be drawn to indicate the areas of the Community which are extreme in terms of affluence or poverty. The figures are also used to determine whether a region should receive money from the various structural funds of the European Union as detailed in Chapter 9.

In general, the more-mature economies of Europe such as the United Kingdom (average annual growth rate 2.2 per cent 1960–85 and 1.6 per cent 1987–92) grew more slowly than the less-mature such as Spain (3.7 per cent 1987–92) and Portugal (5.1 per cent 1960–85 and 3.5 per cent 1987–92). The more-mature economies also showed less volatility in growth rates than, for example, Spain.

In the future, longer term, it is expected that changes involved in the existence of a more genuine single market since the end of 1992 will be a major stimulus to economic growth. It was expected that labour and capital would become more mobile and that costs of production and movement of goods would be significantly lower. The recession after 1990, from which member states emerged at different times, made it more difficult to judge whether this was happening, but the liberalisation of capital markets and financial services is having an obvious impact. High levels of unemployment and higher numbers of non-EU migrant workers have already adversely affected labour mobility between member states.

Employment Comparisons

Since 1975 both the United States and Japan have coped much more effectively with unemployment than Europe although there have been improvements since 1985 in the Union's record. Between 1982 and 1984 the average growth rate of the 12 member states was 1.6 per cent per year and the number of jobs was falling by 600 000 each year. The annual growth rate rose to about 3.5 per cent and 8 million jobs were created between 1985 and 1991. The recession that began to affect member states at different times and rates after 1990 was a major set-back to this improvement. The figures given in Table 6.6 are for unemployment in the various states. We have to assume that 'unemployment' means the same thing in each area. In a perfect world the figures would all conform to the International Labour Organisation (ILO) standard classification and would be comparable without qualification. So we make this very simplifying assumption realising that the alternative is two pages of footnotes and definitions! The interested reader should consult the OECD half-yearly reports to understand the complexities of the definitions, or read *Unemployment and Job Creation* by Andy Beharrell (Macmillan, 1992).

TABLE 6.6
Unemployment Rate (%) (annual average)

	Europe 12	Japan	United States
1975	2.9	1.9	8.5
1981	7.8	2.2	7.6
1985	10.6	2.6	7.2
1986	10.7	2.8	7.0
1987	9.7	2.8	6.1
1988	8.9	2.5	5.4
1989	8.3	2.3	5.2
1990	10.8	2.1	5.4
1991	8.8	2.1	6.6
1992	9.6	2.2	7.3
1993	10.6	2.5	7.2
1994 (est)	11.8	2.9	6.1
1995 (est)	11.4	3.0	5.6

Europe 12 figures are harmonised unemployment rates for the EC. Japan and the USA are OECD standardised unemployment rates

SOURCES Eurostat, *Basic Statistics of the Community/Union*, 25th, 31st and 32nd edn (Luxembourg: Office for Official Publications of the European Communities, 1988, 1994, 1995)

The European statistics represent an average of a very wide range of unemployment in the member states. In 1994, the unemployment rates, not seasonally adjusted, as a percentage of civilian working population were:

Austria	4.4	Italy	11.3
Belgium	12.6	Luxembourg	2.4
Denmark	12.0	Netherlands	9.3
Finland	18.3	Portugal	6.8
France	12.6	Spain	24.3
Germany	9.6	Sweden	7.9
Greece	9.7	United Kingdom	9.4
Ireland	15.8		

European Union unemployment seems to have reached a peak of 11 per cent in mid-1994. The average rate for the Twelve has fallen since then, at different rates in each member state, and the 1994 seasonally adjusted rate is estimated at 10.9 per cent compared with 10.5 per cent in 1993. A particularly worrying aspect of the unemployment figures has been the high proportion of the unemployed who are under 25 and the growing incidence of long- term unemployment. In 1993, for example, over 20 per cent of the labour force aged under 25 in the Twelve was unemployed. In Spain 37.5 per cent of their under 25 labour force was unemployed, and in Italy 30.6 per cent. At the other extreme, in Germany, unemployment among the under 25s was only 4.9 per cent, a figure which reflects well on German approaches to education and training. Unemployment in the female labour force was 12.3 per cent whilst that among males was 9.3 per cent. The United Kingdom, whose overall unemployment rate was 10.5 per cent was the only member whose male unemployment, 12.2 per cent, exceeded its female unemployment, 8.1 per cent. These general statistics give cause for great concern and explain the emphasis in the Union on regional and convergence programmes and cohesion funds.

Some economists and politicians prefer the emphasis to be placed on job-creation rates rather than on unemployment. They also prefer discussion to be in terms of labour market flexibility and deregulation. There is an increasing amount of literature analysing the number and type of jobs created over recent years in both the United States and Europe and on the effects of labour market deregulation, especially in the United Kingdom where young workers had employment and minimum pay protections removed in 1986, and Wages Councils for adult workers were abolished in 1993. The conclusions from the research are often ambiguous or even contradictory. The interpretation of such studies may result in value judgements about the new jobs in the tertiary sector, especially in personal services, as being 'inferior' to the lost jobs in manufacturing industry. The new jobs may be part-time, seasonal, low-wage and unskilled. The recessions of the 1980s and early 1990s have partially recreated the low-waged and insecurely protected service classes of the pre-1914 world. You may, of course, regard this as a good thing if you are financially able to take advantage of the change. The best test of whether such job creation is satisfactory is to look at the skill and experience of the remaining unemployed and see whether it is matched to any extent by the nature of vacant jobs. It may be that there has been a long-term structural decline in an industry, as in coal mining. This means that few relevant new jobs will appear and that retraining is the only solution to the problem. In the United Kingdom, analysis of ex-miners' post-redundancy activity is not encouraging. Some have become self-employed in a variety of occupations. Most have significantly lower average earnings than they received in mining. Few have retrained and many are in unskilled, low-paid jobs such as minicab driving. From the origins of the European Union in the Coal and Steel Community there has been a need to retrain workers as their industries went into structural decline. Retraining has been one of the roles of the Social Fund and Regional Development Funds of the Union. See Chapter 9.

The European Union's role with respect to unemployment generally until 1990 was peripheral because it was regarded as a function of national governments to control their own internal economies and thus their own levels of unemployment. Since the movement towards the Single Market, however, the Union has begun to play an increasingly important part in employment policy where it impinges on the Social Charter. The growing role of the European Union can be seen in the 1993 White Paper on Growth, Competitiveness and Employment.

The White Paper on Growth, Competitiveness and Employment

The White Paper, commissioned six-months earlier, was presented by Jacques Delors, President of the Commission, to the European Council meeting in Brussels, in December 1993. It was aimed at the medium and longer-term reduction of unemployment by creating about 15 million new jobs by the end of the century, thus halving current unemployment rates. It recommended a target growth rate for the Twelve's GDP of 3 per cent per year. The proposals for achieving this included raising capital spending and reducing obstacles to job creation such as high non-wage costs. It supported greater flexibility in labour markets, and the fostering of greater international competitiveness. It argued in favour of supporting recent trends by referring to the benefits of job sharing and more variation of working hours and practices. In this way a greater number of full and part-time workers would be employed. The

White Paper recommended that more resources be put into research and development, training, trans-European networks and into funds to help small businesses.

The White Paper expressed concern about the rate of investment in the European Union, and wanted it raised to about 23 to 24 per cent of GDP as opposed to the prevailing 19 per cent level. It wanted a higher rate of saving, especially from correcting public sector deficits, more stable macro-economic policies, and more attention given to confidence-building in commerce and industry. It provided a detailed comparative analysis of economic growth and job creation showing that the European Union had had a lower job-creation content in its growth than the USA and Japan. It wanted, therefore, an effort to create more jobs to accompany economic growth than had been the case since 1990. The background was that in the second half of the 1980s the economies of the Twelve grew by an annual average of 3.2 per cent and about 9 million new jobs were created.

The costs of the proposals and the methods of financing them aroused great controversy. The White Paper started from the position that the current extremely high levels of unemployment then prevailing were themselves very costly. A conservative estimate put the cost of unemployment to member governments in 1993 at ECU 210 billion. The growth of unemployment had been partly a result of cyclical factors in the recession, partly technological and, to a degree that caused concern, structural. The Delors proposals estimated a financial commitment for the trans-European networks of ECU 20 billion a year from 1994 to 1999. The money would come from three sources. First, about ECU 5.3 billion had already been appropriated in the budget in the form of structural funds, the Cohesion Fund, and money allocated to networks. Second, about ECU 6.7 billion annually was already being spent by the European Investment Bank (EIB) on these areas. Third, the remaining ECU 8 billion could, the White paper suggested, be obtained by the European Commission borrowing money in the bond markets by issuing ECU 7 billion in 'Union Bonds' and obtaining ECU 1 billion from the EIB.

The last proposal, to raise money from Union Bonds, proved controversial, particularly in the light of the growing public debts of most of the member states and their attempts to create better convergence conditions ready for Stage 3 of Monetary Union. In many instances the borrowed money might be re-lent to private-sector firms working on infrastructure schemes. The private sector will also be putting huge sums into networks. A calculation was done of the amount of money to be spent by the European Union and the private sector up to the end of the century. It estimated that ECU 250 billion would be spent on trans-European energy and transport networks and another ECU 150 billion on telecommunication networks. A further ECU 174 billion would go to environmental schemes.

The White Paper contained many detailed proposals and general statements of policy about how to create more jobs and generate economic growth. M. Delors had to keep a balance between job-creating spending of the Keynesian counter-cyclical type and the need to keep a tight rein on monetary aspects such as inflation, interest rates and government deficits. The White Paper was fixed firmly on the goal of monetary union and asked, very sensibly, why spend ECU 210 billion to keep people unemployed when the money could be spent on wealth and job creation. The proposals in the White Paper were approved at the Brussels Council in December 1993 and, with modifications and some retiming, are being implemented. The Cohesion Fund, authorised by the Treaty on Union, came into official existence in May 1994 but had already allocated ECU 1.5 billion for 1993. In addition, the first group of trans-European networks, or TENS as they have come to be known, has been authorised and money allocated. See Chapter 12. It can be argued, therefore, that something can be done at European Union level to reduce unemployment but the speed of implementation of policies has been too slow. In mid-1995 President Chirac of France was arguing at the Cannes summit that greater urgency was required.

The Service Sector

The service, or tertiary, sector consists of commerce, transport, banking, insurance, administration, distribution and personal services. In the Community, in 1975, about 60 million people were engaged in the tertiary sector. This was about 49 per cent of the total civilian labour force. By 1992 84.9 million people were employed in the tertiary sector and the percentage had risen to 61.4

per cent. In the same period, 1975 to 1992, the share of the sector in the GDP rose from 47 to 63.7 per cent. These changes may appear rapid but they were even more pronounced in Japan and the United States. In 1992 about 72.5 per cent of American and 59 per cent of Japanese workers were employed in the service sector. Most of the increase in employment in the Twelve between 1986 and 1992, from 122 million to 139 million in total was in the service sector where employment rose by 18.7 per cent from 71.5 to 84.9 million. The growth of this sector is often seen as a major sign of an economy moving into a post-industrial phase. This is something of an oversimplification because some undeveloped economies have large personal service employment simply because labour is exceptionally cheap. They do not, however, have large employment in banking and financial services.

Many of the manufacturing jobs have been lost through improvements in technology and through transfer to developing countries. The resultant decline of skilled and semi-skilled employment in manufacturing is a cause for concern because there is a limit to which the personal services sector can absorb the unwanted labour. We cannot all survive by taking in each other's washing. Once again, there is a need for a retraining programme to raise the level of workers' skill and mobility. There is also evidence that some countries such as the United Kingdom, France, Italy and Spain require improvements to their labour markets to reduce structural rigidities and involuntary unemployment. They also need to encourage wage bargaining systems which are less fragmented and decentralised and where pay rises are linked more closely to improvements in productivity.

Trade Comparisons

Successive enlargements and the adoption of the Single Market legislation have made the collation and analysis of European trade statistics very difficult. Care should be taken as to whether statistics refer to Europe 12 or to Europe 15, or to the EEA. An additional problem arises from the unification of Germany in 1990 because the East German figures are not regarded as reliable compared with West Germany's, and it is necessary to specify whether a unified Germany is referred to. The creation of the single market led to a serious hiatus in the publication of trade statistics between members because, logically, it is no longer 'foreign' trade in the usual sense. When statistics were resumed they were based on the new system of VAT returns and on business returns. It should be remembered that, in any case, trade statistics have always been subject to subsequent revision, often of an extensive nature and occasionally after a lapse of years.

The original Community was formed with the intention of easing and stimulating trade between its members by reducing all barriers between them. The tariff barriers were quickly removed by 1968 and most of the non-tariff barriers were removed by the end of 1992. It was also expected that the Community's internal market would expand and enable firms to benefit from the considerable economies of scale available in a market which is now, in the European Union of 15 members, 370 million, and in the European Economic Area 373 million, relatively affluent people. The cost-reducing benefits from such a large internal market would, it was anticipated, enable Community firms to compete effectively in world markets. The Japanese, by comparison, have a home market of only 125 million, the United States of 255 million. The North American Free Trade Association of the USA, Canada and Mexico had 372 million in 1992, almost the same as the EEA. The USSR had 287 million and the new Commonwealth of Independent States (CIS), formed in December 1991, has 275 million. Mercosur, the association formed in 1991 by the South American states, Argentina, Brazil, Uruguay and Paraguay has 200 million people. The promised benefits from the huge market have never fully materialised but the European Union is, by most standards, the most important trading group in the world.

How has intra-Community trade developed?

Trade between members, intra-Community trade, has grown much faster since 1958 than trade with non-members. Between 1958 and 1987 trade between members increased by 37 times (8 times in real terms) whereas trade with non-members rose 16 times (3.5 times in real terms). The pattern varies but for all members intra-Community trade accounts for over half their total trade. The details are given in Table 6.7. The countries most dependent on intra-Community trade are Ireland, Portugal, Belgium, Luxembourg and

France. The dependency of The Netherlands has fallen. The United Kingdom used to be the least dependent on the other members for both imports and exports. In 1992 its imports were still the lowest at 51 per cent, apart from those of the new entrant Finland, but her exports had risen steadily over the years to 56 per cent in 1992 which is a greater degree of dependency than Germany's. When she joined in 1958, only about 16 per cent of the United Kingdom's exports and 20 per cent of her imports arose from trade with the Community. The figures in Table 6.7 indicate why Austria, Finland and Sweden joined the European Union

TABLE 6.7

Total Imports and Exports by Partner Country, Europe 12, 1993 (per cent)

Country	Imports	Exports
Belgium/Lux	71	74
Denmark	54	54
Germany	51	50
Greece	60	56
Spain	61	62
France	64	61
Ireland	70	69
Italy	55	53
Netherlands	66	74
Portugal	72	75
United Kingdom	49	53
Austria	67	60
Finland	46	45
Sweden	55	53
EEA (1992)	59	61
USA	16.8	13.3
Japan	12.6	15.6
EUR 12 Intra (1992) 59.3		61.3

SOURCE Eurostat, Basic Statistics of the Union, 32nd Edition 1995 (Luxembourg: Office for Official Publications of the European Communities, 1995)

How has the European Union's external trade changed?

There have been major changes over the years in the composition of the imports. Initially, the original Community was predominantly an importer of raw materials and processed them into manufactured goods for consumption and export. Gradually the position altered and an increasing proportion of imports were semi-finished goods and manufactured articles. Thus, by 1993, more than half the Twelve's imports were manufactured goods, machinery and transport equipment. The United Kingdom's trade has, of course, altered in the same way so that it now has a very large deficit on visible trade in manufactures despite the significant depreciation of the pound sterling since 1992.

TABLE 6.8
The European Union's Main Trading Partners 1993

%	USA	Japan	EFTA	ACP
Imports	17.8	9.8	22.6	3.0
Exports	17.4	4.7	22.0	3.4

SOURCE *Frontier Free Europe* No. 7, 1994 (Luxembourg: Office for Official Publications of the European Communities, 1994)

TABLE 6.9
The European Union's Balance of Trade in Goods, 1985 and 1993 (ECU billions)

	USA	Japan	EFTA	ACP	Rest of World
1985	16.6	−18.1	2.5	10.9	−29.9
1993	−2.2	−25.0	−3.3	1.9	−3.4

SOURCE *Frontier Free Europe* No. 7, 1994 (Luxembourg: Office for Official Publications of the European Communities, 1994)

One of the main variables in trade has been oil and natural gas. Some of this has been derived from within the Twelve, that is, from the United Kingdom and The Netherlands, but most is bought on world markets where the price is very volatile. The trade is normally in US dollars. Large quantities of gas are bought from Russia. In common with other countries the Twelve's trade volume has altered as oil and energy prices have fluctuated. The heavy reliance upon oil imports pushed the overall visible trade balance into deeper deficit until the large reduction of oil prices occurred in

1985. On visible trade, the Community of 12 was in deficit from 1958 until 1986 when a surplus was achieved. The advent of the world recession then caused the external trade balance to return to a deficit of ECU 52 billion in 1992. In 1993 trade improved and the deficit fell to an estimated ECU 3.4 billion. The oil price changes also had an impact on 'invisible' payments in the form of interest, dividends, profits and the purchase of financial and transport services. Table 6.8 shows the Union's main trading partners and Table 6.9 shows how the balance of trade with different trading areas changed between 1985 and 1993. Table 6.10 shows the composition of imports and exports in 1985 compared with 1993.

TABLE 6.10
Extra-Community Imports/Exports by Product Class, 1985 and 1993

	Food, drink, tobacco	Crude materials	Fuel products	Chemicals	Other Manufac- tures	Machinery & transport equipment
			% of Imports			
1985	9.5	10.1	28.4	5.6	26.9	19.5
1993	7.6	6.5	12.7	7.0	35.5	30.7
			% of Exports			
1985	7.5	2.6	5.0	11.2	36.9	36.8
1993	7.5	2.2	3.2	13.1	31.7	42.3

SOURCE *Frontier Free Europe* No. 7, 1994 (Luxembourg: Office for Official Publications of the European Communities, 1994)

The changes in the European Union's current account balances

A country's balance of payments on current account is made up of two main components. The first is payments for visible imports and exports of goods and is called the 'balance of trade'. The second is called the 'invisible balance' and consists of payments into and out of a country for services and other transfers. The most important of these invisible imports and exports are payments for banking, insurance and other financial services. The other main flow of money is interest, profits and dividends from investments in other countries or paid out to foreigners who have made financial investments in the country. Tourism and travel give rise to large invisible flows and so does the purchase of shipping and air services. There are, in addition, private transfers to or from individuals living in different countries. Some countries such as the United Kingdom earn large surpluses on their invisible accounts because of the activities of their financial and commodity markets and because of the large holdings of property and financial investments abroad. This is despite the expansion of foreign holdings of assets in Europe which create an outflow of interest, profits and dividends each year. It should be noted in this context that, if one country's prevailing interest rate levels are high compared with those in other countries, there will tend to be an enlarged flow of foreign capital into that country. This will necessitate larger future outflows of interest payments unless the interest is reinvested in that country. Significant differences in national interest rates have already begun to disappear as the pace of economic and monetary union gathers pace in preparation for a single currency after 1999. This process of convergence is explained in Chapter 8.

When the two components, the balance of visible trade and the balance of invisibles, are added together we have the 'balance of payments on current account' or 'current balance'. There is also an account, called 'transactions in assets and liabilities', of movements of capital into and out of a country. These may consist of flows originating from individuals, firms or governments. They may be moved either on a short-term or long-term basis. The transfer of such funds affects the foreign exchange markets. The overall balance of payments account always balances in the sense that the current balance is matched by the transactions in assets and liabilities.

The establishment of a single market and the removal of border checks on flows of goods has led to the sources of statistics shifting mainly to VAT returns made by traders and to business returns. Logically, if the European Union is a single market, the concept of 'foreign' trade between members is not applicable. As a result, imports between members have been renamed as 'arrivals' and exports between members are now called 'shipments'. The changes have had a practical effect. In February 1995, Eurostat which manages Intrastat, an office that collects data on internal European Union trade, said that by October 1994 only seven of the 12 members had provided their statistics covering the first six months of 1994. Another problem is that many businesses do not forward information about their purchases in other member countries. As a result 'arrivals' are under-recorded compared with 'shipments'.

Visible trade

Each member of the Union has its own accounts for visible and invisible trade and therefore an individual balance of payments on current account, although there may come a time when these national accounts become unnecessary or even impossible to calculate accurately. The accounts show great variety. The United Kingdom, for example, now shows its accounts in terms of EU, non-EU and World categories. In 1992, only Germany, Denmark and Ireland had surpluses in visible trade. The importance of Germany in the European Union can be clearly seen from the figures in Table 6.11.

TABLE 6.11
Balance of Trade, 1992, with the Rest of the World including EU Members

Country	Imports		Exports		
	Billion ECU	*% of GDP*	*Billion ECU*	*% of GDP*	*Balance million Ecu*
Belgium/Lux	102	60	95	56	−6478
Denmark	27	24	31	28	+4310
Germany	316	21	331	22	+15 264
Greece	18	30	7	12	−10 163
Spain	75	17	53	12	−21 830
France	199	20	192	19	−7000
Ireland	17	43	22	56	+5020
Italy	146	15	138	15	−8196
Netherlands	114	46	109	44	−5359
Portugal	23	31	14	19	−9012
UK	171	21	145	18	−26 888
12, Intra + Extra	1207	22	1136	21	−70 782
12, Extra	487	9	435	8	−52 070
USA	409	9	344	8	−64577
Japan	179	6	262	10	+82483

SOURCE Eurostat, *Basic Statistics of the Community*, 31st edn (Luxembourg: Office for Official Publications of the European Communities, 1994)

Invisible trade and current account balances

In 1992, only Denmark, France, Ireland and The Netherlands had current account surpluses. The United Kingdom, Germany and Italy had large current account deficits. The United Kingdom had a large invisible surplus but it was not sufficient to match the visible deficit. The Community as a whole had moved into current account deficit in 1978–79 and continued in deficit until 1983. Thereafter a surplus was achieved from 1983 to 1987, except for a deficit in 1985. Since 1988 the Twelve have had a deficit on visible trade as shown in Table 6.12.

TABLE 6.12
Balance of Visible Trade (Million ECU)

	1988	1989	1990	1991	1992
Intra + Extra	−23.8	−30.3	−50.9	−80.1	−70.8
Extra			−40.2	−70.5	−50.1

There are major influences on the trend of the current account. The most important are the value of the ECU against the dollar and the yen, and world oil prices. As these change the costs of production of European goods alters and their competitiveness in home and foreign markets is affected. The Japanese have been building up balance of payments on current account surpluses ($87 billion in 1987, $35 billion in 1990, $130 billion in 1994), and the United States has been struggling to reduce its deficit ($160 billion in 1987, $92 billion in 1990, $4 billion in 1991, and an estimated $156 billion in 1994). The changes in these totals and the measures taken to disperse the surplus or reduce the deficit affect interest rates and exchange rates. It can be seen, therefore, that European Union trade is heavily influenced by Japanese and American policies. As a general rule, countries with surpluses are reluctant to take swift action to reduce them. Countries in deficit are also slow to take remedial action although, in theory, a country with a floating exchange rate can simply leave the workings of the markets to eliminate surpluses and deficits. If it has borrowed from the IMF it may need to take additional measures in order to satisfy the terms of the loan.

Trade performance needs to be seen against the background of the Uruguay Round of GATT talks which ground to a halt in late 1990, resumed in 1991, failed to reach a conclusion, resumed again in the first half of 1992, collapsed again and finally reached a conclusion in December 1993. Other background features are the unification of the two parts of Germany which affected the flows of capital in Europe, the Fourth Lomé convention with ACP countries, the creation of genuinely independent Central European states and the breakdown of Comecon in 1990, the dissolution of the USSR in December 1991 and its replacement by the Commonwealth of Independent States, and the general world recession. The creation of the European Economic Area, the development of monetary union within the enlarged European Union and the probable future enlargement of membership will also have very important impacts on trade. Another factor is the creation of a six-member Association of South East Asian Nations (ASEAN), which may have considerable impact on world trade because of its high growth rate. In January 1992 they endorsed a plan to establish a regional free trade zone over the next 15 years. ASEAN was formed in 1967 by Singapore, Malaysia, Brunei, Indonesia, Philippines and Thailand. Vietnam and Laos may join this Asean Free Trade Area (AFTA), and it will, if it is ever accomplished, be a market of over 360 million people.

In January 1993, a North American Free Trade Association (NAFTA) was formed between the USA, Canada and Mexico. Other Latin American countries are interested in joining. Its population of 372 million is almost the same as that of the EEA. In South America a grouping called MERCOSUR was formed in March 1991 by Argentina, Brazil, Uruguay and Paraguay. Chile and Bolivia may join later. Mercosur has 200 million people and a collective GDP of US$ 600 billion. The European Union is Mercosur's most important trading partner.

These groupings obviously carry with them the opportunity for increased trade if the spirit of the Uruguay Round is matched by deeds, but they also represent the potential threat of trade wars and restrictions. In order to counteract the threat the European Union has been having talks with all three organisations, NAFTA, ASEAN and MERCOSUR with a view to liberalising trade and developing cooperation. The talks with NAFTA are dominated by the USA which seems keen to reach some sort of formal agreement with the European Union.

The Uruguay Round of GATT talks ended, at long last, in December 1993 and the agreement was signed in April 1994. The GATT has now been succeeded by the World Trade Organisation (WTO). The agreements covered industrial tariffs, agriculture, textiles, patents, anti-dumping measures and some services. It was decided to negotiate later on financial services and telecommunications. In June 1995 the talks on financial services, banking and insurance collapsed when the USA withdrew. Some early predictions said that the overall impact of the Uruguay Round would be to benefit the developed countries most, but World Bank studies in April 1995 contradict these and show that developing countries will benefit most in terms of percentage change in GDP. The European Union, according to OECD estimates, should benefit from a large increase in GNP by AD 2002 of between US$ 70 and US$ 80 billion at 1991 prices. The talks were significant in the development of the European Union because the members were represented as a body in the negotiations by the Commission rather than by national representatives.

Money

What Determines the Value of the Various European Currencies?

A number of factors influence the value of a currency compared with another. These factors change in relative importance over time. They include the supply and demand of the currency in world foreign exchange markets, the extent and nature of official controls on movements of money in or out of a country, government policy and the possible existence of international agreements on foreign exchange rates. An example of this last factor was the Bretton Woods agreement on fixed parities which survived from 1947 to 1971. Another is the European Monetary System (EMS), or more specifically the Exchange Rate Mechanism (ERM) which is part of it.

Economists try to explain the fundamental relationship of two currencies in terms of the 'purchasing power parity' theory (PPP). This formidable title disguises a fairly simple idea, although, needless to say, it can be expressed in a variety of ways and with different degrees of sophistication. At its simplest the theory says that a given collection or 'basket' of goods will have a certain price in each of two countries. This price will, of course, be expressed in the two different currencies. The PPP then says that the foreign exchange rate between the two currencies will tend towards that existing in the prices of the basket of goods in the two countries. So, if our basket costs £20 in the United Kingdom and $30 in the United States, the foreign exchange rate will tend to be around

£1 = $1.5. This is because the competitive nature of the markets leads to shifts in the supply and demand for goods and services as price differences become apparent.

How Well does the Purchasing Power Parity Theory Apply?

This theory seems to show basic common sense and can be seen in operation in cross-border trade between neighbouring developing countries. It does, however, become less applicable in the short and medium terms in developed economies although the PPP's long-run applicability remains valid. The PPP theory is much harder to apply when capital as well as goods and services enter into trade and when speculation is rife. There are several monetarist models of exchange rate determination that take into account these capital and speculative flows. The three main types are *flexible price*, *sticky price* and *real interest rate differential* models. The interested reader should consult *International Finance* by Keith Pilbeam (Macmillan, 1992, ISBN 0–333–54528–1).

Another major problem which arises is the fact that certain important items of expenditure do not entail trade or international exchange. Such items may be power, such as electricity, housing services, a wide range of personal services and local or central government services. More sophisticated versions of the theory try to take this into account and there is sound evidence that the PPP theory of an exchange rate between two countries is valid over time, albeit with short-term aberrations.

Where does the Non-Speculative Demand and Supply of a Currency Come From?

It is easier to answer this question if we take one country, such as Britain as an example. The demand for the pound, on the one hand, comes from foreigners who wish to buy British exports and need to pay British companies in sterling. This demand arises from both visible exports and invisible exports of services such as tourism, banking, insurance, and so on. Obviously this demand relates to the volume of such trade which, in itself, is affected by comparative rates of inflation. Other things being equal, a high exchange rate for the pound will reduce the demand for the United Kingdom's exports. The extent of the reduction will depend on the price elasticity of demand for the exports. Price elasticity of demand measures the responsiveness of demand to price changes. In effect, within certain exchange rate limits, United Kingdom exports yield greater total revenue as the exchange rate of the pound drops.

The other non-speculative demand for the pound arises when foreign companies and individuals wish to transfer capital to Britain for investment purposes. This may be physical investment in the Keynesian sense of expenditure on capital goods such as factories or plant. It may, however, be the transfer of money capital for deposit in a wide range of short-term or long-term financial assets. This type of monetary flow is influenced by the interest rate levels prevailing within the United Kingdom compared with those in other similar economies. It also responds to changes in the comparative rates of inflation and to expectations of movements in foreign exchange rates in different countries. The money is used to buy bills of exchange, Treasury Bills, short- and long-dated government stock, local authority bonds, various types of certificates of deposit and company shares.

The United Kingdom has long been a major international financial centre although the pre-eminence of the City of London is fading despite, to some extent, its importance being maintained by the presence of US, Swiss, Hong Kong, Dutch and German banks who have taken over long-established United Kingdom financial institutions such as merchant banks and high-street banks. As a result of its role there are extremely large flows of capital into and out of sterling. The 'City', meaning the banks and financial institutions, earns large fees and commissions on such transfers. Those paid by foreigners are part of the United Kingdom's invisible earnings on the balance of international payments. Some of these flows into short-dated bills or bonds are very 'liquid', that is convertible into cash, and are transferred easily and quickly, though at some expense, into other currencies if conditions change. These funds which move quickly for very short-term gains are sometimes called 'hot money' – an inescapable element in the foreign exchange markets. It is also frequently an undesirable element.

The supply of pounds, on the other hand, is produced by the reverse elements of the factors described above. That is to say, importers need to sell pounds in order to get the foreign currency required by their overseas suppliers. British tourists are selling pounds to buy the currency they need for their holidays. There is also a large supply of pounds arising from the great volume of investment abroad by British firms and individuals. This investment has, over the years, reached a huge total and economists take an intense interest in its destinations. In recent years, to 1995, North America has been a favourite destination for British overseas investment. Some of this transfer originates in the fashion for take-overs of American firms as a quick way of getting into the North American market.

What is the Role of Speculation in the Fixing of Exchange Rates?

Most of the currency bought and sold in the foreign exchange markets is dealt in with a speculative profit in mind or with the intention of avoiding loss. That is to say, the buyers and sellers do not want the currency to finance visible or invisible trade or capital movements. They are hoping for a profit after the costs of transfer are met from buying or selling. The simplest form of speculation is to buy in the hope or expectation of the price rising in the future so that a capital gain can be made. A more complicated alternative is to sell, at a high price, something that you do not yet possess in the hope that you can buy it at a lower price in order to meet your obligation to deliver it. Markets vary in the scope that they give speculators to operate. Some are strongly supervised but, as the experience of the Barings collapse caused by injudicious speculation in Far Eastern financial derivatives markets in 1995 shows, the supervision is not always effective.

Speculation is made a normal activity in the foreign exchange markets by the existence, side by side, of a 'spot' market and a 'forward' market. A spot market refers, as its name suggests, to a deal based on the current prices prevailing as the deal is fixed. A forward market is often called a 'futures' market when commodities are concerned. It allows dealers to reach agreement on price at one moment on a deal to be concluded in the future – days, weeks or months ahead. The bargain is made. The price to be paid is fixed and must be honoured when the date arrives. Such forward markets do serve a very useful function, enabling buyers and sellers of goods to fix their costs in advance. Thus, for example, an importer of raw materials makes a forward deal so that the cost of production arising from the purchase of foreign exchange to pay for the materials can be calculated exactly.

The existence of forward markets is a great stimulus to speculation but this does not necessarily create greater fluctuation in exchange rates. Indeed, some economists argue that an efficient, well informed speculative market may iron out the peaks and troughs of foreign exchange rate movements. This will reduce the range of fluctuation because speculators need to take their profits while they can and there are always some who try to get out of a rising market by selling before it peaks. Alternatively, they may buy in a falling market before it bottoms out. By so doing they will, if they do it in sufficient volume, cause the rise to cease or the fall to halt. There is also an activity called 'hedging' which involves forgoing high profits but ensures a small profit or prevents a loss. It is also normally employed by people who wish to be certain of the price that they will eventually pay for currency or commodities. Hedging involves precautionary buying or selling, contrary to the speculator's original expectations, in case the market begins to behave differently from the manner anticipated. Risk can be largely avoided by both buying and selling forward at the same time, a course of action followed by those who actually want the currency or commodities traded. The currency speculator may be constantly adjusting buying and selling and making new forward deals in order to avoid loss or to make certain of some profit.

Most speculation, especially in commodities or on the newer markets in options to buy or sell (derivatives), can be fraught with danger since millions of pounds can be lost in a very short period unless the basic rules of precautionary behaviour are obeyed. Financial institutions and banks need to keep a very strict control over their forward dealings. So do companies who buy commodities since they are forced to participate in the markets if they wish to obtain the raw materials to remain in business.

Are there any Controls in the Foreign Exchange Markets?

The United Kingdom abolished its exchange controls in 1979 as part of its efforts to reduce regulation and to expose the economy to free competition. Until then there had been a mixture of controls applied to the export and import of capital and the purchase of foreign exchange to finance deals. These controls stemmed from the war and the period of the postwar dollar shortage. Their intensity and extensiveness varied according to the nation's economic problems. At times, there were draconian restrictions on the amount that British tourists could take abroad. Most of the controls were aimed at outflows of capital. They inevitably generated a supervisory and regulatory bureaucracy and introduced an element of delay and uncertainty into commercial transactions. Most people were glad that they were abolished although there appeared to be a striking increase in the outflow of capital from the United Kingdom after they were ended. Other countries have also abolished exchange controls on capital movements in accordance with a Directive of June 1988, for example, Germany, the Netherlands, Belgium, Denmark, France, Italy and Luxembourg. They achieved this by the target date of 1 July 1990. Of the more advanced member countries France had the most extensive controls on capital which limited the ability of its citizens to hold bank accounts abroad. They also required permission to open foreign currency accounts in French banks and there were restrictions on the ability of French banks to lend to non-residents. Some of these controls stemmed from the early period of socialist government under President Mitterrand when there was a flight of capital out of France. Inevitably, Greece, Spain and Portugal and Ireland which have underdeveloped financial sectors had a higher degree of control over capital movements. They were granted a reprieve until the end of 1992 for full implementation of the directive, and all controls had gone by the end of 1994. There is a safeguard whereby a country can control short-term capital movements if there is a serious problem with its monetary or exchange rate policy. Ireland and Spain introduced temporary controls after the September 1992 exchange rate crisis.

None of the Community countries, however, approached the now dissolved Eastern bloc system of complete control of the inflow and outflow of currency. It was this control that enabled the Soviet Union, for example, to impose a blatantly unrealistic exchange rate for the rouble on foreign visitors. Tourists quickly found that the 'free' market, or the 'black' market, exchange rate was many times more favourable, although taking advantage of it was illegal.

It is intended that the relaxation of controls over capital movements should extend outside the European Union and the European Economic Area to movements to and from non-EU countries. Such relaxation was discussed during the Uruguay Round of GATT talks but left aside for future agreements in 1995 in the context of liberalisation of financial services. The first talks broke down in June 1995. The long-term hope, therefore, is that trade, investments and financial markets will all benefit although it is now recognised that international capital flows are so huge that no country or group of countries can any longer do more than temporarily influence foreign exchange rates. The rapid fluctuation of the exchange rates of the US dollar, the yen and the pound sterling in early 1995 has emphasised this loss of control. Gradually the freeing of capital movements has helped to integrate the financial aspects of the Union. It has introduced more pressure to harmonise the rules and framework under which the banks and financial markets operate. The Second Banking Directive of 1989 which came into force in January 1993 goes a long way to achieving an open market in financial services and so do the other financial and insurance directives passed recently. The achievement of harmony in financial services is essential in the movement towards a common European currency and central bank as proposed in the 1991 Maastricht agreement and at the June 1995 Cannes summit which fixed 1999 as the deadline for a single currency.

Do Governments Allow their Exchange Rates to Float Freely?

Very few governments leave their foreign exchange rates completely to the vagaries of the international markets. Some, like the now dissolved USSR, whose controls collapsed in 1991, went to the opposite extreme and tried to control them completely. Others intervene in the markets when it suits their policy, but generally leave their currency to find its own level. Some, like most of the members of the European Union, get together and operate a coordinated or linked scheme to influence their rates. This scheme is called the Exchange Rate Mechanism (ERM) of the European Monetary System (EMS).

Perhaps the most extensive and effective system of control of foreign exchange rates was that arising from the Bretton Woods agreement of 1944. This survived until 1971, although it suffered many vicissitudes. The agreement required countries to fix their exchange rates at a certain level which was notified to the International Monetary Fund (IMF). This rate was set at a level in relation to the price of gold but was, in effect, setting it against the dollar because the United States fixed the world price of gold in intergovernmental exchange. The country then needed to use its reserves to intervene in the foreign exchange markets to keep the rate within a band of 1 per cent above or below the central (par) rate. For example, the United Kingdom between 1949 and 1967 kept the pound between $2.82 and $2.78 with a central, or 'par' value of £1 = $2.80. For much of the time the rate was closer to the 'floor' price of $2.78 than to the 'par value'. In 1931, in the middle of the great international financial crisis the United Kingdom had left the old gold standard. It set up the Exchange Equalisation Account which contained the country's gold and other currency reserves. This fund of reserves was used, and still is, to enter the foreign exchange markets to buy and sell currencies, including sterling, in order to influence the rate against the dollar. The markets were usually aware of the intervention but not of its extent. This system is essentially the same as the operation of 'buffer stock' buying and selling as in some world commodity agreements or in the Common Agricultural Policy.

Under the Bretton Woods agreement all the signatories used equivalents of the Exchange Equalisation Account to intervene in markets to influence their own rates of exchange. If they got into difficulties in this respect, or into balance-of-payments problems, they could ask the IMF for short-term loans to give them time to correct the situation and restore equilibrium. In the last resort they could devalue their currency. The United Kingdom, for example, devalued the pound, overnight, from £1 = $2.80 to £1 = $2.40 in November 1967. The loans from the IMF were, and are, given provided that the country concerned took action to remove or reduce the fundamental causes of the problem. These might be high internal inflation, excessive government expenditure, or high costs of production reducing export competitiveness. The methods needed to tackle these problems, tax increases and cuts in government spending, were politically unpopular. The terms imposed by the IMF on the 1974–79 Labour government when it asked for loans were an important contributory factor to the unpopularity that led to its defeat in the 1979 election. In contrast no one took much notice when the Conservative government borrowed to support sterling in the ERM crisis of 1992.

The Bretton Woods system of fixed (but adjustable) parities which had to be defended, gradually broke down. Some countries such as Canada floated their currency. Others, like the United Kingdom, were very slow to devalue until forced. Stronger economies, like the West German were very slow to revalue, that is to raise the value of their currency. Governments increasingly felt that fixed foreign exchange rates imposed far too heavy a restraint on their internal economic policies. It was inevitable, therefore, that the growing international financial problems of the late 1960s and early 1970s should induce countries to try a new panacea, freely floating foreign exchange rates accompanied by some intervention buying and selling.

This complete freedom was not, however, entirely suitable for the members of the European Community. They adopted temporary expedients of common exchange rate controls in the early 1970s. These were various versions of what became known as the 'snake in the tunnel'. This was a framework under which each country would have an upper and lower target limit for its exchange rate. Within this 'tunnel' the exchange rate could fluctuate. As the rate came near the outer limits the country needed to take corrective action. The rates of each participating country were interlinked or weighted in calculating the rates against the dollar. The system was modified over time but was not completely satisfactory because some countries were too slow, or ineffective, in taking remedial measures to correct problems. They were slow because the necessary measures were bound to be politically unpopular, since they usually included restraints on public and private expenditure. West Germany was sometimes slow to react despite the persistent strength of its economy and balance of payments because it would have had to revalue the Deutschmark upwards which would have cut the competitiveness of its exports. It was therefore necessary to develop another, more effective system.

Floating Exchange Rates, Monetarism and the Evolution of the EMS

The politicians of the major economies succumbed to the siren songs of the economists who recommended floating exchanges rates. They had reached their wits' end on measures to control inflation, rising unemployment, growing balance of payments deficits and budget deficits. When they were told that they could, in effect, have their cake and eat it, they seized on floating rates as the panacea for all their ills. They thought that they would free themselves from the shackles of having to make unpalatable and unpopular decisions about their internal economies in order to restore a balance of payments equilibrium or to maintain a narrow range of exchange rates. At the same time the new priesthood of the resurrected theory of monetarism joined in the chorus.

This is not the place for a detailed explanation of what is called monetarism, a term that has come to have several meanings with the passage of time. In this context, however, we do need to know that the monetarists saw a direct relationship between changes in the quantity of money in circulation and the rate of change of the price level (inflation). Keynesian economists saw an indirect link because they allowed for excess demand and supply of money to be absorbed in a sort of 'buffer' in the shape of purchases and sales of bonds. The problem confronting the monetarists in practice was deciding what to count as 'money' and then how to control it. The financial world is such that as soon as you try to control something, the participants in the markets switch their assets or holdings into another type. Money takes many forms apart from the cash and notes with which we are all familiar. It includes all sorts of bills and bonds, bank deposits and liquid financial assets such as building society deposits, some of which are held in sterling and some in foreign currencies. In the United Kingdom one of the major problems of the pre-1979 period was that the government had a very large borrowing requirement which was financed by the issue of long-term stock and by the sale of short-term bills (Treasury Bills). Several other member states had similar debt burdens. The methods they adopted were, according to the monetarists, the equivalent, to some extent, of 'printing money'. Thus any attempt to control the growth of the money supply involved the curtailing of government borrowing and, inevitably, cut-backs in public expenditure. This was successfully achieved in Britain by 1988 and the Treasury, with the help of the sale of public assets from the nationalised industries, enjoyed a large surplus of revenue over expenditure and it was able to reduce the National Debt. This process was also supposed to have left extra funds available for the private sector to borrow for investment, that is, it ended what was called 'crowding out'. This was the name given to the process whereby the government, which was always able to pay as high an interest rate as was needed to get loans, could outbid the private sector. Not all economists supported the crowding-out hypothesis.

From the perspective of the United Kingdom a major aspect of the money supply problem was the movement into, and out of, the country of foreign funds. This movement is heavily influenced by the rate of interest prevailing in the United Kingdom compared with that in other comparable countries. High rates, other things being equal, attract larger deposits, and vice versa. The other influence is the level of the foreign exchange rate and expectations about its movements relative to other currencies in the future. Higher rates attract more foreign money into the country and tend to raise the foreign exchange rate. This cuts the effective price of imports and is deflationary, and tends to cut the demand for exports. There follows a detrimental effect on the balance of payments (depending on the relative elasticities of supply and demand of imports and exports) which can contribute to large current account deficits.

Worse still was the significance of exchange rate intervention. Positive official financing involved buying pounds and selling foreign currency from the reserves in order to alter the exchange rate. An inevitable result was for domestic money supply also to be reduced, or to be increased by negative financing. Thus exchange rate policy constrained monetary policy in what, to monetarists, was an unacceptable way.

The United Kingdom adopted policies in the 1980s that were said to be monetarist, although many monetarists thought they were half-hearted and insufficient. The main remaining weapon left to the Chancellor by 1988 was the ability to influence the interest rate. This was aimed at affecting the demand for money. Almost all the other controls over bank lending and asset ratios were abandoned. This was in contrast with West Germany which had an extensive and powerful set of controls over its banking sector. It could, as a result, control the supply of money as well. Consequently, Germany was able to have a low rate of inflation, a low level of interest rates and a heavy inflow of foreign capital. Its position was strengthened by the existence of a sound labour relations structure that kept wage demands within the bounds of what could be afforded from economic growth and increased productivity. Moreover, German banks used Luxembourg, which had a much freer banking regulation structure, as a base for some of their operations for capital transfers when their own home regulations became too oppressive. The monetarists offered what appeared to be a simple explanation of inflation and an apparently straightforward set of solutions. All that governments had to do was to control their money supply and to reduce their government spending and borrowing and everything would be all right. At the same time, they should try to improve the underlying efficiency of the economy by reducing costs on enterprise. These 'supply-side' improvements would reinvigorate a flagging national economy and generate a climate in which enterprise would flourish. Governments would be absolved from responsibility for balance-of-payments equilibrium and exchange rate levels. The system would be self-levelling and self-adjusting and no more politically unpopular measures resulting from balance-of-payments problems would be necessary.

These ideas were not equally well received in all European countries. Some were tried and rejected or modified. On the whole, the economic policies of Europe remained neo-Keynesian with some modifications. It can be argued, of course, that neo-Keynesian policies did not fail in the 1960s and 1970s but that the political will and nerve of politicians collapsed when it came to taking the remedial action required. They did too little, too late, or they acted in response to their electoral cycles rather than to economic imperatives. The United States, which remained the power house of the international economy, was embroiled in the Vietnam War. Its mounting expenditure and deficits at home and abroad fuelled international inflation and disrupted money markets. Another problem was the mounting volume of oil revenues seeking investment outlets. Third World debt was also increasing rapidly. The growing oil revenues resulting from the price rises of the early 1970s shifted about the world looking for high returns and security. Their existence and movement affected exchange rates and interest rates. In the circumstances, it is no surprise that freely floating exchange rates were not fully adopted since most nations intervene to influence their foreign exchange rate. This covert intervention is often called 'dirty floating' and its effectiveness depends to some extent on the size of the reserves with which the country can intervene. The Community adopted its own system arising from the need to make payments between members and to achieve some stability of its currencies in relation to each other. The European Monetary System was born.

What is the European Monetary System?

The EMS was established in 1979 and comprised a European Monetary Cooperation Fund (EMCF), an Exchange Rate Mechanism (ERM) and a currency, or unit of account, called an ECU, and a Very Short Term Facility (VSTF) whereby each central bank could make credit facilities available in its own currency to the other members. ECU stands for European Currency Unit in English but it was also a medieval French gold coin. The need for the role exercised by the EMCF should disappear in the late 1990s as a single currency is achieved and its functions have already been assumed by the European Monetary Institute (EMI) since January 1994 when Stage 2 of Economic and Monetary Union (EMU) began. The United Kingdom did not join the ERM until October 1990 and left again in September 1992 but participated from the start in the EMCF and ECU elements. The Spanish peseta and Portuguese escudo were included for the first time in the calculation of the value of the ECU when its base was recalculated in September 1989.

The European Monetary Cooperation Fund and EMI

The EMCF was set up in 1973 and and its functions are now exercised by the European Monetary Institute (EMI). It operated as a mixture between the IMF and a Community central bank. The participants in the EMS deposit 20 per cent of their gold reserves and 20 per cent of their dollar reserves with the EMCF/EMI. In return they are credited with ECUs, the quantity of which credited to each country will change as the price of gold and dollars alters on world markets. The gold portion of the deposit with the EMCF is valued using six-monthly averages of London gold prices and the dollar portion is valued at the market rate two days before the date of valuation. Thus both the world price of gold and the price of the dollar affect the quantity of ECUs created. Once credited to a country these ECUs can then be used to settle payments between members. The system is a foundation, via the ECU, for both a currency and an international reserve unit. The details of the deposits and their valuation in terms of dollars are reviewed every two years. The technicalities of the scheme are highly complex but there is no doubting the effectiveness of the institution. The number of ECUs in existence increases yearly and in 1994 the EMI issued ECU 56 billion to central banks. There were ECU 175 billion stocks and bonds in the financial markets in September 1994. The EMCF/EMI has a disadvantage in that it cannot control the creation of ECUs because that is determined by the gold price and rate of the dollar.

The EMCF/EMI also has the function of making the Exchange Rate Mechanism work in the sense of facilitating payments between members. The intervention mechanism which is designed to make the ERM work obliges countries' central banks to give each other unlimited, very short-term credit facilities to finance required interventions. These loans and debts are paid through the EMCF in ECUs and interest is also paid in ECUs. In August and September 1992, for example, Germany provided enormous assistance to Italy and the United Kingdom to support their currencies but to no avail. As the single market developed to 1992, more and more restrictions on banking and on movements of money were relaxed. Under Stage 2 of the plan for monetary union regulations are being harmonised. The agreement reached at Maastricht in December 1991 in the Treaty on Union shows that the EMCF/EMI and the ECU will both play an increasingly important part in the progress towards a new central bank and a currency for the European Union as outlined below. The functions of the EMCF/EMI will no longer be required when the ECU's successor is established as a single currency because there will be no exchange rate fluctuations between the currencies of participating countries. A European Central Bank will be established when a single currency is adopted. Presumably, the EMCF function, or some variant, will still be required for any country still outside the single currency but within the remains, if any, of the ERM.

The European Currency Unit

The ECU was a new name for the European Unit of Account (EUA), introduced in 1975, and has taken over all the functions of the EUA. From 1950 there had been a unit of account introduced by the European Payments Union (EPU) which was very straightforward in that it was based on the weight of gold in one US dollar. It was converted into national currencies at the official central rates for a member's currency, as determined by the Bretton Woods agreement. When that agreement began to break down in the early 1970s a number of different units of account were adopted, based on a variety of measures, some relatively stable, some fluctuating. The EUA replaced all these and was based on a specific quantity of each of the members' currencies. This was a copy of the Special Drawing Rights (SDRs) introduced by the IMF in 1969. The value of the SDRs was based upon an agreed 'basket' of 16 different currencies weighted according to their relative importance. The ECU then is a 'basket' currency which is used in the Union's budget, in payments between members and between them and African, Caribbean, Asian and Pacific members of the Lomé Convention. It is also used in Common Agricultural Policy payments, in the European Coal and Steel Community and in the European Investment Bank and may be held as a reserve currency at the EMI by non-members of the Union. Apart from these official uses there is a rapidly growing private market for the ECU; loans in ECUs can be raised by companies; you can buy travellers' cheques in ECUs; payments can be made in ECUs, and they are quoted on foreign exchange markets. In 1988, the United Kingdom government began issuing Treasury Bills in ECUs to finance some of its short-term borrowing requirements and in 1991 floated a foreign currency bond denominated in ECU and amounting to 2.5 billion ECU. It has continued to issue ECU Treasury Bills at regular intervals and in April 1995 there were ECU 3.5 billion outstanding. The United Kingdom government's total outstanding debt in ECU-denominated bills and bonds was ECU 11.5 billion. Many other European Union members such as France, Austria, Italy and Denmark and some supranational organisations and corporate bodies also issue debt denominated in ECU. The European market in ECU bond issues developed quickly but suffered a setback after the 1992 ERM crisis. The ECU is a genuine currency in international payments. It is not available as notes or coin, except for collectors, but is a unit of account, a store of value and a medium of exchange, that is it performs the traditional functions of money. The Isle of Man has issued a legal tender ECU gold coin but that is not of great monetary significance. There is every possibility that, at the end of the century, a version of the ECU, with a different name, will be *the* currency of the Union of a number of member states, although its nature will have changed and there would be a European Central Bank to control its issue. The United Kingdom made an attempt in 1990 and 1991 to have the ECU adopted as an *extra* currency alongside the others and usable at the individual's discretion as well as for interstate transfers. This proposal for the so-called 'hard' ECU never appealed to most of the other members because it showed a lack of commitment to monetary union and was regarded as a typical British attempt to stall the implementation of the programme recommended in the Delors Committee Report on Economic and Monetary Union of April 1989. The idea was briefly revived in early 1995 by the United Kingdom Prime Minister.

How the ECU 'basket' is made up

The quantity of each currency in the basket was re-examined every five years, in 1984 and 1989, but has been frozen from the date that the Treaty on Union came into force, 1 November 1993. The amounts are given in Table 7.1. The last reconstitution was in September 1989 to include the escudo and the peseta. The Greek drachma was included in September 1984. The weight of each currency can vary a little day by day and more over time because of the appreciation and depreciation of currencies against one another. The weight of a currency is calculated by dividing the amount of the currency by its official ECU exchange rate which is worked out at specific times of each day. The weights given in Table 7.1 are those on 1 February 1994.

You can look up the value of the pound in ECUs in the foreign exchange section of a newspaper. In October 1995, £1 = ECU 1.2161, or 82 pence. In 1994 the rate averaged £1 = 1.2924 ECU, or one ECU was worth about 77 pence.

The ECU is bought and sold on the foreign exchanges just like any other currency and also features in futures and options markets. Billions are dealt in every day on the exchanges and their use is growing and extending. One of their attractions is their relative stability in the markets which tends to reduce some of the risks of international trading and financial transfers.

TABLE 7.1

Composition of the ECU and its Weights 1 February 1994

Currency	One ECU comprises the following fixed amount of national currencies:	Weight %	ECU Exchange rate
Deutschmark	0.6242	32.1	1.9451
French franc	1.332	20.2	6.604
Sterling	0.08784	11.8	0.7461
Dutch guilder	0.2198	10.1	2.1792
Belgian/Lux franc	3.431	8.6	40.107
Italian lira	151.8	8.0	1896.4
Spanish peseta	6.885	3.5	195.52
Danish krone	0.1976	2.6	7.5493
Irish pound	0.008552	1.1	0.7765
Portuguese escudo	1.393	0.9	157.4
Greek drachma	1.44	0.5	279.71

NOTES 1. The amounts of currencies in an ECU were frozen on 1 November 1993 and will not be altered, even if new members join
2. The weights can vary each day and over time as currencies appreciate or depreciate
3. The official ECU exchange rate is fixed at certain times each day
4. The weight $= \dfrac{\text{The amount of a currency}}{\text{Official ECU exchange rate}} \times 100$

SOURCE Bank of England Fact Sheet, May 1994

In order to calculate the value of the ECU, the central bank in each member state works out a representative market rate for its currency against the dollar. These rates together can then be used to calculate the dollar equivalent of the basket of European Union currencies. The ECU is thus valued at the sum of the dollar equivalents of the currencies in the basket.

The Exchange Rate Mechanism

The mechanism was designed to help create what was called, when it was introduced in March 1979. 'a zone of monetary stability'. In order to create stability in the relationships of the exchange rates of the members, it was decided to replace the early 1970s' versions of the 'snake in the tunnel' systems referred to above with a grid system. Each participant establishes a central rate for its currency which is expressed in ECUs. The rate set has to be approved by all the members and is not set solely at the individual country's discretion. Greece has not yet been a member of the ERM. Spain joined the mechanism in June 1989 and Portugal in April 1992. The United Kingdom joined, after intense debate, in October 1990 and was forced out, together with Italy in September 1992. Austria joined in January 1995. In normal circumstances new entrants adopted 'wide' bands of 6 per cent permitted divergence from their central rates as opposed to the usual 2.25 per cent. Italy, which operated a wide, 6 per cent band, adopted the narrower band in January 1990 before being forced out of the ERM in September 1992. The United Kingdom operated under the wide 6 per cent bond whilst it was a member. In August 1993, after more massive speculation in foreign exchange markets, the ERM bands were extended to 15 per cent and many commentators declared the ERM and the prospect of monetary union dead. However, after realignments of some currencies to new, lower central rates and even after more destabilisation caused by the strength of the Yen and Deutschmark and fluctuations of the US dollar, most of the currencies settled back into the 'narrow' 2.25 per cent bands, albeit with the occasional dip outside. Germany and the Netherlands have a bilateral agreement to keep to 2.25 per cent narrow bands.

After fixing a central rate, the next step is to use these ECU expressed rates to work out a grid of bilateral exchange rates, for example between the Deutschmark and the French franc. See Table 7.2 for details of the grid. Once these bilateral rates are established a restriction is put upon the extent to which the market rates may diverge from the bilateral rates – normally up to 2.25 per cent on either side. These margins on either side of the bilateral rate are accompanied by a central rate fixed against the ECU which enables 'divergence indicators' to be established (see below). It is likely that Greece, Sweden and Finland will initially be given a 6 per cent margin on either side of their central rates if their currency joins the ERM, assuming that the 15 per cent no longer applies. Before the United Kingdom joined there was considerable debate about the desirable level of divergence to be granted and the length of the transition period. The crucial question, however, was the level of the bilateral rate against the German mark, which was eventually set at £1 = DM 2.95. Many economists regarded this as too high a rate and one which might prove indefensible in the long run. They were proved correct and sterling fell by over 20 per cent against the Deutschmark between September 1992 and July 1995 after leaving the ERM. It had recovered slightly in September 1995 until another bout of speculation struck the markets during an ECOFIN meeting to discuss the single currency.

TABLE 7.2

The Currency Grid (bilateral central rates and selling and buying rates in the EMS exchange rate mechanism for four countries from the nine in the system, from 6 March 1995)

		Belg/Lux 100 francs	*Danish 100 krone*	*French 100 francs*	*German 100 DM*
Belgium/	S	—	627.880	714.030	2395.20
Luxembourg	C	—	540.723	614.977	2062.55
B/L francs	B	—	465.665	529.660	1776.20
Denmark	S	21.4747	—	132.066	442.968
D. Krone	C	18.4938	—	113.732	381.443
	B	15.9266	—	97.943	328.461
France	S	18.8800	102.100	—	389.480
FF. francs	C	16.2608	87.9257	—	335.386
	B	14.0050	75.7200	—	288.810
Germany	S	5.63000	30.4450	34.6250	—
deutschmarks	C	4.84837	26.2162	29.8164	—
	B	4.17500	22.5750	25.6750	—

C = Bilateral central rate

S/B = Exchange rate at which the central bank of the country in the left-hand column will sell/buy the currency identified in the row at the top of the table

SOURCE   Bank of England Fact Sheet, May 1994 updated

Although the narrow band is fixed at 2.25 per cent on either side of a central rate, this does not mean that a particular currency could necessarily fluctuate against another by a full 4.5 per cent. This is because it is part of a grid against all the other currencies within the ERM. For example, the Belgian franc might reach its limit against the peseta before it could make full use of its range against the French franc. The consequence of this impact of the grid is that the band in practice is less than 4.5 per cent and appears nearer half that.

Since 1979 there have been periods in which one or more countries' currencies have got into difficulties, leading to 19 realignments of the central rates between 1979 and 1995. Table 7.3 gives a brief history of the ERM. These realignments, in the early days, usually involved revaluing the deutschmark and guilder and devaluing the lira and French francs. Recent realignments in 1995 have been of the peseta and escudo. The French have been pursuing a *franc fort* policy and have withstood realignments at great cost as their level of unemployment has risen in consequence. Such readjustments must be done by agreement because every country's ECU-related central rate is dependent on the rates of the other countries. The sequence of events, therefore, is for the bilateral rates to be renegotiated first after which the central rate is recalculated. There will probably be a final realignment of currencies during State 2 of EMU before 1999 as member states move to narrower bands within the ERM to enable a single currency to be established. The United Kingdom may have re-entered the ERM by then, depending on which party is in government. Italy too may have rejoined if it has reduced its political instability. It expressed a keen desire to re-enter the ERM so that the lira could be ready for the single currency but the German Finance Minister, speaking in September 1995, was not very convinced of Italy's entry in 1999.

TABLE 7.3
An ERM Chronology: Developments in ERM Central Rates (1979–95)

There have been nineteen realignments since the EMS was founded

Year	Date	Currency	% Realignment
1979	13 March	Start of the EMS (+/− 2.25% for all participants except LIT at +/− 6%)	
	24 September	DM	+2
		DKR	−2.9
	30 November	DKR	−4.76
1981	23 March	LIT	−6
	5 October	DM, DFL	+5.5
		FFC, LIT	−3

TABLE 7.3 *Continued*

Year	Date	Currency	% Realignment
There have been nineteen realignments since the EMS was founded			
1982	22 February	BFC	−3.5
		DKR	−3
	14 June	DM, DFL	+4.25
		LIT	−2.75
		FFC	−5.75
1983	21 March	DM	+5.5
		DFL	+3.5
		DKR	+2.5
		BFC	+1.5
		FFC, LIT	−2.5
		IR£	−3.5
1985	22 July	BFC, DKR, DM, FFC, IR£, DFL	+2
		LIT	−6
1986	7 April	DM, DFL	+3
		BFC, DKR	+1
		FFC	−3
	4 August	IR£	−8
1987	12 January	DM, DFL	+3
		BFC	+2
1989	19 June	Entry of Spanish peseta (+/− 6%)	
1990	8 January	LIT (adoption of narrow band)	−3.7
	8 October	Entry of pound sterling (+/− 6% band)	
1992	6 April	Entry of Portuguese escudo (+/− 6% band)	
	14 September	BFC, DM, DFL, DKR, ESC, FFC, IR£, PTA, UK£	+3.5
		LIT	−3.5
	17 September	UK£, LIT Suspend ERM membership	
		PTA	−5
	23 November	ESC, PTA	−6
1993	1 February	IR£	−10
	14 May	PTA	−8

		ESC	−6.5
	2 August	Widening of fluctuation margins to +/−15% for all ERM currencies	
	9 January	Entry of Austrian schilling	
1995	4 March	PTA	−7
	6 March	ESC	−3.5

The net change in a particular central rate is approximately equal to the difference in the percentage changes shown against the two currencies concerned. For example, in March 1983 the Deutsche mark was revalued by 2% against the guilder and 9% against the Irish pound

SOURCE Bank of England Fact Sheet, May 1994 with additions

What are the divergence indicators for?

Divergence indicators are intended, first, to act as an early warning that a particular currency is deviating too much from the average, and, secondly, to provoke an early response before the gap grows too large. It is presumed in the EMS that a country will take appropriate action to restore the level of its currency and to remove or restrain the cause of its divergence. The system should encourage economic discipline and make governments work harder at controlling their inflation rates and public sector spending. They have not been completely successful in this because of the political reluctance of some governments to take the necessary measures. This is one reason why there have been realignments over the years.

What happens if a divergence indicator is reached?

If a currency touches its 2.25 per cent, 6 per cent or 15 per cent margin above or below its bilateral rate against another country, it must take specific actions in its economic policies to readjust the relationship over time. The divergence indicator is set at a level within these outer limits to give it early warning to take action. In the short run it will indulge in intervention buying and selling, and is helped by the other country involved. In addition the central bank with the strong currency buys the weak currency, and the central bank with the weak currency sells the strong currency. It may borrow from the 'strong' central bank if it does not have enough reserves to sell. These manipulations are conducted with the help of the EMI (EMCF before 1994) and all the dealings are in ECUs. The Very Short Term Financing mechanism (VSTF) is the device used by the EMI for lending to members to help support their exchange rate. Any interest on loans is also paid in ECUs. The use of ECUs has the effect of sharing between the two countries the risk of any loss on the foreign exchange dealings. This intervention is compulsory once the divergence thresholds are reached, but a country may choose to take earlier action and indulge in what is called *intramarginal* intervention. The 'strong' currency has often been the Deutschmark and Germany has sometimes been reluctant to persist with assistance for an obviously overvalued currency and has recommended realignment instead. Italy took this advice, unavailingly, in 1992 but the United Kingdom refused and was forced out of the ERM. Germany had spent an estimated DM 24 billion assisting the lira and very large sums helping sterling.

What has been the Effect of the Exchange Rate Mechanism since 1979?

The participants have very diverse economies with varying degrees of reliance upon foreign trade, and their balance-of-payments positions and rates of inflation differ greatly. Germany has dominated the ERM because of its low inflation, steady growth and its usually very healthy balance-of-payments surpluses. Italy tended to be a problem, despite the greater 6 per cent range of latitude for the lira until 1990. The French economy has gone through bad patches but has recovered. Belgium, the Netherlands and Austria, and to some extent Denmark have kept their exchange rates very stable against the Deutschmark. In 1991 Sweden, before joining the European Union, tried to keep its currency exchange rate as if it were already in the ERM but was forced to abandon the policy. In the face of this variety the ERM has, on the whole, achieved a remarkable degree of stability of exchange rates for its participants in a period when world exchange rates have been volatile. The study of comparative exchange rate movements is beset with statistical problems, but the rates of the currencies within the grid seem to have been less subject to the extremes of fluctuation than those outside it. This is not necessarily entirely due to them being in the

ERM, but the supporters of the EMS believe that it is. It can be argued that there is a zone of Deutschmark stability rather than a full ERM zone. The exceptional volatility of exchange rates since early 1992 has caused some economists to say that monetary union is impossible but has inspired others, especially in Germany and France, to argue that it means that monetary union should be speeded up. Most of the problems have been a spill-over from the fluctuations of the yen against the US dollar, from speculation arising from anticipated interest changes, and from the use of the Deutschmark as a haven.

Why did the United Kingdom Not Join the ERM until 1990?

The Labour government of 1974 to 1979 was a weak government reliant on the support of minority parties. Despite the referendum which strongly supported the United Kingdom's continued membership there was a powerful element in the party and Cabinet which regarded the Community as an alien authority. They feared deeper involvement in any enterprise which appeared to them to be non-socialist in aspiration or from which they could not easily escape. The government faced severe difficulties in its economic management. The inflation rate and level of unemployment were rising rapidly. A succession of incomes policies was tried and found wanting, culminating in the breakdown of the 'social contract' and the subsequent 'winter of discontent'. The balance of payments and the value of the pound were both subject to unusual pressures because of the inflow of capital to exploit North Sea oil development. Large loans had been raised from the IMF and other groups of international lenders. It was thus not thought to be a good time to embark on what was seen as another uncertainty by joining the ERM. It may be that the government was not willing to accept the required levels of discipline to make the pound fit within the ERM, regarding it as a surrender of sovereignty over its economic policies. The arguments since 1990 over whether sterling should join a single currency are strongly reminiscent of the debate in the late 1970s.

Between 1979 and 1990 the pound fluctuated between wide extremes. As a result there was a sharp conflict between those whose interest was in having a low exchange rate, mainly against the dollar (that is exporters), and those who favoured a high rate (that is importers). For a time the pound, on a tide of oil, reached the 1967 devaluation rate of £1 = $2.40. This had a devastating effect on manufacturing industry and was partially responsible, together with high interest rates, for the destruction of the United Kingdom's manufacturing base in the early 1980s. Then, for a while, the pound fell so low that experts were predicting a £1 = $1 exchange rate. There were, however, reasons for this greater volatility of the pound. Sterling is more important than the other European currencies in international trade and finance. The general point of importance, though, is that there was no real agreement on what is a reasonable, workable rate of exchange against the dollar and the yen. The United Kingdom government had no genuinely consistent policy with relation to the exchange rate except to let it float in accordance with market forces. It did, periodically, intervene to halt a movement or to nudge it in a certain direction and its interest rate policies sometimes had an exchange rate dimension, in that it was aimed at influencing the flow of capital into and out of sterling.

Although there was a lack of a coherent, interventionist policy, a consensus of opinion grew up that strongly favoured the United Kingdom's entry into the ERM. Thus, by 1987, it appeared that Mrs Thatcher, with a few loyal supporters, was the only obstacle to joining, and there was a major difference of opinion between her and the Treasury and the Bank of England. This position gradually changed after mid-1988 as more economists analysed the hypothetical effects of the United Kingdom's joining. They became more cautious in their support and some became critical of the possible effects. One cause of the change was the revelation that Mr Lawson, the Chancellor of the Exchequer, had been following a policy of keeping sterling in step with the German mark for about a year, with a view to joining the ERM. A number of economic events undermined this policy and Mrs Thatcher disapproved of the degree of intervention required in the foreign exchange markets.

In the final analysis, however, the main reason why the United Kingdom did not join the Exchange Rate Mechanism was the fear of loss of economic sovereignty and the reluctance to accept externally imposed discipline over economic policy. There was a lack of agreement about what level to set for the pound against the mark, and there were problems about the percentage allowed initially for divergence from the central rate. These were resolved when the United Kingdom joined the ERM on 8 October 1990 at a central rate against the Deutschmark of £1 = DM 2.95, within a wide band of 6 per cent. After some initial difficulties the pound settled down within its bands and did not come under real pressure until the end of 1991, when the United Kingdom showed a lack of commitment to the EMS when it chose to demand an opt-out clause from the Union Treaty draft at the Maastricht summit in December 1991. The pound was also unsettled by the failure of the economy to rise out of its recession and by the strength of the US dollar. The real difficulty for some sections of British opinion in adopting a full commitment to the European monetary union is a psychological one related to national pride, independence and sovereignty. There had also been some disenchantment with the price that had to be paid for membership of the ERM in terms of an externally imposed discipline that resulted in an inability to manipulate aggregate demand or interest rates in preparation for a general election in 1991 and in an ominous rise in unemployment.

The 'impossibility theorem'

The last statement of the previous paragraph makes the point that politicians and the public were slow to wake up to the reality of what economists call the 'impossibility theorem'. This states that the bodies responsible for economic and financial policies cannot simul-taneously and continuously follow the three objectives of: (1) free mobility of capital; (2) fixed exchange rates; and (3) an independent monetary policy. The integration of world capital markets means that, in practice, monetary authorities have to obtain the best trade-off between the second and third, exchange rates and domestic monetary independence. This idea is very important when discussing the development of European monetary union.

Why was the United Kingdom forced out of the Exchange Rate Mechanism?

In August and September 1992 a tidal wave of speculative transfer of currencies forced the United Kingdom and Italy, on 16 and 17 September, to withdraw the pound sterling and the lira from the ERM, and threatened the very existence of the mechanism itself.

The financial turmoil took place against a background of uncertainty about the ratification of the Maastricht Treaty on European Union, especially in respect of the French referendum of
20 September. The events in the currency markets sent shock
waves through the political world. The media reacted by giving
more emphasis than usual to those who predicted the total collapse
of the ERM and the demise of the Maastricht agreement. It was,
for the United Kingdom Government, a traumatic period because
it was forced to abandon the central plank of its economic policy,
that is the achievement of low inflation by the discipline of the
ERM. In what was inevitably called a 'U-turn', it returned to a
floating, depreciating pound, to the prospect of higher inflation
and to a short-term deterioration of the balance of payments.
The only political rewards lay in the ability, up to a point, to cut
interest rates, in the hope that the falling exchange rate would help
trade and reduce unemployment and in the encouragement of the
belief that it could now resume an independent economic policy.
This independence is partly an illusion and the United Kingdom
has paid a penalty for being outside the ERM in the form of an
interest rate that has been approximately 2 per cent above Germany's and that of the other core countries. The differential is
likely to continue as long as the United Kingdom remains outside
the ERM.

When German reunification took place the Federal Government
under Chancellor Kohl took the decision, against the advice of the
Deutsche Bundesbank, to adopt an exchange rate of one Deutschmark for one East German Mark. For technical reasons the real
rate was closer to 1 DM for 1.5 East Marks. It also decided to
finance the immense cost of reunification not from increased
taxation but from reserves and borrowing. (A 'unification tax' was
imposed later.) These decisions were taken for sensible political
reasons but had an inflationary effect. The Bundesbank responded
dutifully by tightening its monetary policy and raising its interest
rates. On 16 July 1992 it added 0.75 per cent to the Lombard rate
to reach a 10 per cent level, the highest since 1932. At the same
time, the United States was following a low-interest-rate policy in
a desperate attempt to pull its economy out of recession in the run
up to the November Presidential election.

The conjunction of high (10 per cent) interest rates in Germany
and Europe, and low (3 per cent) rates in the United States

stimulated the transfer of capital from US dollar holdings into other currencies, especially the Deutschmark and the Dutch guilder which was closely tied to it. The yen was also favoured after the Japanese government injected money into its flagging economy. Other European countries were forced to raise their interest rates in line with Germany in order to minimise outflows of capital. Some countries such as Sweden, Finland and Norway which had aligned their currencies with the ECU, and thereby to the Deutschmark, were also forced to raise interest rates. The volume of money that is available for movement in international currency markets is immense and has been growing since the progressive abolition of controls on capital movements after 1979. In September 1992 a spokesman for the United States Treasury estimated the figure passing through the foreign exchange markets at $1000 billion *daily*. Of this, about 7–10 per cent related to trade transactions in visibles, to invisibles and to capital movements for investment in real assets. The rest was 'hot' money seeking to maximise interest rate yields and short-term capital gains in so far as that was commensurate with security. In contrast, he estimated that the six leading countries' reserves available for intervention in currency markets totalled only $250 billion.

The United Kingdom entered the ERM at a central rate of £1 = DM 2.95, a level regarded as too high by many economists. Its permitted floor in the 6 per cent wide band of divergence was DM 2.7780. By mid-August 1992 it had fallen to the psychologically important low of DM 2.80 mainly because the United Kingdom had not raised interest rates to follow the latest German rise. This was because of the basic underlying weakness of the United Kingdom economy signified by a failure to recover from the recession after the April General Election. The balance of payments was deteriorating rapidly despite the recession, a time when it should have improved. A rise in domestic interest rates would have been politically damaging. The Government comforted itself with the lower inflation rates being achieved and by the strength of sterling against the dollar. The rate reached £1 = $1.99 in late August on the same day it fell to DM 2.79. The British public was assured that it was the dollar that had problems not the pound.

In the last week of August the currency markets became very active as French opinion polls began to predict a 'No' vote in their referendum on the Maastricht Treaty. Some intervention buying occurred to help the pound and pressure was put on Germany to cut its interest rates. The United Kingdom borrowed ECU 10 billion to support the pound by an intricate method that received admiration from the money markets until it dawned on them that, despite its cleverness, it was not really different from the much maligned loan from the IMF in 1978. After four days of relative calm the Finnish markka was devalued and floated after breaking its link to the Deutschmark. Sweden and Norway raised some interest rates to very high levels. The pound fell to near its floor on 9 September but the Prime Minister ruled out devaluation or realignment as 'a soft option' and said that the United Kingdom would keep the DM 2.95 central rate even if other countries in the ERM realigned. On 13 September Germany persuaded Italy to realign the lira downwards with an effective devaluation of 7 per cent. Germany had spent about DM 24 billion supporting the lira under the ERM system. In return it promised that the Bundesbank would cut interest rates. The United Kingdom, in a fateful decision, decided not to take the opportunity of realigning the pound.

The promised cut in the German Lombard rate was a disappointing 0.25 per cent. The Bundesbank was asserting its independence and regarded a greater change as unjustifiable in terms of German needs. The markets reacted very strongly. The lira could not maintain its new parity and sterling fell to its floor. The United Kingdom Chancellor, Norman Lamont, tried, very belatedly, to raise interest rates to stem the speculative flows. Minimum Lending Rate was reinstated to raise rates by 2 per cent on the morning of 16 September, and when that had no effect, by a further 3 per cent in the afternoon. The 15 per cent rate had no effect and the pound was suspended from the ERM. The 3 per cent rise was immediately removed, followed next day by the removal of the 2 per cent increase. Rates returned to 10 per cent. The currency dealers rejoiced at their profits which were estimated at £900 million over the week.

The lira also left the ERM and Spain devalued the peseta by 5 per cent. Italy said it would rejoin the ERM within a few days but later changed that to 'at the first opportunity'. The United Kingdom's Prime Minister said, at first, that sterling 'would resume membership of the ERM as soon as circumstances allow'. He later told Parliament that he had a list of conditions that must be met before sterling rejoined. He has since changed the timescale and said that sterling would not rejoin the ERM until after the next general election, that is probably not until 1997. The United Kingdom quickly cut its interest rates by 1 per cent to 9 per cent in order to stimulate the domestic economy. Further cuts followed. The pound rapidly fell to £1 = DM 2.50 with the expectation that it might fall further. By June 1995 it had fallen to an all-time low of £1 = DM 2.18 because of more speculation about the US economy and interest rate changes. A rate between DM 2.20 and DM 2.30 seems a likely longer-term level. The dollar strengthened after late 1992 as funds flowed back but has since weakened in 1994 and 1995. The devaluation of sterling against the Deutschmark and other core European currencies will be inflationary over the next few years, but the short and medium effect on employment has been beneficial. It is, of course, hard to separate the effect of sterling leaving the ERM from the more generalised impact of the world economic recovery. The initial response of the media was to label the 16 September 1992 as 'black Wednesday', but many prefer to call it 'white Wednesday'. The latter is favoured by the Eurosceptics and those who prefer to forget that an increase in inflation lags about two years behind foreign exchange rate depreciation.

The currency speculators, fresh from their triumph over sterling and the lira, switched their attention to the French franc but determined Franco-German resistance in the form of intervention buying drove them off until after the French referendum. They returned but were again repulsed but were more successful against the peseta, escudo and punt in early 1995. There is a constant risk that they will return to the fray especially as the ERM bands are narrowed closer to the establishment of a single currency. In 1992 Ireland, Spain and Portugal, who all suffered from speculative attention, imposed short-lived controls on capital movements. Their success has encouraged the discussion of methods of revamping the ERM to include controls on capital movements. Some experts say that the new electronic markets make this impossible but others argue that it might make the flows easier to restrict or penalise.

Will the Single Market have much Impact on Money and Banking?

Several Directives have come into effect and will gradually have an enormous effect, although some are in several respects weaker than originally envisaged. The Capital Adequacy Directive (CAD) and the Investment Services Directives both came into effect on 1 January 1996. The main Directives on banking have been in force longer than those for insurance and investment services but often years elapse between the passing of a Directive and it coming into force. The Second Banking Directive, for example, was passed in 1989 but only came into effect in 1993. The main approach has been to provide what is called a 'passport' which establishes that authorisation from the regulatory body in a firm's home state enables that firm to operate throughout the Union without further authorisation. There are still gaps in the liberalisation programme relating to pensions, insolvency laws, legal services, auditors' liability, borrowing and lending techniques in the real estate sector, and collective investment schemes in transferable securities. There are still problems remaining from the transposition of the Directives into national laws. Some states transpose on the basis of broad principles whilst others apply a detailed and strict interpretation.

It is the intention that the movement of services and capital as well as that of goods and people should be freed from artificial restrictions. This has involved the dismantling, in most states, of a range of restrictions on the holding and transfer of capital and currency. The United Kingdom had relatively few controls except those required to prevent fraud and to protect the customer, the shareholder and the depositor. It was partly this lack of controls, matched only by Luxembourg, that enabled the City of London to retain its pre-eminence in European financial markets. However there is a long-term threat to this position as the European markets are also freed. The French, German and Italian stock exchanges and other continental financial markets are being modernised. Continental banks, especially German banks, are becoming more international as can be seen by their purchase of banks and financial institutions in the United Kingdom.

There is a real risk that the City of London will fail to put enough resources into European financial centres to exploit the new markets. A proposal for an early linking of major financial centres with a common electronic dealing system has foundered although new attempts are being made. It is expected that all EU members will have domestic real-time gross settlement systems by the end of 1996. The EMI, since 1994, has been working with national central banks to link these domestic systems. The EMI has approved a new payment mechanism to be known inevitably by yet another acronym, TARGET (Trans-European Automated Real-Time Gross Settlement Express Transfer System). Assuming that it comes into existence and does not simply join the expanding graveyard of acronyms, it will be run by the EMI with national central bank assistance. It is a matter of dispute as to whether the delays that have occurred will help perpetuate London's pre-eminence or allow the other major European centres to prosper more quickly. There is also a threat to the City in that the new Union rules may, in some respects, make London less attractive to non-European banks such as the Japanese, Arabian and American. A decisive influence may prove to be the decision to locate in Frankfurt the new European Monetary Institute (EMI) which it is intended will become the European Central Bank (ECB) during Stage 3 of monetary union. The development of information technology may mean that its Frankfurt head office where decisions are made will not be the place in which its activities occur. Mr Major opted out of commitment to Stage 3 of monetary union at the Maastricht summit in December 1991 and thereby forfeited any supportable claim to the EMI and ECB being established in London. He seemed remarkably blasé in the House of Commons at the prospect of not securing this important insurance to the continuing dominance of the City of London, but a great deal of disquiet was expressed by others at the long-term consequences of the Central Bank going to Frankfurt.

There have also been significant changes in the framework within which insurance services operate. These changes, theoretically, provide great opportunities in Europe for British companies which already have a major international role but some early indications are that continental insurers are moving into the United Kingdom market via rescue operations and take-overs. A general fear of some British commentators is that the single market will impose a more bureaucratic regulatory framework than exists in the United Kingdom today. This, it is argued, partly defeats the objective of freeing the European Union from restrictions.

The liberalisation of the financial services within the European Union has, to some extent, been paralleled by an effort to liberalise world markets. The December 1993 Uruguay Round of GATT agreement included what is called GATS, or General Agreement on Trade in Services. Over the next few years the World Trade Organisation set up by the Uruguay Round to replace GATT, will work to eliminate obstacles to free trade in financial services. The central principle is that of the 'most favoured nation' (MFN) which prevents countries discriminating between the service suppliers of other members of the WTO. Unfortunately, the first talks in June 1995 on the details of liberalisation collapsed when the USA withdrew. They were resumed and reached agreement without the USA in July 1995.

These rather mundane areas of early advance were overshadowed by the row that developed in 1988 between Mrs Thatcher, then Prime Minister of the United Kingdom, and other members of the Community, notably Jacques Delors, the President of the Commission. This concerned the idea that the Single Market and the freeing of capital movements made inevitable the creation of a Community central bank and a single Community currency. Mrs Thatcher dismissed this idea as nonsense despite public opinion polls at the time that indicated that the British people would not mind a European currency. M. Delors was, of course, right. A single market for capital, a European Monetary System based on the ECU and an Exchange Rate Mechanism all suggest the need for a single, or super, European Central Bank and a single currency. Mrs Thatcher and her successor Mr Major may have delayed the introduction, and the United Kingdom and some other members may never join, but the single currency and European Central Bank will almost certainly arrive in due course. The next chapter deals with the debate about a single currency and monetary union.

One Market, One Money? 8

The Single European Act (SEA) of 1986 which created the 1992 single market plan included economic and monetary union as a formal objective and imposed on the members an obligation to work towards a convergence of domestic policies in order to achieve it. The Treaty, however, required any future institutional changes in respect of monetary policy to be done by amendment to the Treaty, a process which required unanimity. Those who opposed or who were doubtful about a future common monetary policy thought that this procedure would satisfactorily delay any change. They were disappointed and what followed is an object lesson for those who fail to take account of the steamroller like capability of the Commission and European Union to grind onwards to a conclusion. M. Delors and the Community central bankers met in committee and produced in April 1989 what came to be called 'the Delors Committee Report'. This was to lead to a powerful surge towards fuller economic and monetary union and to a new treaty. An incidental effect of the surge was to carry away Mrs Thatcher from the office of Prime Minister in November 1990 as her opposition to monetary union caused her to adopt an embarrassingly strident tone which was out of tune with important elements in her party and cabinet.

The Delors Committee Report

In June 1988 the Hanover summit meeting agreed to Jacques Delors, President of the Commission, forming a committee of 17 members including governors of central banks from members of the Community. The Governor of the Bank of England attended in a 'personal capacity'. Its task was to study the steps needed to achieve a monetary union as defined in the SEA though its terms of reference did not, at Mrs Thatcher's insistence, include mention of a single currency for Europe or a European Central Bank. The committee started meeting in September 1988 and produced a unanimous report in April 1989 which was accepted by the Madrid summit in June 1989.

The report defined monetary union as 'a currency area in which policies are managed jointly with a view to obtaining common macro-economic objectives' and laid down three conditions for achieving one. These three points have been central to the discussions ever since and will remain so for the rest of the decade. They were, first, total and irreversible convertibility of currencies; second, the complete liberalisation of capital markets and the integration of financial markets; and third, the irrevocable locking of exchange rate parities. The committee said that once these three conditions had been achieved individual national currencies would become substitutes and that interest rates would tend to equalise between every member state. As a result it would be possible to have a single currency for the Community and that this would be desirable though not strictly necessary. The report went on to state the need for a common monetary policy with a new institution to implement it, that is a federal European System of Central Banks (ESCB) which would have a Council appointed by the Council of Ministers and be independent of national governments. It would govern national central banks whose functions would gradually wither away as monetary union developed.

The report included a list of the four basic elements required for economic growth. Three of these caused no surprise because they were simply restatements of previously held beliefs; that is, a Single Market with free movement of goods, persons, capital and services; a competition policy and other measures to strengthen markets, and common policies directed at structural change and regional development. The fourth, however, was the coordination of macro-economic policies including binding rules for budgetary policies. This raised all sorts of fears and spectres in the hearts of those who were concerned about economic sovereignty and the ability of national governments to use budgetary policies to steer the economic cycle for electoral purposes. It also led to the development of discussions about the nature and degree of convergence of national economies required before monetary union could take place.

The committee outlined a timetable for the attainment of economic and monetary union, or EMU as it came to be called, and proposed three stages. Stage 1, which actually started in July 1990 following an agreement at the Madrid summit in June 1989, and has been completed, involved concentrating on the completion of the single market from its starting date of 1 January 1993 and on increasing monetary cooperation. The coordination of policies has been improved through the working of the Council of Economic and Finance Ministers, which is called ECOFIN in Euro-jargon. Those members not in the ERM were expected to join and the United Kingdom (1990–92), Spain and Portugal did so, leaving only Greece, plus later members Sweden and Finland outside. Austria joined in January 1995. No time-scale was fixed for this stage but the committee thought that seven years would be sufficient. During Stage one each nation was expected to supervise its own economic performance in the light of agreed economic objectives. After July 1990 there was an increase in cooperation and consultation and some countries such as Denmark, Belgium and the Netherlands began to operate within a narrower self-imposed band within the ERM, trying to keep their exchange rates more stable against the Deutschmark.

Stages 2 and 3, which were eventually incorporated in modified form in the Treaty on Union at Maastricht, were not given definite starting dates or time spans in the report. During Stage 2 changes to the Treaty of Rome could be made, or a new treaty agreed. Decision-making would become collective and the European System of Central Banks (ESCB) would be set up. The emphasis would be on setting medium-term objectives by the use of majority voting but other collective decisions on budget deficits, exchange rate and other monetary policies would need unanimous decisions. Gradually, during Stage 2, fluctuations of currencies within the ERM grid would be eliminated. All this would involve a substantial transfer of economic power from national governments to the ESCB. It was this proposed transfer that most concerned the objectors to the plan. Stage 3 of the Delors committee plan would have given the ESCB the power to put constraints on national budgets in order to preserve monetary stability or to increase Community revenues or to force members to make their economic adjustments more effective. At this point the Community could adopt a single currency, such as the ECU, and national currencies could be phased out.

The Madrid summit meeting, in a compromise, decided, as stated above, to implement Stage 1 of the Delors report on 1 July 1990 and to establish an Inter-Governmental Conference (IGC) to plan for economic and monetary union. This IGC was to run parallel with another one on Political Union and both were to prepare reports and draft treaties for a final decision to be made at the Maastricht summit in December 1991. The discussion of economic and monetary union and political union side by side was essential because the proposals to have a single currency and single central bank for the Community seemed to produce the inevitable conclusion that some sort of a federal union would eventually develop, to replace the separate national states. There was still a debate going on in the United Kingdom in 1994 and 1995 as to whether a single currency inevitably implied political union or not. Cabinet ministers appeared to take different views. Those who were dubious about the Delors report hoped that the IGCs would fail to produce an agreement that could be put into treaty form but they underestimated the political drive towards economic and monetary union that had been generated by the logic of the creation of the single market. They naïvely thought that they could settle for an enormous free trade area without any necessity for closer political and economic union. In practice, the decision to adopt Stage 1 of the Delors committee report was also a decision to adopt the later stages because the path to monetary union was clearly shown by the report, and by the earlier Werner report of 1970, to be a single, continuous one. This did not mean, of course, that there would not be any modifications of the Delors plan, and the Maastricht agreement produced several.

Maastricht and Economic and Monetary Union

Maastricht is a small town in the Netherlands built in a loop of the river Maas or Meuse close to the borders with Germany and Belgium. Many of its market traders accept any currency from the European Union countries. The difficulty inherent in such multicurrency dealings highlights the reasons for the determination of many Europeans to aim for a single currency. Maastricht was the centre for the Council of Europe meetings in early December 1991 that agreed the draft Treaty on Union because the Netherlands were currently holding the Presidency of the Community. The meetings were enlarged by the presence not only of the foreign ministers who usually attend such Councils, but also of the Finance Ministers. Representatives of the media attended in huge numbers. Most of the work had been done before the national leaders met and draft treaties were well-publicised beforehand, and national political stances were fully advertised. The nature of such meetings is that every leader must appear, for the benefit of the folks back home, to have negotiated strongly and effectively. 'Face' is very important and the media is massaged on a regular basis to ensure that the headlines reflect what the politicians desire. The truth behind the final outcome may take many years to emerge as the agreements are put into practice and the European Court of Justice interprets them.

The decisions in respect of economic and monetary union were as follows. In February 1992 the formal Union Treaty on economic, monetary and political union was initialled and was eventually ratified by national parliaments and came into force on 1 November 1993. The delay in ratification did not prevent early preparations being made to implement EMU and the European Monetary Institute in particular. In June 1992 there was a revision of the Community's financing discussed at the Lisbon summit. The Single Market with free movement of capital, goods and services, but not entirely of people, came into force on 1 January 1993. In January 1994, Stage 2 of economic and monetary union started. (Stage 1 began in July 1990.) During this stage, on 1 January 1994, a European Monetary Institute (EMI) was set up to prepare for the final stage of EMU. The EMI is the forerunner of the European Central Bank (ECB) and its role is outlined below.

During Stage 2 of EMU the member countries are supposed, despite the problems of the ERM in September 1992, August 1993 and March 1995, to bring their exchange rates into narrower bands and begin the process of making their economies converge to certain accepted limits in relation to some key indicators. These so called convergence tests are:

1. *Inflation.* The country must have had an inflation rate which is no more than 1.5 per cent higher than that of the three members of the ERM with the lowest rates in the previous year.

2. *Interest rates.* The country must have had long-term interest rates (long bond rates) no more than 2 per cent higher than the lowest three members in the previous year.
3. *Exchange rate.* The country must have been in the normal band of the ERM for two years and not to have realigned (devalued) in that time.
4. *Budget deficit.* The country's budget deficit must not exceed 3 per cent of Gross Domestic Product.
5. *Debt stock.* The country's outstanding stock of public debt must be less than 60 per cent of GDP.

TABLE 8.1(a)   Economic Indicators and the Maastricht Treaty Convergence Criteria

		Inflation[a]	*Long-term interest rate*[b]	*General government lending (+) or borrowing (−)*[c][d]	*General government gross debt*[c][d]
Belgium	1993	2.8	7.2	−6.6	138.9
	1994	2.4	7.7	−5.5	140.1
Denmark	1993	* 1.3	* 7.3	−4.4	79.5[e]
	1994	** 2.0	** 7.8	−4.3	78.0[e]
Germany	1993	4.1[f]	6.5	−3.3 #	48.1
	1994	3.0[f]	7.0 #	−2.9 #	51.0
Greece	1993	14.5	23.4	−13.3	115.2
	1994	10.8	20.8	−14.1	121.3
Spain	1993	4.6	10.2	−7.5 #	59.8
	1994	4.7	10.0	−7.0	63.5
France	1993	2.1	6.8	−5.8 #	45.8
	1994	* 1.6	* 7.2	−5.6 #	50.4
Ireland	1993	** 1.5	** 7.7 #	−2.5	96.1
	1994	2.4	7.9 #	−2.4	89.0
Italy	1993	4.3	11.3	−9.5	118.6
	1994	3.9	10.6	−9.6	123.7
Luxembourg	1993	3.6	6.9 #	1.1 #	7.8
	1994	*** 2.1	*** 6.4 #	1.3 #	9.2
Netherlands	1993	2.6	6.4	−3.3	81.4
	1994	2.7	6.9	−3.8	78.8

Portugal	1993		6.5		10.0	−7.2		66.9
	1994		5.2		10.4	−6.2		70.4
United	1993	***	1.6$^{(g)}$	***	7.5	−7.8	#	48.3
Kingdom	1994		2.4$^{(g)}$		8.1	−6.3	#	50.4

*,**,*** = first, second and third best performer in terms of price stability.

= public deficit not exceeding 3% of GDP; public debt not exceeding 60% of GDP.

(a) Annual rates.

(b) In percentages, annual average.

(c) As a percentage of GDP.

(d) Provisional for 1994.

(e) General government gross debt figures not adjusted for the assets held by the Danish Social Pension Fund against sectors outside general government, government deposits at the Central Bank for the management of foreign exchange reserves, and government debt from the financing of public undertakings. In accordance with the Council's and Commission's statements concerning Article 1(4) of Council Regulation 3605/93 of 22nd November 1993, for Denmark these items shall be stated separately. After this adjustment the debt level at end-year is 52.1% of GDP in 1993, and 53.5% of GDP in 1994.

(f) Western German consumer price inflation.

(g) The UK's inflation objective is set in terms of the CPI excluding interest payments (RPIX). This measure, which is closer to the harmonised definition of consumer prices currently under consideration, rose at an annual rate of 3.0% in 1993 and 2.4% in 1994.

SOURCES: National data (inflation (CPI), long-term interest rates), European Commission (general government lending or borrowing, general government gross debt; see also footnote (e) below). The statistical data to be used in assessing whether the Member States meet the convergence criteria shall be provided by the European Commission. Adapted from *European Monetary Institute Annual Report 1994* (April 1995, Frankfurt am Main).

The extent to which the member states matched these convergence criteria in 1995 is shown in Table 8.1 (a and b). The interpretation of the figures is not straightforward and the EMI is developing an agreed set of measurements of, for example, consumer price inflation (CPI) to apply after 1997. The measurement of CPI will be close to the United Kingdom system of RPIX which is the Retail

Price Index without mortgage interest payments. Some states, led by Sweden, think that an unemployment criterion should be added. A small industry has grown up analysing whether the criteria will be met. The best source of information as opposed to speculation, the 'horse's mouth', is the *Annual Report of the European Monetary Institute.*

TABLE 8.1(b)   The Economic Situation of the New EU Member States*

		Real GDP[a]	Inflation [b]	Nominal effective exchange rate (1991 = 100)	Long-term interest rate[c]	General government lending (+) or borrowing (-)[d]	General government gross debt [d][e]
Austria	1993	−0.3	3.6	103.2	6.8	−4.1	63.5
	1994	2.8	3.0	103.8	7.0	−4.4	65.0
	1995	3.1	2.5	105.0	—	−4.9	—
Finland	1993	−2.6	2.2	75.0	8.8	−7.2	61.8
	1994	3.7	1.1	81.2	9.1	−4.7	70.0
	1995	5.0	2.0	85.8	—	−5.0	76.0
Sweden	1993	−2.1	4.7	81.1	8.6	−13.3	74.4
	1994	2.2	2.4	80.2	9.5	−11.7	81.0
	1995	2.7	2.9	80.5	—	−9.6	—

SOURCES: European Commission (real GDP, general government lending or borrowing, general government gross debt), national data (inflation (CPI), long-term interest rates, OECD (effective exchange rates). Figures for 1995 are drawn from the European Commission – Autumn forecasts 1994. The data may be subject to revision. Adapted from *European Monetary Institute Annual Report 1994* (April 1995, Frankfurt am Main).

* Austria, Finland and Sweden joined the European Union on 1 January 1995, following the positive outcomes of referenda held on 12 June, 16 October and 13 November 1994 respectively.

(a) Annual percentage changes. (b) Annual rates. (c) In percentages, annual average. (d) As a percentage of GDP. (e) Data not completely in line with the Maastricht definition.

During Stage 2 the members have started the process leading to the independence of the Community's central bank by setting up the EMI. According to the Treaty, 'The currency composition of the ECU basket shall not be changed, and from the start of Stage 3 the value of the ECU shall be irrevocably fixed.' The single currency will not be the present 'basket' ECU but a new currency representing the irrevocably fixed values of existing currencies. In theory, Stage 3 could have started as early as 1 January 1997 but the Cannes summit of June 1995 accepted an ECOFIN recommendation that this date was unrealistic and that the alternative of 1999 was the target to aim at.

By the end of 1996 the European Commission and the EMI will produce a report stating which members have met the agreed criteria for joining a full currency union, although it will presumably be of largely academic interest since the starting date for Stage 3 is now 1999. In 1996 also, an IGC will have been held and the European Union leaders will have reviewed the Union Treaty although further Treaty changes are unlikely to become effective until late 1997 or the following year when ratification is completed. After studying the report of the Commission and EMI, there would have been a decision by qualified majority vote on whether to move to Stage 3 of EMU in 1997 and the date for its inception. When it is agreed on a start for 1999 then exchange rates will be irrevocably fixed and a European Central Bank will take over the functions of the European Monetary Institute.

The United Kingdom is committed to all the clauses relating to EMU up to and including Stage 2, but was granted an opt-out protocol at Maastricht which enabled it to make a separate and delayed choice about Stage 3, the commitment to a common currency and to the ECB. Denmark was granted a protocol that enables it to submit any advance to Stage 3 to a national referendum. The United Kingdom made a great fuss over the need to consult parliament about adopting a common currency but the real reason for the demand for an opt-out clause was the fear of a split in the Conservative party led by the Thatcherite 'Eurosceptics' in the run-up to a general election in 1992.

The Treaty said that if it were decided in 1996 (it has already been decided in 1995) that it is too early for any countries to embark on Stage 3 in 1997 and no plan for a single currency has been introduced, then by the end of 1998 the Council of Ministers will decide by a qualified majority which economies are strong enough to begin on EMU. The designated countries will begin Stage 3 of

EMU by 1 January 1999 at the latest. This does not mean that national currencies will immediately be replaced by the new European Union currency because the task of replacing existing notes and coin is a mammoth one. Over time, however, a common currency would be introduced after 1999 and would consist of note designs denominated in the common currency, which the Treaty specifies as the (new) ECU, together with some reference to the original, established currency. In late 1994 a working party published a report on the alternative practical routes to a single currency. Inter-bank operations would probably be undertaken at the new irrevocably fixed parities for a period before notes and coins came into circulation. Most experts agree that there should be as short a time as possible between the two events. The name of the new currency was decided at the December 1995 Council meeting. It will be called the Euro.

The details of the methods of implementing the single currency and monetary union have been intensively discussed and in May 1995 the Commission published a Green Paper, *On Introducing the Single Currency*.

The 1995 Green Paper on Introducing a Single Currency

The Green Paper, which was accepted by the European Council in June 1995, consists of a statement by the Commission of its ideas of how the transition to a single currency should take place and an analysis of the issues to be confronted. The Paper has an Annex which is a progress report of an independent Expert Group that has been studying the introduction of a single currency under a mandate from the Commission. The Green Paper aimed at reducing the uncertainties that exist about the change-over by presenting what it calls a 'reference scenario'. This is given in Figure 8.1. It also aimed at identifying a comprehensive list of the problems involved and suggested an approach to solving them. Its third aim was to 'define a communication strategy to ensure public support' and explain how the single currency will be introduced. In February 1996 an information and publicity campaign was launched to 'sell' the Euro to the people of Europe. The United

Kingdom government refused to participate in the persuasive advertising aspect of this campaign.

A three phase approach is proposed, as is shown in Figure 8.1:

- *Phase A:* The Council decides to launch the single currency and announces the participating countries.
- *Phase B:* This will start not more than a year after the start of Phase A. Parities will be irrevocably fixed. During Phase B there would be a 'critical mass' of financial activities in the single currency built around a single monetary policy and the issue of new public debt.
- *Phase C:* This would start not more than three years after the start of Phase B. It would complete the transition with a rapid introduction of new notes and coins and the general change-over of the means of payment. It suggests a few weeks as the time period for the introduction of new notes and coins.

According to the Treaty, Phase B should start, at the latest, on 1 January 1999 for those members who meet the convergence criteria. The Commission recommends that the periods mentioned should be maximum periods and that the Council should fix the dates as deadlines.

The Green Paper justifies its 'reference scenario' on the following grounds. It says it is sensitive to the needs of European citizens. It allows sufficient time to conduct a comprehensive exercise to tell the public about the advantages of a single currency and to reassure them about the transition and its effects on their lives. It says the scenario is pragmatic and will reduce costs for all concerned. It is also 'economically robust'; that is, it will require a high degree of sustained convergence. The convergence criteria will be strictly adhered to. The critical mass approach will, it says, ensure the credibility and irreversibility of the changes. It argues that it meets the needs of the banks, especially in the very short period of existence of parallel circulation of two currencies. Banks will have time to convert computer systems and will have lower administrative costs than if they had to run two currencies for a longer period. The Green Paper argues that its proposals follow the democratic requirements of the Treaty on Union.

FIGURE 8.1

Introduction of a Single Currency – Sequence of Events

PHASE A Launch of EMU	PHASE B Start of EMU	PHASE C Single currency fully introduced
Start of the phase:	*Start of the phase:*	*Start of the phase:*
• List of participating Member States	• Fixing of conversion rates	• ECU notes and coins introduced
• Date of start of EMU announced (or confirmed)	• ECU becomes a currency in its own right	• Banks have completed the changeover (retail business payment systems)
• Deadline for the final changeover to the single currency	• Monetary and exchange-rate policy in ECU	• Notes and coins denominated in national currency are withdrawn
• Setting up of the ESCB and the ECB	• Inter bank, monetary, capital, and exchange markets in ECU	• Public and private operators complete the changeover
• Start of production of notes and coins	• New government debt issued in ECU	• Only the ECU is used
	• Corresponding wholesale payment systems in ECU	
Throughout the phase:	*Throughout the phase:*	
Stepping-up of preparations and implementation of measures that will, if possible, have been adopted beforehand:	• Banks and financial institutions continue the changeover	
• Legal framework	• Public and private operators other than banks proceed with the changeover circumstances permitting	
• National steering structure		
• Banking and financial community changeover plan		
1 year maximum	3 years maximum	Several weeks

SOURCE The European Commission, Green Paper on Introducing the Single Currency, May 1995

The Green Paper's justification of a single currency

The Green paper lists the benefits forcefully along the lines of the original Delors Committee Report. It summarises them as follows:

1. A more efficient single market without disruptions to trade and investment caused by exchange rate fluctuations.
2. A stimulation to growth and employment arising from greater price stability and the integration of financial markets. Borrowing conditions should be improved.
3. The removal of currency conversion costs between member currencies.
4. Greater international stability following from the new currency's inevitable role as a world reserve currency equal to the dollar and yen.
5. Collective management by a single monetary authority will enhance the monetary sovereignty of the Union beyond that possible for a national currency. The single currency will be one of the best and strongest in the world.

Other points in the Green Paper

It also dwells on legal and technical issues and considers, but rejects, other possible scenarios for the transfer. It also strongly advocates the need for a communications strategy of a decentralised nature according to the principle of subsidiarity. It wants member governments, financial bodies and others to prepare the way by informing their customers and training their staff. There was a meeting in the Autumn of 1995 of the EMI, member states, the European Parliament and private-sector representative to develop the communications strategy. There should be large sums of money in it eventually for advertising agencies. The campaign began in February 1996.

Given the very long lead time to the introduction of the single currency and the need to avoid chaos, member states must commit themselves well before 1999 in order to participate in the preparations. The inner core, who will meet the convergence criteria, will find the commitment easy. The remainder, especially the United Kingdom with its Stage 3 opt-out, may find they are in an invidious position. Will they participate wholeheartedly and risk the waste of the large sums of money involved in the education programmes if they do not fulfil the criteria for entry, or will they decide at an early stage not to join in? At the unofficial summit at Majorca in September 1995, all the members decided to maintain the Treaty on Union's timetable for a single currency. The United Kingdom was aggressively sceptical about the number who would qualify and reasserted the need to study the prospects of countries not in the first, inner core of members to form a single currency union.

The United Kingdom's Opt-out

The protocol that the United Kingdom negotiated recognises that it 'shall not be obliged or committed to move to the third stage of economic and monetary union without a separate decision to do so by its government and parliament'. The protocol continues, saying that the United Kingdom shall notify the council whether it intends to move to the third stage, and that unless it does, it will be under no obligation to do so. If no date is fixed for the beginning of Stage 3 the United Kingdom may change its notification before 1 January 1998. The United Kingdom will retain its powers in the fields of monetary and exchange rate policy and be free to negotiate international agreements for itself, but it will have no rights to participate in the appointment of the president, vice-president and the other members of the executive board of the European Central Bank. If the United Kingdom changes its mind after the commencement of Stage 3 by other members it may notify its desire to join, but must meet the necessary convergence conditions and pay its dues in terms of capital subscriptions and the transfer of foreign reserve assets to the ECB. Some economists find it unthinkable that the United Kingdom would be able to remain outside the Stage 3 system if it gets under way with important members such as France and Germany and the Benelux countries. Since 1992 the United Kingdom government and the Bank of England have observed all the requirements of the Treaty in terms of membership of the EMI, monetary cooperation and attempts to meet the convergence criteria, with the exception of membership of the ERM. In July and September 1995 the Chancellor of the Exchequer said that the United Kingdom would meet the convergence criteria by 1997 in all respects except membership of the ERM.

Opinion is strongly divided on the adoption of a single currency by the United Kingdom. Some argue that the United Kingdom's trade patterns and financial structures, especially the variable interest rates in the housing markets, make membership of a single currency undesirable. Others predict that the whole scheme will falter as various countries come to count the cost of convergence and the political unpopularity likely to be involved from deflationary policies and possible increases in unemployment. The British government has begun to express concern about the costs and implications for those countries that do not enter the single currency in the first phase. The Commission was given the job in mid-1995 of researching this question. The fear is that there would be large shifts of population or flows of capital, or both, between those countries that did not have an economy in a sufficient state of convergence with the core, single currency states. The need to meet the convergence criteria has assumed great importance and many economists and politicians think that they should be modified to include levels of unemployment.

The European System of Central Banks

The Union Treaty goes into great detail about the establishment of the ESCB, the European Central Bank, their functions and the extent of their independence from national governmental interference. The Treaty says that a ESCB and a ECB shall be established and that 'the primary objective of the ESCB shall be to maintain price stability'. It defines the tasks of the ESCB as, firstly defining and implementing the monetary policy of the Community; secondly conducting foreign exchange operations consistent with treaty provisions; thirdly holding and managing the official foreign reserves of the member states; and fourthly the promotion of smooth operation of payment systems. It is expected to 'contribute to the smooth conduct of policies pursued by the competent authorities relating to the prudential supervision of credit institutions and the stability of the financial system'.

'The ESCB shall be composed of the European Central Bank and of the central banks of the member states'. The decision-making bodies of the ECB will be firstly, the Governing Council, which will comprise the members of the Executive Board and the Governors of the national central banks, and, secondly, the Executive Board.

The President, the vice-President and the other four members of the Executive Board will be appointed for eight years by common accord of the governments of the members, on recommendation of the Council of Ministers and after consulting the European Parliament and the Governing Council of the ECB. They will not be able to serve an additional term. In an attempt to guarantee the independence of the ESCB, the Treaty says that 'neither the ECB nor a national central bank, nor any member of their decision-making bodies shall seek or take instructions from Community institutions or bodies, from any Government of a member state or from any other body'. It goes further and says that Community and Government institutions and bodies undertake to respect this principle and will not seek to influence the members of the decision-making bodies of the ECB. Some countries will have to rewrite the laws governing the roles of their central bank to conform with the Treaty. In effect the Treaty is creating a system which is even more independent than the Bundesbank has been.

Why have a Common Currency?

The Delors Committee report lacked a quantitative assessment of the benefits and costs of EMU so another report was produced which benefited from the advice of economists from outside the Commission. It was called *One Market, One Money* and was considered at the December 1990 Council. It made a case based on the following questions:

- What are the effects on the economy's efficiency, investment and therefore growth from eliminating transactions costs and exchange rate fluctuation?
- What are the benefits deriving from a European Central Bank committed to price stability?
- What other advantages will accrue, for example from a reduction in real interest rates due to the disappearance of the exchange risk premium?
- What are the benefits from the ecu becoming a global currency?
- Will these major benefits outweigh the costs of forgoing the instrument of devaluation of currencies notably for those countries in the process of catching up?

The conclusions were that the potential financial benefits of full monetary union are enormous. The reader is advised to apply a healthy degree of scepticism to the following figures because only the transactions costs can be measured with confidence; the other figures are more speculative and rely on assumptions that not everyone would accept. A major saving would be the removal of the costs of exchanging the currencies of the members. It was estimated that these costs are between ECU 13 billion and ECU 19 billion a year in the Community of 12 as a whole (£9 billion to £12 billion at that time). This was between 0.3 and 0.4 per cent of the Twelve's GDP. Smaller countries would gain more than large, 0.9 as against 0.1–0.2 per cent of GDP. The report also stated that monetary union would mean an increase of production in the Twelve of about 5 per cent of its Gross Domestic Product, arising from the greater confidence induced in investors who will no longer be deterred by exchange rate fluctuations. It also expects that the convergence of inflation rates would stimulate real output by 0.3 per cent of the Twelve's GDP. An additional benefit would be that the members of EMU would no longer need to keep currency reserves in relation to fellow members' currencies and this would save money. A saving of ECU 160 billion was estimated. A further benefit is very hard to quantify but would arise from the greater ease with which trade could occur if there were no currency considerations.

Over the long term the greatest benefits would arise from the convergence of inflation rates and the tendency for interest rates to equalise and fall. It would be easier for enterprises to control costs and there would be greater certainty in their investment decisions. The Report argued that EMU would lower the costs of economic shocks from events such as the 1970s oil price rises and international tensions by reducing fluctuations in growth and inflation. There would still be international currency dealing costs against, for example, the yen or the dollar, which would continue to fluctuate on a free foreign exchange market, assuming that the present floating rates prevail.

There are, however, significant costs in creating a monetary union. The experience of France, Belgium and Spain in the 1990s as they brought their policies into a form that would maintain their currencies within the ERM bands, and the recent experience of the United Kingdom, show that the progress towards economic convergence can be very painful. The evidence from the difficulties of transition in the monetary union of East and West Germany emphasises the point although very special circumstances prevailed there. The pain springs from rising unemployment as the economy adjusts to the fact that slow depreciation of the currency can no longer be used to maintain international competitiveness and to absorb rising production costs, especially wage costs. It will still be possible for real exchange rate changes, that is competitiveness, to occur as the new currency shifts against the dollar and yen but it would be essential to maintain price and wage flexibility.

There is also a painful loss of sovereignty over interest rate changes when a single currency is adopted. Members of the ERM have found it very difficult to avoid following the interest rate changes introduced by the German central bank. The criteria for convergence referred to above impose great budgetary, and therefore political, constraints on governments. It is predictable that unscrupulous politicians of all persuasions will use the ERM and EMU as a scapegoat for their inability to resolve national or sectional problems. EMU will produce long-term benefits whereas politicians are faced by short-term imperatives. On a gloomy note, those with experience of the French introduction of the 'new' or 'heavy' franc and of the United Kingdom's introduction of decimal coinage can only blench at the thought of the tide of ignorance and prejudice that will flood the popular press as the new currency is introduced. The hysterical reaction in some quarters in the United Kingdom in October 1995 when, at long last, metrication was more effectively enforced will appear as a mere whisper in comparison with the typhoon that will strike if a single currency is ever introduced. For some people the issue of monetary union is limited to the question of whether the Queen's head will disappear from the currency.

The Single Currency and Employment

Critics of EMU began to attack the idea of a single currency on the grounds that it would create economic shocks to some regions and generate high unemployment. The Commission replied to these charges in October 1995 in a paper entitled 'European Strategy for Employment' compiled by the two Commissioners for Economic Affairs and for Social Affairs. The paper asserted that, if the

Maastricht convergence criteria were adhered to and if investment led growth of between 3 and 3.5 per cent a year were maintained, there would be a fall in unemployment from 10.7 to 5 per cent by the year 2000. The process would create 11 million new jobs and links in closely with the proposals of the White Paper on *Growth, Competitiveness and Employment* which is discussed in Chapter 6. The general thrust of the paper was to encourage France's efforts to meet the criteria and to refute suggestions that a single currency will destroy jobs. Some commentators regard the conclusions as over optimistic because they are based on the premise that the convergence criteria will be successfully adhered to. The paper does, however, sound a warning note that if they are not achieved unemployment would decline temporarily to 9.75 per cent in 1997 and begin rising again to 11 per cent in the year 2000.

The Theory of an Optimum Currency Area

It is generally agreed that a single market does not necessarily require a single currency but many economists argue that it is desirable. There is a section of economic theory which deals with whether an area would benefit from a single currency. Modern versions developed from an article by R. A. Mundell (1961) in the *American Economic Review*, Vol. 51, 'A Theory of Optimum Currency Areas'. OCAs as they came to be called became the subject of academic discussion and the European Union and EMU can be considered in the light of the theory. The overall conclusion of the OCA theory is that whether the benefits from EMU are more likely to exceed the costs depends on four main elements:

● The degree of interdependence between members;
● The degree of capital and labour mobility;
● The similarity of the members' economies so that what are called economic shocks have roughly the same effects on all; and
● The flexibility of wages and prices.

The higher the degree of the first two elements and the greater the similarity of economies and the greater the flexibility of wages and prices, the more likely EMU is to succeed. This conclusion explains the great stress placed upon the application of the convergence criteria since 1990. It also explains the growing belief that only a small core or inner ring of members will benefit from EMU if it is begun in 1999. Some commentators think that there are three 'rings'. The first would be Germany, Austria, France, the Netherlands, and Belgium and Luxembourg (who have had a currency union for 75 years). There is some doubt about France and Belgium's debt percentages. They have had close links with the Deutschmark for some years even in disturbed times. The other two rings are less easy to determine because the United Kingdom and Denmark are wild cards because of their opt-outs. The second ring might be Italy, Spain, Ireland, Sweden, Finland and Denmark. The third would be Portugal and Greece. Denmark is close to meeting the convergence criteria and Ireland and Spain are keen to be in the inner core. Ireland is likely to meet the convergence criteria but would find it difficult to participate in EMU if the United Kingdom remained outside. Italy is eager to be in the centre but its political problems and large debt factor are likely to keep it out. There was a row at the unofficial summit meeting in Majorca in September 1995 after the German Finance Minister said that Italy would not meet the convergence criteria. A speculative surge swept through the foreign exchange markets. The United Kingdom, if it rejoined the ERM in time, will meet the convergence criteria and could join and, for once, be in at the start of an important change.

The Future

In 1970 the Community said that it would create a monetary union by 1980. It failed, and on the basis of that experience many people think that the Maastricht agreement will also fail to produce EMU. Such thinking fails to appreciate the subtlety and significance of the Treaty details. The third and final stage of EMU will start definitely by 1 January 1999, according to a reassertion of the agreement by national leaders in September 1995, and the European Central Bank will have been set up by 1 July 1998, or at least six months before a single currency comes into existence. The single currency would not necessarily be in circulation but exchange rates would have been fixed irrevocably and would be used in inter-bank transfers. The economic convergence criteria are given great weight by the Treaty and, in 1996, a majority of the 15 members would have had to be 'fit' for the currency union to proceed (if that date had not been abandoned as a target). After 1996, however, there is no need for this so called 'critical mass' of fit countries to be achieved. All that the Community leaders must do in 1998 is to decide which countries are ready for EMU, which will proceed anyway six months later. The number of qualifying states then will be at least three because of the way the convergence criteria are stated. In practice more are likely to be fit to proceed, especially those who have been aligning their economies closely to Germany's.

It should be remembered that Germany was a powerful supporter of the Maastricht agreement on monetary union although it wanted greater progress on the political front, especially an increase in the democratic controls exercised by the European Parliament. Germany would like to share the burden of having an international reserve currency into which speculators crowd during disturbed times. The proposed management structure of the European Central Bank appears to guarantee its independence from outside political interference and some commentators say it will be even more independent than the Deutsche Bundesbank. When the German constitutional court permitted its government's ratification of the Maastricht Treaty it issued warnings about the nature of the future monetary union. Chancellor Kohl had a hard task in selling the agreement to the German people who will insist on the new European currency being at least as good as the present Deutschmark. Public opinion has become cooler on the proposal and many politicians have adopted a populist, anti-single currency policy. As for the United Kingdom, whose leadership has been surprised at the degree of commitment of the other members, and has been isolated by its opt-out clause, it will either be a member of the group in the slow lane to EMU, with the considerable disadvantages that entails, or, as many commentators think, it will find the pressures to join the full EMU irresistible. In the background is the important influence of how multinational companies will react if a single currency zone is created within Europe and from which the United Kingdom is excluded. They are likely to transfer their new investments and some of their activities into that zone. The United Kingdom's opt-out would then be seen as short-sighted and lacking in vision.

It can be argued that we would all benefit from a single currency. A Euro MP once explained to the European Parliament that if you started with £100 in cash and changed it into francs and then into lira and so on until you had successively bought all the currencies of the Community, and then bought back pounds, you would only have £26 left. Thus £74 would have gone on commission without you having bought anything! (There seem to be a number of versions of this measurement and £45 is an alternative remainder that is quoted. Presumably the arithmetic depends on whether you are buying and selling at individual or corporate rates. Many banks charge a minimum 2 per cent or £2 commission on each transaction.) The logic of a single currency will eventually get through. Indeed, there has already been considerable growth in the use of the ECU by private business and some individuals. There is a danger of a two or three-speed Europe developing in the field of monetary union with some of the other major countries of the Community going ahead without the United Kingdom. In 1995 the British prime minister, Mr Major, persuaded the new President of France, M. Chirac, to support his request that the Commission investigate the effect of a single currency grouping on the non-members of the group. The December 1996 European Council has initiated such as investigation. It is becoming evident that exclusion from a single currency might be very harmful in terms of unemployment, higher interest rates and inflation and flows of capital and people. In contrast, those who might join a single currency are worried about the outsiders using competitive devaluation of their currencies to maintain trade and employment.

The creation of a central bank for the Union might pose more problems, especially for economic nationalists. The United Kingdom is again very concerned about economic sovereignty. The Germans, for their part, are increasingly concerned about the prospect of sacrificing the strong Deutschmark to an uncertain 'Euro' over which they will have significantly less control. Some German authorities are arguing for the revision of the Treaty on Union to include effective sanctions or 'fines' against members who fail to maintain fiscal prudence after the single currency starts. That would involve some direct intervention in internal financial affairs. The impartial observer might say that the European performance, especially that of the German Bundesbank, is superior to that of the Bank of England in recent years. Thus the United Kingdom would do well to pool what little of the sovereignty remains to the Bank of England and Treasury with the Europeans. Many economists say that this sovereignty is, in any case, very severely constrained. It is impossible for the United Kingdom to operate an independent policy in the face of the other economic forces in the world, such as the Deutschmark, the dollar and the yen. Britain is, moreover, reduced to having only one shot left in its locker – interest rate changes, and even in this respect is largely constrained by the need to follow what is done by Germany. The City of London and leaders of commerce and industry, if not certain politicians of the Thatcherite persuasion, appear to be recognising that their future self-interest lies in a European commitment, including a single currency and European Central Bank. They are certainly increasingly anxious about the penalties of being left out.

The debate about a single currency in the United Kingdom has, with the exception of academic and financial circles, been conducted in a cloud of emotion, dogmatism and ignorance. The arguments are finely balanced economically because only one of the points at issue, savings on transactions costs, can be properly quantified. Unfortunately the vital debate on the other largely non-quantifiable areas has been drowned out by the outpourings of nationalist extremists who seem to wish to reconstruct the nineteenth-century nation-state. While the argument has raged, the Bank of England has quietly been putting itself and its affairs into a position to be able to join once the political decision was made. It is participating fully in Stage 2 of EMU and has adjusted some of its financial aggregates and measures to fit the new requirements of the EMI. It is also implementing the various Directives on banking, insurance and financial services which will ease the path to monetary union. It is likely to meet the convergence criteria with the exception, perhaps temporary, of membership of the ERM. If the single currency goes ahead after 1999, there is a strong possibility, depending on the state of the Conservative Party and the result of a general election, that sterling will be part of it. There might, however, be a referendum on entry and even convinced democrats must quail at the thought of such a complex issue being the subject of a single question requiring a simple 'Yes' or 'No' answer.

Postscript: One Market, One Money?

In December 1995 the European Council in Madrid fixed 1 January 1999 as the date for the start of the single currency and decided that it should be called the Euro. In mid-1998 a decision will be made by qualified majority vote on which countries are qualified to join in. The Council agreed to the United Kingdom's request that a study be made of the consequences of the single currency and EMU on those members who remained outside.

In January 1996 it was revealed that the slow-down in the German economy and the rise in unemployment (to 4.1 million in February), had caused its percentage of debt to the GDP to rise to 3.6 per cent, thus calling into question whether Germany would meet the Maastricht convergence criteria of 3 per cent by mid 1998. The French government, too, was in political difficulties as a result of strikes and demonstrations against its proposals to cut public spending and social security benefits as a means of meeting the Maastricht criteria.

The German and French governments responded with a strong reassertion of their commitment to the 1999 date for launching Stage 3 of EMU. They also adopted a joint programme at the end of January 1996 to reduce unemployment and their deficits. The four-year joint action programme is intended to trigger an upswing in investment and employment by a very mixed bag of measures. The package was not received very favourably by analysts and trade unions in the two countries.

A war of words developed and British politicians took the opportunity to criticise the timetable for EMU and, in some cases, the whole concept. The Chancellor of the Exchequer stressed the need to maintain the convergence criteria, a view that was already being heavily stated by German central bankers and the Finance Minister. The United Kingdom Foreign Secretary expressed doubts about the realism of the single currency timetable. Mr Redwood, the ex-Cabinet minister who had challenged Mr Major for the leadership of the Conservative Party, criticised the whole concept of EMU and seemed to advocate the benefits to members with weak economies of retaining the option of competitive devaluations.

The German Bundesbank spokesmen argued strongly in favour of keeping strictly to the Maastricht criteria on the grounds that the German people would not otherwise accept the Euro in place of the mark. They also wanted agreement on a system of penalties to apply to members who adopted the single currency but subsequently failed to keep fiscal and monetary rectitude in respect of borrowing.

The war of words developed at the World Economic Forum at Davos in February 1996. The theme was 'Sustaining Globalisation'. Chancellor Kohl made a speech restating his European integration-ist ideals and was critical, without naming names, of the United Kingdom as 'the slowest ship in the convoy which must not be allowed to determine the speed of the convoy'. Railway metaphors are obviously giving place to naval ones. He argued that greater integration is necessary to avoid future conflict in Europe. In a controversial passage, which was badly received in the British media, he said, 'The policy of European integration is in reality a question of war and peace in the 21st century.' He quoted 'my late friend François Mitterrand', who had told the European Parliament before he died, 'Nationalism – that is war.' The Chancellor also said, 'Nobody wants a centralised superstate. It does not exist and never will exist.'

No doubt the war of words will continue as the members adjust their positions for the 1996 Intergovernmental Conference. In the meantime other events have taken place that will affect EMU. In early February 1996 the Commission launched an information campaign across the European Union to familiarise the public with the concept of the Euro and the practical implications of its introduction. It will finance a large-scale TV and press advertising campaign. The United Kingdom, although helping to finance the advertising, has said it wants nothing to do with the persuasive advertising aspects of the campaign. Few protests were raised at this censorship. In October 1995 the Commission published a paper called *European Strategy for Employment*, which is an answer to the critics who say that EMU can succeed only at the expense of jobs and economic growth. The paper argues that member governments could take active measures to create about 11 million new jobs by AD 2000 if they adopted investment-led growth. In February 1996 President Santer called for a 'confidence pact' between employers and trade unions to help expand growth and employment. He will visit each member state in the hope of having a summit meeting in May 1996 dedicated to the creation of jobs in the European Union. The general theme that will be pressed is that a single currency will help to create jobs.

There are strong pressures from some quarters to postpone the starting date for the single currency but, in early 1996, France and Germany were resisting the pressures. There were also suggestions that the Maastricht convergence criteria should be softened to help Belgium and possibly France. There were even suggestions that Italy and Spain should be given 'associate status' in the single currency. There was also a revival of the rumour that France and Germany would go for a sudden joint merger of the mark and the franc ahead of 1999.

The Social and Economic Integration of Europe

9

Introduction

The nations of Europe are likely to retain their distinctive characters for many centuries to come, but the very existence of the European Union will tend to create greater uniformity of approach in vital areas of daily life. This will happen largely because of institutional and legal pressures to conform, but there will also be a considerable informal pressure arising from the natural human characteristic of copying successful methods and procedures. The process has already gone a long way in the original Six members despite the differentiating marks of language and history. It is continuing with the subsequent groups of members. In this context two areas in particular are worth looking at in greater depth, regional policy and social policy itself. Closely linked with these are environmental policy which is dealt with in Chapter 10, and law and justice which are dealt with in Chapter 11.

The Social Policy of the European Community

The social policies of the European Community originated in the European Coal and Steel Community (ECSC) which was intended to rationalise the two industries so it was inevitable that the social implications should be considered. Thus one of the ECSC's objectives was 'to promote improved living and working conditions for the workers' and involved provisions for redeployment, safety, retraining, resettlement, guaranteed adequate wages, free movement of workers and safeguarded entitlement to social security benefits.

The European Community took over these objectives although they were not always expressed in exactly the same form. There were also important additions, notably the adoption of the principle of equal pay for equal work for men and women and an emphasis on harmonisation of standards among member states. The Community also set up a Social Fund whose objective was to promote employment opportunities and geographical and occupational mobility for workers within the Community. An area of particular interest was social security for migrant workers. Minimum health and safety standards were also established by the Euratom Treaty. Since then there have been a number of committees and action plans together with a series of directives aimed at improving health, hygiene and safety at work. The Treaty on Union established a new Committee of the Regions which first met in March 1994. It has 222 members, mainly elected representatives of local and regional authorities, and must be consulted on matters involving education, culture, public health, trans-European networks and economic and social cohesion. Its work supplements that of the long-established Economic and Social Committee which also has 222 members from business, trade unions, farming and consumers and which must also be consulted on a range of issues, Both committees have the right to produce opinions on their own initiative.

The European Structural Funds

There are three structural funds that provide money in the effort to reduce regional disparities and increase economic and social cohesion. These are the European Regional Development Fund (ERDF), the European Social Fund (ESF) and the Guidance section of the European Agricultural Guarantee and and Guidance Fund (EAGGF). The ESF was set up by the Treaty of Rome in Articles 123 to 127. The Fund has been reformed on several occasions since, in 1971, in 1977 and 1983; in 1988 a major review led to the introduction of new rules from January 1990 not only for the ESF but also for the Regional Fund (ERDF) and the Farm Fund (EAGGF). There was a further revision in January 1994 and a special Financial Instrument for Fisheries Guidance (FIFG) was introduced in 1993 as an additional help to struggling fishing communities. The three funds and the FIFG have been given five principal Objectives. A sixth, to cover Arctic and sub-Arctic regions was added when Sweden and Finland were admitted in 1995. There had been a campaign, rejected by the Council of Ministers, to make the fishing industry the subject of a separate sixth objective. The post-1994 framework, indicating which funds are applicable, includes the following objectives:

1. Helping less-developed regions that are lagging behind; that is, those with a gross domestic product per head of less than 75 per cent of the Union average or where there are special reasons for including them in this objective. This definition covers the whole of Ireland including Northern Ireland, Portugal, Greece, South and West Spain, the Mezzogiorno of Italy, and the overseas territories of France. Since 1994 it has included one region of Belgium, Hainaut and its neighbouring French areas, the Flevoland region of The Netherlands, all the East German Lander, Merseyside and the Scottish Highlands and Islands. The only region to be removed from the list was Abruzzi in Italy. (ERDF, ESF, EAGGF)

2. The economic conversion of declining industrial areas where the unemployment rate and the rate of industrial employment are higher than average and the rate of industrial employment is declining. (ERDF, ESF)

3. Reducing long-term unemployment and facilitating the integration into work of young people and those socially excluded from the labour market. (ESF)

4. Facilitating the adaptation of workers to industrial changes and to changes in production systems through preventative measures against unemployment. (ESF)

5a. Promoting rural development and helping to adjust production, processing and marketing structures in fishing and in agriculture and forestry as part of the CAP reform process. (EAGGF, FIFG)

5b. Assisting development and economic diversification in vulnerable rural areas affected by structural decline. They must satisfy two of the following three criteria: a high share of agricultural employment, a low level of agricultural income,

and low population density and/or a significant trend towards depopulation.   (EAGGF, ESF, ERDF)
6.   Helping regions with a population density of less than eight inhabitants per square kilometre and meeting certain criteria on GDP. Arctic and sub-Arctic areas of Sweden and Finland will benefit.

Strictly speaking, the regional objectives are 1, 2, 5b and 6 whilst the others, 2, 3 and 5a cover the entire Union. The Social Fund concentrates on objectives 3 and 4, reducing long-term unemployment and integrating young people aged under 25 into work. The Map, Figure 9.1, indicates the areas to which the Funds are directed.

The structural funds obtain their money from the Union budget and the amount allocated to them has grown steadily since the late 1980s. In the 1970s and the early 1980s the demands of the CAP expanded rapidly, especially on the price guarantee side, and prevented any significant growth in the Social or Regional Funds. The European Parliament and Community politicians found this increasingly frustrating. Their frustration partly explains the willingness, as described in Chapter 5, to curtail agricultural spending. There was a slow growth in expenditure by both the ESF and the ERDF but this did not match the problems that arose from widespread unemployment and industrial decline after 1973. The difference in emphasis on the programmes can be seen from the 1985 budget which appropriated about 67 per cent of the total for agricultural guarantees and another 2.5 per cent for agricultural guidance and other specific measures. In contrast, the appropriation for the Regional Fund was a mere 7.5 per cent of the total budget and 6.5 per cent for the Social Fund. The other areas which received relatively little support in many people's view was assistance to developing countries and food aid.

The decision was made, therefore, that more money should be devoted to the Social Fund, the Regional Fund and overseas aid. (In 1995 the overseas aid budget was reconstituted and effectively reduced.) The resources allocated to the two funds were doubled from 7 billion ECU in 1988 to almost 14 billion ECU by the beginning of 1993. Between 1994 and 1999 about 142 billion ECU at 1992 prices will be spent on the structural funds of which 70 per cent will go towards Objective 1 plans. By 1999 about 36 per cent of the total budget commitment appropriations will be for structu-

FIGURE 9.1
Regions Eligible for Aid under Objectives 1, 2 and 5b, 1994–1999

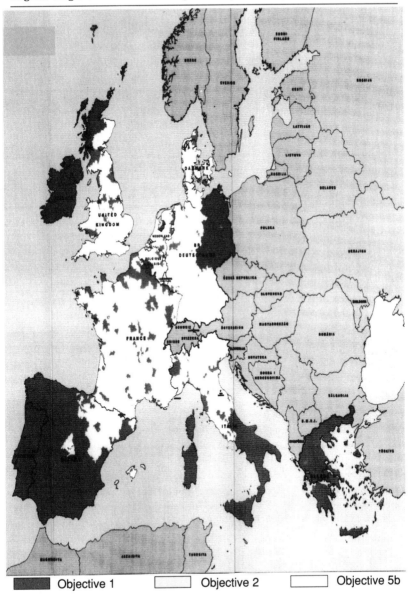

Objective 1   Objective 2   Objective 5b

ral operations. Decisions on the increases were delayed because of the conflict of interest between the 'rich' northern members of the Community, who would contribute most of the money to the funds, and the relatively poorer, southern states.

On the financial side of the social policy, one of the recent problems has been created by the accession of Greece, Spain and Portugal. These have, in varying degrees, higher unemployment, lower incomes per head and lower standards of social provision. The Community responded by raising the budget for expenditure from the Regional and Agricultural Guidance Funds. Overall, between 60 and 70 per cent of the total funds have been spent in Portugal, Greece and parts of Spain and Italy. Ireland is also included in this group. In 1985 there were also established some special schemes called Integrated Mediterranean Programmes which have been used to develop the Mediterranean areas of France, Italy and Greece. They aimed at reducing high unemployment and economic weakness, and raising living standards. They have provided training facilities, protected the environment and improved agriculture, fishing and the infrastructure. There has been another programme to help Portugal, called PEDIP, which was intended to improve Portuguese productivity and the quality of its goods. The continued relative economic weakness of these areas was recognised when the Treaty on Union established a Cohesion Fund to help Greece, Ireland, Portugal and Spain meet the convergence requirements of economic and monetary union as described in Chapter 8. Cynics regarded the Cohesion Fund as the price that had to be paid for those countries agreeing to the Maastricht treaty changes.

The Cohesion Fund

The Cohesion Fund was set up by the Treaty on Union and came into official existence in May 1994 but had been operating informally since the 1992 Edinburgh Council. The purpose of the fund is to remove excessive economic and social differences between the members of the Union so that economic and monetary union can be achieved by the end of the century. The fund is aimed at four members, Spain, Portugal, Greece and Ireland. The money provided is in addition to that given under the objectives of regional policies and represents a major shift of resources from the 'rich northern' countries to the less-developed 'south'. The Treaty on

Union contains a protocol on economic and social cohesion and designates the fund to those countries with a per capita GNP of less than 90 per cent of the Community average. Each country must have an approved programme indicating its policies to achieve the convergence criteria for economic and monetary union. The money allocated by the Cohesion Fund is approved by the Commission and granted on a project-by-project basis according to strict conditions related to the convergence programme. The money will only be given for environment and transport infrastructures. The recipients must also undertake not to reduce their own investments in these areas. The projects must 'be of a sufficient scale to have a significant impact in the field of environmental protection or in the improvement of trans-European communications networks (TENS)'. The cost of each project or group of projects will normally be above ECU 10 million. Each project will be thoroughly appraised, usually by the European Investment Bank (EIB) to make sure that the medium-term economic and social benefits are commensurate with the resources deployed. The assistance given will vary between 80 and 85 per cent of the total cost of the project but preliminary studies and technical assistance provided by the Commission qualify for 100 per cent grants. The Cohesion Fund regulation order allocates the fund between the four countries as follows: Spain, 52–58 per cent; Greece, 16–20 per cent; Portugal, 16–20 per cent; Ireland, 7–10 per cent. Table 9.1 shows how much is allocated over the years to 1999 and Table 9.2 shows the distribution of the money allocated in 1993.

TABLE 9.1
Resources Committed to the Cohesion Fund

1993: ECU 1.50 billion (ECU 1.565 billion at 1993 prices)
1994: ECU 1.75 billion (ECU 1.853 billion at 1994 prices)
1995: ECU 2.00 billion (ECU 2.152 billion at 1995 prices)
1996: ECU 2.25 billion (ECU 2.421 billion at 1995 prices)
1997: ECU 2.50 billion (ECU 2.690 billion at 1995 prices)
1998: ECU 2.55 billion (ECU 2.744 billion at 1995 prices)
1999: ECU 2.60 billion (ECU 2.798 billion at 1995 prices)

Total: ECU 15.1 billion (more than ECU 16.223 billion in adjusted prices)

SOURCE *The European Union's Cohesion Fund* (Luxembourg: Office for Official Publications of the European Communities, 1994)

TABLE 9.2
Assistance from the Cohesion Fund in 1993 (ecus)

Member state	Total	%	Environment	%	Transport	%
Spain	858 450 703	54.90	252 083 242	29.0	606 367 461	71.0
Portugal	283 568 700	18.10	122 794 100	43.0	160 774 600	57.0
Greece	280 364 000	17.90	175 222 400	62.0	105 141 600	38.0
Ireland	141 887 100	9.10	55 917 250	39.0	85 969 850	61.0
Technical assistance	374 125	0.02				
Total	1 564 644 628	100.00	606 016 992	38.7	958 253 511	61.3

SOURCE *The European Union's Cohesion Fund* (Luxembourg: Office for Official Publications of European Communities, 1994)

What principles lie behind the distribution of Structural Funds?

In 1989 a set of four principles was established to determine action through the structural funds and these were reinforced by new rules adopted in 1993. First, action must concentrate on the six objectives. Second, there must be partnership and close cooperation between the Commission and the local, regional and national bodies concerned. Third, the principle of additionality must apply; that is, that the member state should not reduce its own spending but should use Union funds to supplement it. Except in special circumstances the member must at least maintain the previous level of public spending for each objective. Fourth, there should be proper programming through partnership over a specified number of years.

The United Kingdom has experienced some problems over the years with the third principle of additionality because it has attempted to substitute Community money for national funds. The Commission has, on several occasions, reprimanded the United Kingdom government and withheld money until it was satisfied that the principle was being met. Most of the structural fund money, about 90 per cent, is spent via national programmes which are agreed between the Commission, regional and local authorities and national governments. About 9 per cent is spent as a result of European Community programmes and initiatives.

Most of these over the years to 1999 will concentrate on a number of schemes with the usual variety of Eurospeak titles. INTERREG helps cross-border cooperation and energy networks. LEADER supports local rural development. REGIS deals with outermost regions. EMPLOI refers to the occupational integration of women, young people and the underprivileged. Others such as ADAPT, SME, RECHAR, KONVER, RESIDER, RETEX deal with adjustment to industrial change. URBAN concerns urban policy. Restructuring the fishing industry has the charming name of PESCA.

One might justifiably ask if all this expenditure and variety of schemes are achieving their objectives. Over the years many attempts have been made to measure the effectiveness of various national regional policies and location of industry policies. Unfortunately for the researcher the policies are continually changing and so is the macro-economic climate. The conclusions are usually inconclusive or assert that each new job created cost the tax payer a vast sum of money, or that the new firms would have been forced by market pressures to relocate anyway and that large sums are absorbed by the bureaucracy that administers the funds. It is obvious from simple observation that many localities in Europe have benefited from the expenditure. Most of the sponsored schemes now sport large, blue European Union flagged notice boards declaring the European origin of finance for all sorts of improvements schemes from impressive bridges to small traditionally built fishing boats. The locals and the tourists must feel the benefit although a project such as the bridge to Skye arouses controversy. Some projects in the Iberian peninsula are even more controversial. Figure 9.2 shows the variation of gross domestic product among the richest and poorest regions in the European Union.

What Areas does Social Policy Cover?

The following list will give some idea of the pervasiveness of the policy although these items cannot be discussed individually in any depth. It will be obvious, however, that simply listing the items reveals a great possibility of conflict between governments and the Union. Most members are able to accept these policies with little

FIGURE 9.2

Per capita Gross Domestic Product (GDP) in the Richest and Poorest Regions in the EU Member States

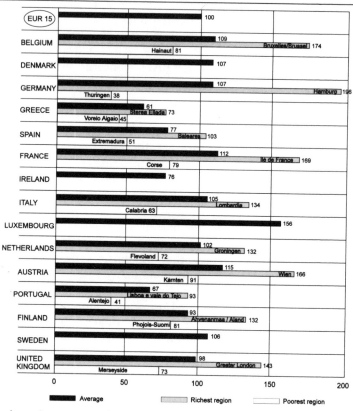

The chart shows per capita GDP expressed in purchasing power standards. The 1992 figures are measured against the EU average for the 15 Member States (= 100); thus values above 100 indicate that GDP per head is better than the average, while values below 100 mean that it is below average. The chart gives the overall national figure for each country and the figures for the richest and poorest regions in each (where details were supplied). The names of regions are shown in the national languages. Denmark, Ireland, Luxembourg and Sweden have one figure only, the national figure

SOURCE Eurostat (1995), *European Integration* Periodical 1995, Klaus-Dieter Borchardt (Luxembourg: Office for Official Publications of European Communities)

difficulty and 11 signed the Social Charter in December 1989. But the prevailing pro-market, anti-interventionist policy in the United Kingdom was very different from the social democratic, interventionist tone of the Community's social policy and the United Kingdom refused to sign. The difference of opinion was a problem in the negotiations at Maastricht in 1991 leading up to the Treaty on Union.

The areas covered by the policy include:

- Free movement of workers;
- Social security for migrant workers;
- Promotion of workers' geographical and occupational mobility;
- Equal pay for men and women;
- Safety at work;
- Health protection in the nuclear industry;
- Working hours and holidays;
- Vocational retraining;
- Handicapped persons, elderly workers;
- Youth unemployment;
- Full and better employment – coordinating national policies;
- Redeployment of workers in declining industries;
- Leisure of workers, housing;
- Accident prevention and health protection;
- Integration of migrant workers;
- Help for the neediest – homeless, old, vagrants, one parent families;
- Industrial democracy, workers' participation;
- Rights of working women.

The penultimate item in the list, industrial democracy and workers' participation, created problems for the United Kingdom government. Having 'defeated' the unions between 1979 and 1986, it faced the unwelcome prospect of the Community legislating for Works Councils and possibly putting trade unionists on the board of management of all companies above a certain size. The fact that most European countries saw this as right, sensible and constructive seemed to escape the British government. There was also a misinformed fear that signing the Social Charter would lead to the imposition of a national minimum wage in the United Kingdom.

From the lengthy list given above it may be useful to examine one area in detail, the rights of working women.

How has the Social Policy Affected the Rights of Working Women?

Article 119 of the Treaty of Rome said that pay differentials between men and women should be abolished by the end of 1961. This deadline was not achieved and it was reset at the end of 1964. The delay was despite the fact that most of the written constitutions of the members include guarantees of the equality of the sexes. It became apparent as time passed that women remained in a relatively unprivileged position both in the labour market and socially. In 1975, therefore, the Council of Ministers adopted a directive which required member states to repeal all laws, regulations and administrative provisions that were not compatible with the principle of equal pay. They were also ordered to ensure that the principle was integrated into collective agreements and individual contracts. They were to enable any woman to claim her rights before the courts without fear of dismissal. A year later, in 1976, a supplement to this directive gave members two and a half years to give equal treatment to men and women in access to employment, vocational training, promotion and working conditions. They had to abolish all legal provisions and any terms of collective agreements that were prejudicial to working women. These directives led to extensive changes to British and other member states' law.

There still remained, however, areas of discrimination, for example in the application of social security. At the end of 1987 member states were given a six-year period in which to introduce equality of treatment. This includes the abolition of discrimination in respect of sex, marital or family status, the coverage of social security schemes, the obligation to pay contributions and the calculation of benefits and allowances.

Since then the Commission has insisted on receiving regular reports from each country on its progress in implementing the directives. It has followed up any failures to do so by threatening reference to the Court of Justice and has, on several occasions, brought actions against recalcitrant member states. Private individuals have also brought cases before their national courts and later appealed to the European Court of Justice.

As an extension of its efforts the Commission organised an action programme between 1982 and 1985 on promoting equal opportunities for women. Another programme was implemented between 1986 and 1990. The adoption of the Charter of Fundamental Social Rights for Workers (the Social Charter) in 1989 led to a third action programme aimed to run from 1991 to 1995. It was intended to produce a more integrated and comprehensive strategy for action and to develop new schemes to help women in vocational training and employment. This included the protection of pregnant women at work and of those who have recently given birth. There have been a number of other initiatives such as the NOW scheme to provide new opportunities for women by setting up exemplar projects on vocational training. The United Kingdom objected to some of the provisions relating to the remuneration of pregnant women during their time off work because the other members, in order to circumvent the United Kingdom's veto, made proposals for the Social Charter under the 'health and safety' rules which required only a qualified majority in the Council. The United Kingdom resented this manipulation of the Single European Act.

A fourth action plan to cover the years 1996 to 2000 has been adopted and will focus on the participation of women at all levels and in all spheres of society. The Commissioner for Social Policy said that the Commission would try to ensure that equality would be built into the design and implementation of all relevant programmes and policies. The Commission employs a team of lawyers to develop and draft legislation for employment, and social affairs ministers to discuss and approve. It also monitors how equality-related laws work in practice. No one pretends that equality has yet been achieved especially when the evidence of inequality of earnings, and so on, is seen, but the Union has made effective progress towards creating a proper legislative framework for equality. This has probably gone much further than some individual governments, including that of the United Kingdom, left to their own devices would have done. It was, for example, an appeal to the European Court of Justice in 1991 that led to a reversal in the United Kingdom armed forces' policy of dismissing servicewomen who became pregnant and to the payment of large sums in compensation.

The Social Charter

It quickly became apparent after the passing of the Single European Act in 1986 and its implementation after July 1987, that the removal of barriers to trade needed to be balanced by some progress towards the harmonisation of social conditions and social legislation in the member states. The Commission, therefore, asked the Economic and Social Committee (see Chapter 1) to draw up a 'European Charter of Basic Social Rights'. The committee, made up of representatives of employers, workers, professions, farmers, and small and medium-sized businesses, produced a draft in February 1989. Its efforts were supported by a resolution in the European Parliament in March 1989 calling for significant advances on the social aspects of the Community.

The draft proposals were considerably modified in the version produced by the Commission in its submission to the Council of Ministers in May 1989. The ministers responsible for social affairs and employment discussed the proposed Social Charter in June 1989 and it was the subject of further consultations with industry and trade unions before its final version was accepted by 11 members of the European Council at Strasbourg in December 1989. The United Kingdom refused to adopt it despite important changes made during the discussions. In 1990 the Commission put forward an action plan to carry out the charter. It is fair to say that very little was achieved before the Maastricht summit in December 1991 and this partly explains why the 11 'opted themselves out' in the Social Chapter protocol of the Treaty on Union to form what is usually called the Agreement on Social Policy. The '11' is now the '14' because the new members, Austria, Finland and Sweden have all accepted the Social Charter and the Social Chapter protocol of the Treaty on Union.

There was a significant change in the title of the charter as it passed through the consultative process but the media still call it the 'Social Charter'. The name adopted was the 'Charter of Fundamental Rights for Workers'. The substitution of the words 'rights for workers' for 'basic social rights' reflected a narrowing of the scope of the charter. The original conception was of a charter that would apply to all, irrespective of whether they were actually in work or not. One of the areas to be discussed at the 1996 Intergovernmental Conference will be the need for a statement of rights for all citizens of the Union.

A second important alteration was to shift the emphasis from providing solutions at a Community level to increasing the role of the member states. This was partly a recognition of the principle of 'subsidiarity', that is legal changes being instituted at the level of decision-making most appropriate to the matter involved. In other words, responsibility for most of the rules and legislation affecting workers' rights devolves on to the individual member states. There would still be plenty of scope for Community action but a great deal of national variation in provision remains. The European Parliament criticised this change of emphasis away from citizens to workers and the general vagueness of the charter itself.

The impact of the Social Charter

The Charter is based on the fundamental principles relating to 12 main themes, or rights:

1. Free movement of workers based on the principle of equal treatment in access to employment and social protection.
2. Employment and remuneration based on the principle of fair remuneration; that is a decent basic wage, receipt of a fair wage, and fair treatment for part-time workers.
3. Improvement in living and working conditions. This is concerned mainly with working hours, holiday entitlement, shift working, rest periods and redundancy procedures, among other things.
4. Social protection based on the rules and practices proper to each country. (It is this section that makes the controversial reference to a guaranteed minimum wage and to social assistance to those who lack adequate means of subsistence although there is not an intention to *impose* a minimum wage across the board.)
5. Freedom of association and collective bargaining.
6. Vocational training. This refers to the right to continue vocational training throughout one's working life, including the right to have leave from work in order to undertake such training.
7. Equal treatment for men and women. This aims at equality of access to employment, social protection, education, vocational training and career opportunities.

8. Information, consultation and participation of workers. This has proved to be a very controversial proposal because it aims particularly at those employed in transnational companies. It intends that they be given the right to be informed and even consulted about major events affecting the company that may influence working conditions and employment.

9. Protection of health and safety in the work-place. This area has led to the issue of several Directives following the issue of a Framework Directive in 1989. These are an attempt to create Union-wide standards of good practice. The fishing, mining and construction industries are the major targets for improvements in health and safety practices but people working in offices have also been affected by legislation on, for example, the use of display-screen equipment.

10. Protection of children and adolescents. This aims at a minimum working age of 16 with youth employment being subject to labour regulations geared to the needs of young people. It also intends to establish the right to two years of vocational training after the end of compulsory education.

11. The elderly. This asserts that those reaching retirement, or early retirement ages are entitled to a pension which provides a 'decent' standard of living. Those not entitled to a pension should be given a minimum income, social protection, and social and medical help.

12. The disabled. This aims at giving every disabled person the right to benefit from measures for training, rehabilitation, and social and occupational integration.

The action plan put forward by the Commission included a list of directives, regulations, decisions and recommendations under each of the 12 headings. (See Chapter 1 for an explanation of the different applications of these terms.) Its intention was to concentrate on areas where it thought legislation was required to create the social dimension of the single internal market or to contribute to the economic and social cohesion of the Community. The Commission proposed playing a very minor part in the sections relating to freedom of association and collective bargaining, preferring to leave changes to the decision of individual governments. The intention was to present all the proposals before the end of 1992 and to follow up with further measures as necessary after 1993. The

FIGURE 9.3

The Application of the Qualified Majority Vote to Social Policy

Summary table of the chief legal bases for social policy instruments

PROTOCOL NO. 14 ON SOCIAL POLICY	EC TREATY
Qualified majority possible	**Qualified majority possible**
(Article 2(1))	Article 49: free movement of workers
Improvement of the working environment to protect the health and safety of workers	Article 54: right of establishment
Working conditions	Article 57: mutual recognition of qualifications
Informing and consulting workers	Article 125 (new): ESF (implementing decision)
Equal opportunities – labour-market and treatment at work	Article 127 (new): vocational training
Integration of persons excluded from the labour-market	Article 118a: health and safety at work
	Article 100a, Article 43: agriculture, Article 75: transport
Unanimity (14) required	**Unanimity (15) required**
(Article 2(3))	Article 51: social security (measures needed for free movement)
Social security and social protection for workers	Article 100: internal market
Protection of workers in the event of termination of employment contract	Article 130d: tasks, priority objectives and organization of Structural Funds
Representation and collective defence of workers' and employers' interests, including co-determination	Article 235
Conditions of employment of nationals of non-member countries residing lawfully in the Community	
Financial contributions for promotion of employment and job-creation	
Explicitly outside Community powers	
(Article 2(6)) Remuneration Right of association, right to strike, right to impose lock-outs	

SOURCE *Intergovernmental Conference 1996, Commission Report for the Reflection Group, Annex 14* (Luxembourg: Office for Official Publications of the European Communities, 1995) delays in ratifying the Treaty on Union from 1992 to 1993 resulted in very slow progress being made on implementing the Social Charter. However, the United Kingdom, which was the major cause of delays, opted out of the Social Chapter of the Treaty on Union. To be more precise, the other 11 members (now 14) formed their Agreement in Protocol 14 of the Treaty under which they can debate and vote by qualified majority vote on many areas of social policy without the United Kingdom participating or voting. Figure 9.3 shows the complex procedural arrangements arising from social policy being governed by two legal bases; first Title II of the Treaty on Union (mainly the original Treaty of Rome and amendments), and second the Agreement under Protocol No 14 which allows the Fourteen to legislate at European level without the United Kingdom.

Conclusion on the Social Charter

The Social Charter has a basic weakness in that it uses terms such as 'decent', 'fair' and 'equitable' without adequate definition or reference to monetary levels. This is bound to cause problems because such use of subjective terms always starts off a discussion in confusion. Eventually, no doubt, a consensus will develop about the meaning of these terms in relation to absolute levels of income, benefits and provision but, in the meantime, there is ample scope for the development of several interpretations based on national or party self-interest.

Underlying the demand for a Social Charter is a fear which is prevalent in the more affluent countries with better social provisions, that the advent of the single internal market will, if unchecked, cause what is called 'social dumping'. This phrase, like all community jargon, takes on several meanings, but two predominate. The first is the idea that, given free movement of workers and their families within the Union, they will gravitate to those countries with the highest standards of provision, thus placing a heavy burden on those countries' budgets for social provision as well as creating housing, employment and educational demands. These workers would 'dump' themselves in the affluent regions and be willing to work for lower wages and in worse conditions to the detriment of the existing local work force. Germany, for example, in 1995, was taking action to curb the influx of foreign construction workers who were willing to work illegally for lower wages than provided for in German employer/worker agreements.

The second aspect of 'social dumping' is that, if the differences in wage levels and working conditions persist among member states, industry and commerce will tend to shift its location to those countries, such as Portugal, Spain and Greece with the lowest levels, or to areas with labour forces from outside the European Union. The United Kingdom fits this category because its government seems keen to promote the country as a cheap-labour zone in order to attract foreign firms, although it does tend to couch its language in terms of flexible labour markets rather than emphasising cheap labour. This second aspect of social dumping, of which there is already some evidence, would adversely affect those nations with better provision in the areas covered by the Social Charter. The critics of the argument say that the multinational companies who set up plants in countries such as Spain and Portugal do not run down or close their existing plants elsewhere in the Union.

The United Kingdom refused to sign the Social Charter in 1989 on the grounds that the areas covered by it were the responsibility of individual governments and that the Community was an economic institution, not a social one. Its opposition was important in establishing the greater application of the principle of subsidiarity to the charter. In spite of this, and despite its opt-out from the Social Chapter of the Treaty on Union, the United Kingdom will find itself forced into implementing some regulations and modifying its own laws to give effect to directives passed under the qualified majority voting system applied to measures to implement the single market. The Directive on Works Councils is an example. The evidence is that the United Kingdom had already, before 1990, been forced or dragged along by the Community at a pace faster than it would have adopted on its own. The United Kingdom is still near the bottom of the European league in terms of social security provision, hours of work, inspection of health and safety at work, and overall social welfare. The United Kingdom also remains far behind in relation to worker participation in management and decision-making.

The Social Chapter of the Maastricht Agreement

The divergence between the United Kingdom and the other members in the field of social legislation will widen if the Social Chapter opt-out protocol for the Fourteen in the Union Treaty does actually work as intended. It permits the application of qualified majority voting by the 14 to some significant areas and will speed up progress. This is already happening. The Works Council Directive which was first discussed in 1972 was passed at last in November 1994 under the Agreement of the Fourteen. The United Kingdom took no part in the voting. The European Directive as it is called will come into effect in September 1996. It applies to enterprises and groups which employ at least 1000 people in the 14 countries, with at least two establishments, each of which employs 150 people, in two European Union countries. The directive provides for informing and consulting employees about, for example, relocation projects, plant closures, and collective lay-offs. The procedure is initiated whenever at least 100 employees from two different countries or their representatives request it. The consultation and information system will take the form of Works Councils or some other body, if the management and employees agree.

The directive was the first to be agreed, by the 11, under the Treaty on Union opt-out Agreement. Despite the attitude of the British government, several large United Kingdom firms announced their intention of conforming to the directive and setting up Works Councils; for example Marks and Spencer, BP, United Biscuits, ICI and Courtaulds Textiles. Continental-based multinationals with plants in the United Kingdom will undoubtedly establish Works Councils or the equivalent. In practice, such Councils are simply institutionalising established methods for consultation and exchanging information. The most common method in the United Kingdom is the Joint Consultative Council (JCC) of employees and employers' representatives.

Some observers find it hard to see how the United Kingdom can remain unaffected by this situation, especially as it seems as if multinational firms will have to apply common standards to their establishments in the 14 states and in the United Kingdom. If the United Kingdom did go ahead with the same general approach as the other members, it might pull the United Kingdom's social policies out of the Victorian age. It is remarkable that anyone in a civilised society should believe that employees are not entitled to be informed and consulted about important events affecting their lives and those of their families. The argument against the directive is, of course, based on the possible addition to employers' costs of the improved provisions for their employees and on an alleged potential reduction in employment of workers on low wages. The United Kingdom government is also reluctant to face up to the likely increases in its own expenditures and the tax implications from improvements in its social provisions. There is, of course, a significant increase in productivity to be expected from a work force that feels secure, valued and works in a cooperative, team environment. Evidence of this can be seen at the Rover assembly plant at Longbridge where workers now have strong job guarantees.

During the Maastricht negotiations the United Kingdom insisted on the Social Chapter being removed from the Union Treaty. As a result it was removed into a separate protocol enabling the 11 (14) to continue with the Social Charter's proposals. The assumption is that they will continue trying to get the agreement of all 15 to proposals. The arrangement is that agreements made under the protocol will continue to be taken within the framework of the Community's institutions which will be 'on loan' to the 14 members. If the United Kingdom cannot accept a proposal it will opt out of discussions and decisions. Figure 9.3 shows that there are still some important areas where unanimity of the 15 is still required.

The 14 have agreed that certain issues can be decided by qualified majority vote but they also agreed to keep certain issues for unanimous vote, as listed in Figure 9.3.

The parallel systems of dealing with social policies are working but are proving cumbersome. The 14 members, and the Commission, have expressed the hope that the United Kingdom will change its attitude and reverse the opt-out. The Labour Opposition has already said it would accept the Social Charter and Social Chapter if it came into power.

Towards Sustainability – The Environment 10

The Community and the Environment

The word 'environment' is usually used in a subjective as well as objective sense to refer to the quality of the air, the water, countryside, soil, sea and animal life around us. This quality is heavily influenced by the size of population and its density. This, together with income per head, determines the other major factor influencing the quality of the environment, that is energy use. These three forces, population size, population density and energy use tend to predetermine the nature and scale of environmental problems. These difficulties can, of course, be alleviated or aggravated by European Union policy. Some people allege that the Common Agricultural Policy has been responsible for considerable ecological damage with its stimulation of arable farming and the 'excessive' use of fertiliser and pesticides.

It should always be remembered when discussing environmental issues that they nearly always have an international aspect. The United Kingdom's power station gases may be Western Europe's acid rain. A chemical works putting effluent into the Rhine affects the quality of the North Sea. A Chernobyl disaster, or atmospheric test of a nuclear device, spreads a radioactive swathe across several continents. It is this international feature of environmental affairs that makes the European Union peculiarly valuable because it has the administrative machinery already in place to act quickly in pursuit of a coordinated policy. It must be said, however, that the discussion and implementation of policies seems to take an inordinately long time.

What is the population background?

In 1993, the population density of the 12 members was 146.8 per square kilometre. That of the 15 was lower at 114.5 because of the sparsely populated Arctic areas of Finland and Sweden. This compared with 329 in Japan, 27.6 in the United States and 13 in the old USSR (in 1989). It is expected that all these figures will rise marginally by the year 2000. The figures for European countries show a wide range as is clear from Table 10.1.

Crude measures of overall density are only a start to analysing basic pressures. We also need to have data on urbanisation and population movements over time. It is urbanisation which produces the undesirable concentrations of atmospheric pollution from vehicles and industry, creating the need for extensive systems for the collection and disposal of refuse and sewage. The very act of creating urban areas destroys natural habitats, trees and hedgerows. It requires large volumes of raw materials such as timber and aggregates like sand and gravel. Urban growth is accompanied by extensive road building, power lines, pipelines, reservoirs, pumping stations, sewerage works and railways. The process involves the exploitation of natural resources, many of which are from the Third World. Since there has been relatively little stress on the recycling of materials in most member states, until the 1994 Directive on recycling, this represents a high level of new demand.

The growth of communications and the ownership of the private motor car now ensure that no area is free from exploitation. There has been a remarkable expansion of urbanisation, for example, in the areas of the Union blessed by sun and sea. High incomes and the trend to early retirement have accelerated this movement, nor are inland or mountain areas safe if they are suitable for leisure developments. As a result, seas and lakes are prone to many forms of pollution. Since water touches or crosses many frontiers and derives from rain or melting snow, even a nation which actively pursues a sound environmental policy may be at the mercy of its 'dirty' neighbours. The United Kingdom had the unenviable reputation in the 1970s and 1980s of being the 'dirty man of Europe' because its atmospheric pollution drifts on the prevailing westerly winds over to Scandinavia and Western Europe. Excuses are uttered and the United States is also blamed but only gradually have effective countermeasures been taken.

TABLE 10.1
Population Density in the European Union

	B	DK	D	GR	E	F	IRL	I	L	NL	P	UK	EUR12	A	FIN	S	EUR 15
Area of the Member States, 1993 (1 000 km²)																	
Area	31	43	357	132	505	544	69	301	3	42	92	244	2363	84	338	450	3235
Population of the Member States, 1993 (1 000 inhabitants)																	
Population	10 085	5 189	81 180	10 362	39 141	57 327	3 561	58 098	398	15 290	9 877	58 168	348 676	7 991	5 066	8 719	370 452
Population Density of the Member States, 1993 (per km²)																	
Density	325.3	120.7	227.4	78.5	77.5	105.4	51.6	193.0	132.7	364.0	107.4	238.4	147.6	95.1	15.0	19.4	114.5

SOURCE Frontier Free Europe No. 3, 1995 supplement (Luxembourg: Eurostat)

In the autumn of 1988, Mrs Thatcher donned a 'green' mantle in a major speech and, after the passing of the Environmental Protection Act in 1990, more action has been taken in the United Kingdom on atmospheric pollution from industry, on exhaust emissions, water quality and the disposal of waste into the sea although the environmental lobby is still not satisfied with the depth of the commitment or with the speed of the implementation of measures. The keystone of the United Kingdom's policy is integrated pollution control (IPC), which recognises that all the elements in the environment are inextricably linked. Some experts regard the British Inspectorate of Pollution and the National Rivers Authority as the most vigorous pollution control bodies in Europe. The system of 'command and control' appears to be both tough and fair but there are doubts about its efficiency and effectiveness. There are strong indications from recent government publications that the United Kingdom government is proposing to reduce regulation and introduce more economic incentives to reduce pollution. It is also urging similar policies on its fellow members of the European Union. In November 1994 the Commission recommended the member states to examine all their tax systems and fiscal stimulants in order to reveal and eliminate measures that encourage activities harmful to the environment.

The European Court has not always been satisfied that European law has been complied with. In January 1992 the Advocate General issued a preliminary opinion saying that the United Kingdom was failing to meet Community purity standards for drinking water and specifically that it had failed to implement a 1980 Directive setting standards to be met by a 1982 deadline. There were excessive nitrate levels in 28 water supply zones in the United Kingdom. The Commission proposed taking similar action against all the member states except Denmark, Greece and Portugal. In 1995 the Commission was proposing further action against several members about a variety of environmental failings.

Fortunately, the expected population growth of the Union is marginal although that of some countries in Eastern Europe gives cause for concern. There is an opportunity to implement effective policies that are built into all areas of agricultural, commercial and industrial expansion. It is perhaps as well to keep the issue in perspective. In the Twelve, in 1989, an estimated 9 per cent of land was classified as 'built up'; 54 per cent was agricultural; 26 per cent 'wooded'; 1.6 per cent was 'inland water'; 9 per cent had 'other uses'. If enough money and political will is forthcoming then those elements which arise from within the Union can be controlled. Those elements arising outside the Union, for example the destruction of tropical rain forest, require international action such as that arising from the June 1992 UN Conference on the Environment and Development and its adoption of the '21st Agenda'. The conference is often called the 'Earth Summit'. The April 1995 G7 Environmental Conference in Hamilton also produced some progress. It is fortunate that 'green' politics have become very important, especially in Germany and Scandinavia. The unification of Germany has had a major beneficial effect and has led to the closing down of a large number of East German plants responsible for pollution, although the financial cost has been huge. The European Union is also spending large sums on environmental improvements in Central and Eastern European countries through the PHARE and TACIS programmes. The political will seems to exist to make environmental considerations paramount, although, in The Netherlands the government was brought down in May 1989 because it tried to push control of the private motor car too far. After a quiescent period the 'green' movement reasserted itself in early 1995 by mobilising public opinion to boycott the Shell Company's products after it announced its intention, with the United Kingdom government's approval, of dumping an oil platform in the Atlantic.

FIGURE 10.1
Inland Consumption of Primary Energy per Head, 1991

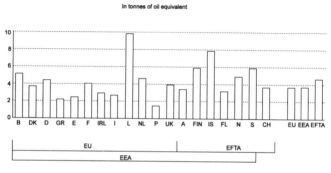

SOURCE   Eurostat, *EFTA News* January, 1994

Shell may have had the environmental balance of argument in its favour but swiftly reversed its plan.

How significant is energy use in the Union in the environmental context?

All the members of the European Union have been net importers of primary energy since 1989. In that year, the United Kingdom's net exports of energy, mainly from North Sea oil and gas, became net imports. A comparison of the consumption of primary energy per head is shown in Figure 10.1 for 1991. Oil accounts for about 44 per cent of European primary energy requirements. The transport and burning of oil is probably the major environmental hazard. Nuclear power is growing in importance especially in France where it was used to generate about 73 per cent of the electricity in 1992. By 1992 nuclear energy was being used to generate 34 per cent of the electricity in the Fifteen. Over the years since the oil crisis of 1973 industry has managed to reduce its share of energy consumption. The reduction is not wholly attributable to the recession but is also related to economies in use and to new technology. In the household and services sector consumption has been a static share of the total. In the field of transport, however, there has been a significant and continued rise which is largely accounted for by the growth of private car ownership, despite the greater fuel efficiency of modern vehicles. The development of energy networks in the trans-European networks programmes should yield considerable benefits in terms of efficiency and lower costs.

Energy consumption has several main implications for the environment. The extraction of coal is usually environmentally harmful. The extraction and transport of oil is accompanied by potential risks as with the *Torrey Canyon*, *Amoco Cadiz* and *Piper Alpha* disasters. Nuclear energy for electricity generation carries the greatest long-term hazard to the environment although enormous expenditures and engineering skills go into reducing the risk factor. The greatest immediate hazards, however, come from the burning of hydrocarbon fuels, coal, oil and natural gas. The emissions from this burning pollute the immediate environment and, through the atmosphere, the environment hundreds or thousands of miles away. In addition, the production, use and dispersal of chemicals and plastics sometimes has an accumulative deleterious effect on the environment.

The European Community implemented a series of environmental action plans over the years. The latest, the Fifth, which is called 'Towards Sustainability', began in 1992 and will last until 2000. Previous plans have been subject to regular review to see if targets were being met. One review in particular, that of 1988, had an important impact. It led to an increased emphasis on the promotion of energy efficiency in a new programme introduced in 1989. The *Thermie* programme provides money for spreading technological information on energy efficiency, renewable energy sources, clean coal technologies, and oil and gas prospecting and development. The *Thermie* programme entered its second phase in 1995 and will last until 1998 although there was a dispute about its funding. In December 1991 45 nations signed a new European Energy Charter incorporating proposals aimed at creating a legal and financial framework to exploit Eastern European energy resources more efficiently. Western members will install modern, environmentally cleaner power stations and equipment. In June 1994 a new version of the Energy Charter was agreed and was signed by the European Union in December 1994. The Union and 48 countries in Eastern and Western Europe and four non-European countries, Japan, the USA, Canada and Australia, have agreed on policies that are intended to act as a catalyst to revive and modernise the energy industries in Central and Eastern Europe.

Has the European Union developed a coherent policy on the environment?

The answer to this question is a qualified 'yes'. There is still a debate about the detail and the timing of initiatives but the need for a policy was recognised as long ago as 1972. The Single European Act of 1986 established legal requirements in the environmental sphere and by 1993 over 200 pieces of legislation applied to the environment. A fundamental problem is that most of the legislation is by means of directives. Individual members are supposed to transpose the spirit and intention of the directive into their own law. Some fail to do this quickly and effectively. The Community undertook action programmes and the fourth, between 1987 and 1991, shifted the emphasis from simply preventing environmental deterioration to incorporating environmental considerations into the basic agricultural, social, regional and economic policies. As a generalisation it can be said that before 1992 policies were *corrective*, that is they dealt with clearing up problems, whilst post-1992 policies have been *preventative*. The latest policies build an environmental approach into all programmes in order to prevent environmental damage. An example of this is the Cohesion Fund for development in Spain, Portugal, Greece and Ireland (see Chapter 9). The current action plan has the fine sounding title 'Towards Sustainability'.

Fine words are not always carried into action, but a positive step was made when the European Council made the 'Dublin Declaration' in June 1990 agreeing that the Community had a special responsibility for the environment both to its own citizens and to the wider world. They called for special protection for Antarctica, and a treaty preventing development there has since been signed. They also urged the acceleration of efforts to reduce depletion of the ozone layer and to revise the Montreal Protocol of 1987 which deals with that issue. The ozone layer is expected to continue its depletion well into the next century and in September 1995 it was discovered that the hole in the layer over Antarctica had doubled in area compared with the previous year. The Council adopted some popular concerns and sought combined efforts to check destruction of tropical rain forests, soil erosion and the spread of deserts. To give credence to their fine words, they said they were willing to put additional financial and technical resources into the effort. They congratulated themselves on the inclusion of such environmental considerations in the Fourth Lomé Convention and expressed great concern at the environmental problems being revealed in Eastern Europe. The '21st Agenda', referred to above, adopted after the 1992 UN Conference on the Environment and Development in Rio de Janeiro, reinforced their commitment to international cooperation.

The European Environment Agency

The Commission made detailed proposals in 1989 for the setting-up of a European Environment Agency (its initials are unfortunately another EEA) to include, if they wished, neighbouring non-member countries. The European Parliament wanted it to be given greater powers than those proposed so its role will be reviewed after two years. The decision was made in May 1990 to adopt the scheme and the Agency was given the job of providing reliable data, objectivity, and the information needed to monitor the application of Community laws on the environment. The hope was expressed that it might eventually become the basis of an *international* agency. The Agency eventually came into being in late 1993 and is based in Copenhagen. The EEA is seen as the culmination of a programme called CORINE that lasted from 1985 to 1990. It was an experimental project on the collection of information on the environment and natural resources. The main aim of the EEA is to make sure that the public is properly informed about the state of the environment. In order to do this it is establishing a European Information and Observation Network. We can expect an upsurge of information over the next few years on environmental matters. The main emphasis to begin with will be on: air quality and atmospheric emissions; water quality, resources and pollutants; the state of the soil, flora, fauna and biotopes; land use and natural resources; waste management; noise emissions; chemical substances harmful to the environment; and coastal protection. To quote the Commission, 'special consideration will be given to transfrontier, pluri-national and global phenomena and the socio-economic dimension'. Perhaps they will also, one day, measure the pollution of the English language!

It is hard for the lay person to find a way through the labyrinth of statistics and propaganda that emanates from governments and pressure groups. It is to be hoped that the new European Environmental Agency will make the task easier. Environmental and ecological pressure groups have multiplied like rabbits over the last 20 years. They all want government, European Union or international action of some sort. Frequently, this involves large expenditure or additional costs on producers or users. The scene is then set for a clash of pressure groups. Usually, the producers' lobby is financially stronger and more skilled at manipulating the political decision-making process. Eventually, the environmental lobby may triumph in whole or in part through the persuasion of public opinion, as in the suspension by most countries of whaling, or in the international agreement in May 1989 to suspend the use of CFCs by the year 2000. Gradually, governments may see votes in appeasing the 'green' lobby. Alternatively, reports from its research institutions may provoke them into belated action as in the banning of CFCs in plastics and aerosols in order to protect the ozone layer, as mentioned above. It is probably fair to say that the United Kingdom has rarely been at the forefront of environmental progress in Europe. Its role, despite recent protestations, has been a cautious, tending to the negative, one as is shown by its opposition to a carbon/energy tax.

How has the European Union Policy Developed?

In 1972, there was a major United Nations Conference on the Environment in Stockholm. The Community Heads of Government later in 1972 acknowledged that economic growth had to be linked to improvements in living standards and the quality of life of its citizens and to protection of the environment and natural resources. They concluded that 'economic expansion is not an end in itself'.

The Heads of Government laid out a 13-point programme and asked the Commission to formulate a Community environment policy. This was done and in late 1973 the Community's first programme began. It lasted four years and was followed by a second and third. The fourth programme began in 1987 and operated until the end of 1991. The fifth began in 1993 and runs until 2000. Over 200 pieces of legislation were enacted by the first four programmes although not all the tight deadlines specified have been met. The Commission had tried to define 'the environment' as 'the combination of elements whose complex interrelationships make up the settings, the surroundings and the conditions of life of the individual and of society, as they are, or as they are felt'. This broad definition includes the man-made environment such as the architectural heritage as well as the natural world.

The Heads of Government had agreed on some very important principles in 1972 that have been included in subsequent statements. For example, the Single European Act of 1986 endorsed those principles mentioned. The main decisions were that preventive rather than curative action should be taken over pollution, that environmental damage should be rectified at source, and that the polluter must pay the costs of prevention and rectification. The SEA included the phrase that 'environmental protection requirements shall be a component of the Community's other policies'. This could be regarded as simply a bland form of words but the Act also said that any future Commission proposals about health, environmental protection and consumer protection would 'take as a base a high level of protection'. This partly explains the wide-ranging measures and disputes over environmental policy that emerged after 1986. A main focus of attention in the late 1990s is likely to be the role and effectiveness of the European Environment Agency described earlier. It is worth noting that a major difficulty has emerged because of the sharp recession in the European economy since 1990. Environmental improvements tend to be costly and are easier to afford and justify in periods of economic growth. The recession also brought with it reduced economic activity and, necessarily, lower levels of energy use and emissions. It is hard to separate the effects of the recession from those of the emission-reducing policies. The policies may not be working at all well.

The Treaty on Union and the environment

The Treaty, in Articles 130r to 130t raised environment action to the status of a policy. It expanded on the principles and guidelines for environmental measures and gave formal recognition to the principle of prevention. The need for a high level of protection was stressed. The idea that other Union policies should take account of environmental considerations was accepted. As part of this commit-ment, the new Cohesion Fund established by the Treaty allocates money for the environment to the four recipients.

The Treaty made decision-making more efficient by replacing unanimity, in most cases, with the Qualified Majority Vote in Council. It also replaced the need merely to consult the European Parliament with the cooperation procedure. The decision-making procedure has not, however, been made more simple because in some cases the codecision procedure is used and in others the Council must reach a unanimous agreement after consulting the Parliament. There is still a grey area between procedures under the Treaty and those under the Single European Act. There is uncertainty, according to the Commission, as to which procedure to adopt, codecision under Article 100a or the cooperation proce-dure under Article 130s. The grey area has created problems particularly in discussions on the disposal of waste.

The Treaty on Union made some important improvements in the development of environmental policy but has created new complications as far as the legal bases of the policies and the clarity of the decision-making procedures are concerned.

Eco-labels

Since 1994 the Commission has adopted sets of ecological criteria for manufacturers to satisfy if they want an Eco-label for their products. The label is a flower made up of the 12 stars of the European Union flag. The criteria are designed to promote environmentally friendly products. Washing machines and dishwashers, domestic fertilisers or soil improvers, paper towels and toilet paper already have a set of criteria. Detergents, paints and varnishes will soon follow. The Eco-label should prove an effective stimulus to manufacturers and to concerned consumers and produce long-term benefit.

Who should Pay to Protect the Environment?

The concept that 'the polluter must pay' is frequently voiced. It sounds clear, straightforward and just. In practice, however, it is by no means simple. It is not always easy to identify a polluter although scientific tests are improving so much that it is now possible to identify the origins of most oil spillages, Even then it is not always easy to identify the spiller. Atmospheric pollution cannot always be traced to its source. Moreover, there is a code of legal practice for waste disposal. People often exceed these legal limits in an undetected or accidental fashion. Even water authorities are sometimes forced to pollute waterways with excessively toxic levels of discharge. There is also a major disagreement sometimes about the safe level of pollutant or discharge. One of the functions of policy is to fix standards of emissions, discharges and additives.

The phrase 'the polluter should pay' frequently means, in practice, that the consumer pays in the form of higher prices. This is the case with water supplies, emissions from power station flues and car exhaust controls. If the supplier is a 'natural monopolist', as with water and electricity, most of the burden of increased cleanliness is passed on to the consumer. If the industry is oligopolistic, as with petroleum, then most of the burden will be borne by the consumer but its extent will depend on the effectiveness of the collusion, tacit or otherwise, among sellers.

The principle of the polluter paying may depend upon the state creating a very effective inspection, supervision and monitoring service backed by effective punishment for malpractice. Most of the costs of this will fall on the taxpayer because the regulatory system, if effective as a deterrent, will not produce sufficient income to pay for itself. The principle eventually boils down to the fact that an industry has to pay for any of the costs needed to equip itself to comply with minimum standards. In the United States there is an interesting scheme that allows power station operators to buy and sell 'licences to pollute'. Those who have modern, efficient non-polluting, plants can sell their quota of licences and thereby cut their selling prices to the consumer or simply recoup part of the cost of the extra investment in cleaner plant. The less efficient have to buy licences, thus raising costs and having to charge customers more. The total of licences will be reduced until they are no longer needed. They will inevitably become dearer over the years as they become scarcer, assuming that demand for them continues.

The alternative to the consumer paying is for the government to cover some costs out of taxation. Another possibility is to identify the polluters and make them pay. At present, many 'polluters' are undetected. They are, in effect, keeping their production costs down by not having effluent or emission control and treatment. They are managing to make someone else pay some of their costs in terms of dirt, noise, unusable land, dead rivers and plant life, or dead animals. These costs are called 'external' costs by economists and are foisted on to the community at large or in particular. Occasionally, there can be external benefits when a firm improves the environment and reduces other people's costs or raises the quality of their lives. The result of the existence of these external costs and benefits means that there is often a divergence between the private and social costs of an economic activity. It may be profitable in terms of private costs and revenues alone. But if externalities are taken into account a deficit between social costs and benefits may outweigh any private profit. That is to say, that the private firm is profitable commercially but society as a whole is losing more than the firm's private profit. Economic terminology varies in this context but it is normally stated as:

Private costs plus external costs equals social costs (cost side);
Private benefit plus external benefit equals social benefit (revenue side).

The European Union has recognised this possible divergence between private and social costs caused by external costs, and has implemented a directive which says that major public or private development projects in agriculture, industry or infrastructure (for example road building) must produce an environmental-impact assessment before the work begins. The instigator must analyse potential pollution or other impact such as noise, on soil, air and water. The effects on wildlife habitats must also be considered. Permission for the project is only granted, and then possibly with conditions attached, after these environmental considerations have been balanced against the social, economic and other benefits of the scheme. There remains, of course, the question of how much weight is placed on the different aspects of the environmental impact assessment.

The private sector may take valuable initiatives in the environmental field. For example, in 1994 three vehicle manufacturers, BMW, Fiat and Renault agreed to use each others' networks for collecting old cars and recycling them. Another example is the swift shift towards the use of unleaded petrol as a result of some fiscal incentives and initiatives from the oil companies. In 1986 only 1 per cent of petrol consumed in the 15 member states was unleaded. By 1994 it had risen to 54 per cent, and was over 90 per cent in Germany. The gradual increase in the use of bio-fuels from oilseeds is another example of private or municipal initiative.

Would energy taxes help?

The issue of whether to have a so-called carbon tax (or carbon dioxide/hydrocarbon fuel tax, or carbon/fuel tax) is one of the longest-running sagas of the European Union. The proposed tax has been at the heart of the Commission's plans to reduce carbon dioxide emissions, so what may turn out to be the final agreement on the tax in December 1994 is an extremely feeble response by the member states. The United Kingdom has led the opposition to the detail of the proposals although it has accepted the general principle. Indeed, the United Kingdom's introduction of VAT on domestic fuel may be seen as partly a softening-up exercise in preparation for a carbon tax.

In September 1991 the Commission produced discussion proposals on the introduction of a completely new tax on energy use in the Community. Shortly afterwards the environment ministers of the 12 welcomed the suggestions and later accepted the principle of a tax to reduce carbon dioxide emissions. The proposals have been discussed at great length by three main groups of ministers; finance, energy, and environment. The final decision was supposed to have been taken in June 1992.

The taxes, if adopted, would have been phased in from 1993 to 2000. They would have applied to non-renewable sources of energy and would have been most heavily applied to those fossil fuels which produce the highest levels of carbon dioxide emissions and contribute to global warming. The aim was to make the taxes 'fiscally neutral' by reducing other taxes. Even so, the Commission predicted that the taxes would raise inflation by about 0.5 per cent, and cut economic growth slightly. The hope was that the United States and Japan would follow suit, although it was admitted that the USA is so tied to relatively profligate energy use that it would find it hard to shake off its old ways. The taxes would have been levied by each individual member state and have two components, one on the non-renewable element, and the other on the degree of contribution to pollution. The figures envisaged would, by the year 2000, have put a tax of $10 a barrel on oil (rising from a $3 tax in 1993). They would have led to a rise in the price of industrial coal by about 60 per cent, petrol by 6 per cent, domestic heating oil by 17 per cent, and domestic electricity by 14 per cent.

One of the main objectives of the proposed tax was to meet the target of maintaining carbon dioxide emissions at 1990 levels in the year 2000. The United Kingdom set itself a later target date of 2005. In mid-1995 it was apparent that only two members, Germany and Belgium, would come anywhere near their self-imposed targets for controlling carbon dioxide emissions. The Commission said other policies would have to be adopted, and suggestions included further speed restrictions on all vehicles, the use of the tax revenues to encourage energy efficiency, raising minimum standards for household appliances and equipment, and financing renewable sources of energy. Progress has been made along these lines, for example the gradual introduction of speed limiters on heavy-goods vehicles after

1994. The Commission reckoned that there was scope for improvement in energy efficiency in the region of 15 per cent throughout the members as a whole on the basis of existing technology. The proposals have met with fierce opposition from vested interests and from the governments of the poorer member states who stand to lose most from the rise in energy costs because of increases in their production costs. The economic downturn has strengthened opposition to the proposals because they are seen as raising costs and reducing international competitiveness.

The amount of revenue raised by the proposed tax would be a staggering 50 billion ECU each year, approximately. Since the Union is responsible for about 15 per cent of the world's emissions of carbon dioxide and has only 6 per cent of the world's population, it was vital that the other nations were persuaded to follow similar policies. (The USA is responsible for about 23 per cent, Japan for about 5 per cent, and the old USSR and Eastern European countries for 25 per cent.) It would have taken great political courage to adopt the tax strategies proposed by the Commission because they were bound to be politically unpopular even when other taxes were reduced to compensate for the carbon taxes. That courage has been lacking. Unfortunately, the politicians who govern our world tend to have short-term, electoral perspectives. Most of them do not expect to be alive when depletion of the ozone layer and global warming have their full effect!

The decision made in December 1994 was a feeble compromise that has rendered the carbon tax virtually dead for the time being. The decision made by the Environment Council was that the Commission should draw up a framework for member states to apply a carbon tax in their own country *if they wish*. The framework was drawn up in May 1995 and would apply from 1 January 1996. Members wishing to apply the carbon/energy tax would have flexibility within common parameters with the aim of harmonising rates by 1 January 2000. The target rates for the tax are the equivalent of $10 per barrel of oil which is a rate of 44.87 ECU per 1000 litres of petrol. Since the whole point of the carbon/energy tax was to introduce it collectively, preferably with parallel action from Japan and the United States, this decision effectively kills off the tax which was at the heart of the policy. Sweden, which already has a carbon tax, will be left to suffer the burden of relatively uncompetitively priced energy.

Environmental groups are very angry at the turn of events, and in early 1995 were accusing the Commission of having abandoned the commitment the European Community made at the Rio Earth Summit in 1992 on stabilising carbon dioxide emissions. The Council of Ministers has refused to commit itself to reducing carbon dioxide emissions after 2000. Evidence submitted to the Commission in early 1995 indicates that carbon dioxide emissions in the Union will not be stabilised but will actually rise by over 6 per cent between 1990 and 2000. They may rise by a further 15 per cent between 2000 and 2015. While the European Union fails to act vigorously, the 36 small nations that form AOSIS, the Alliance of Small Island States, many of which are barely above sea level, are becoming increasingly concerned by the prospect of global warming and rising sea levels.

The Emperor Nero is alleged to have fiddled while Rome burned. The European Union, or some parts of it, appears to be doing the equivalent. If we try to look on the bright side, there are some experts who are trying to persuade us that global warming is: (a) a figment of the gloom-and-doom merchants' fevered imaginations; or (b) would not matter if it did happen; or (c) would be a jolly good thing for some of us. Perhaps the European Union is so deeply immersed in the details of Packaging Directives, Eco-labels, recycling, and banning PCBs and PCTs that it fails to see the larger picture. Perhaps it acts on the adage that the longest journey starts with a single step. Ultimately it may be a replay of the ancient conflict between the selfish 'economic person' dwelling in the free, competitive market, and the socialised, globally-aware citizen of the world or, alternatively, a matter of short-term personal satisfaction versus long-term collective benefit.

Law and Democracy **11**

Law and Justice

It is the application of law which distinguishes civilisation from anarchy. Thus a study of the European Community and Union should probably start from a detailed examination of its legal base. The Community and Union are unique – there has never been a national or international system like it – and are based on a new, autonomous and uniform body of law that is separate from national law. This body of law also transcends national law and is applied directly in all member states.

In order to make sure that there was a uniform interpretation and application of this law the Community set up the Court of Justice based in Luxembourg. Its job is to ensure that the law is observed when the Treaties establishing the Community are applied and interpreted.

The origins of Community law

The major source of Community law lies in the 'primary' legislation created by the members. This consists of the Treaties of Paris and Rome in particular, plus various Conventions and the Treaties of Accession when new members join. It also includes the Treaty on Union which was formally ratified by all members in 1993. Association agreements with non-members such as Turkey (1963) and the First Lomé Convention of 1975 with African, Caribbean and Pacific countries are also sources of primary legislation. These treaties and agreements have had numerous additions made to them as time has passed. These additions are called protocols, schedules or annexes and count as 'primary' legislation.

The other important written source is called 'secondary' legislation, and is the law created by the Community institutions. It usually takes the form of directives, regulations and 'decisions' which may be addressed to states or to individuals.

There are also some international agreements reached by the Community or Union as a whole. The most important of these relate to tariffs and trade negotiated via GATT and now the World Trade Organisation (WTO). These agreements are implemented by directives and decisions and thus become Community law rather than remaining as international law.

Community law has, in addition, an unwritten basis. Various articles of the Treaties of Rome say that the Court of Justice must look at the general principles of law as well as at the written law. The early treaties say nothing about fundamental rights so it is essential to apply general principles in this area. The Treaty on Union 1993 contains a new article on *citizens'* rights such as the right to citizenship of the European Union, to move and reside freely within it and to have consular advice. It also says 'The Union shall respect the rights and freedoms as guaranteed by the European Convention for the Protection of Human Rights and Fundamental Freedoms, and as they result from the constitutional traditions common to the member states as general principles of Community law'.

There is also what is called 'customary law' which results from established practice. The best example has been the right of the European Parliament to question the Council of Ministers. This has derived from custom.

The Court of Justice frequently applies the general rules of international law. These are regarded only as a supplementary source of Community law because they tend to be very generalised.

An important source of law in the Community stems from decisions made by the Council of Ministers. The ministers represent their governments so technically these 'decisions' are governmental agreements and, therefore, international conventions. These decisions are taken by the ability of each state to act under international law, not under power conferred by the Community treaties. There is still some debate as to whether these decisions, based as they are on international conventions, are technically Community law, but they are in practice which is what matters.

The Court of Justice

Since 1995 the court has consisted of 15 judges assisted by nine advocates-general. They each have two assistants, legal clerks who do research for them on the case and on procedure and who prepare documents for them. The judges and advocates-general have their independence guaranteed by law. They are irremovable; they deliberate in secret and are immune from legal proceedings against them unless the court itself waives the immunity. The appointment of members of the court is done by agreement by member governments. The judges sit for six years and may have their term of office renewed. Membership is arranged so that every three years there is a partial replacement of judges. There is no nationality requirement but there is one judge from each state. The judges have a variety of backgrounds apart from recently practising law or being a judge. Some of them have been diplomats, some politicians, some academics and some senior officials. They must be chosen from 'persons whose independence is beyond doubt and who possess the qualifications required for appointment to the highest judicial offices in their respective countries or who are proconsuls of recognised competence'.

The judges choose a president from among themselves. The president acts for three years directing the court, allocating cases, appointing a judge as rapporteur for each case and determining the schedules for hearings. The president may act alone to give judgment in summary proceedings on applications for provisional measures but the decision may be referred to the full court.

The advocates-general are appointed on the same terms as the judges. They are assigned to cases and their job is 'to act with complete impartiality and independence and to make, in open court, reasoned submissions on cases brought before the Court in performance of the tasks assigned to it'.

The court conducts most of its business in plenary session, with a quorum of seven judges. Cases brought by member states or institutions of the Union must be heard in plenary session. The court may, however, operate in 'chambers'. There are four chambers composed of three judges, and two chambers composed of five judges. The chambers take cases in rotation and do not specialise. Cases brought by individuals or firms may be referred to chambers rather than to the full court. The structure of the Court of Justice is summarised in Figure 11.1.

FIGURE 11.1
The European Court of Justice

Governments of the
Member States appoint
the 15 judges
and 9 Advocates-General
by common accord for
a term of six years

COURT OF JUSTICE
Full court of 15 judges
2 chambers with 5 judges
4 chambers with 3 judges

TYPES OF PROCEEDING

| Actions for failure to fulfil obligations under the Treaties (Commission or Member State v. Member State) | Actions for annulment (against Council or Commission) Actions on grounds of failure to act (against Council or Commission) Claims for damages against the Community | References from national courts for preliminary rulings to clarify the meaning and scope of Community law Opinions |

COURT OF FIRST
INSTANCE
15 judges

Direct actions by natural and
legal persons, except
anti-dumping cases
Staff cases
Actions under the ECSC Treaty
Ancillary actions for damages

SOURCE Updated from *The ABC of Community Law*, 4th edn (Luxembourg: Office for Official Publications of the European Communities, 1994)

The Single European Act of February 1986 led, in October 1988, to the attachment of a 'Court of First Instance' to the Court of Justice. It has 15 judges who may also act as advocates-general. It hears cases brought by officials of the Community on staffing matters, actions on competition law, actions concerning the anti-dumping laws and cases under the ECSC Treaty. It does not hear actions brought by member states nor deal with questions referred for preliminary rulings. There is an appeal from its decisions to the Court of Justice on points of law.

It is important to realise that, although the Court of Justice is the Union's supreme judicial body and that there is no appeal against its judgments, other national courts at all levels also apply European Union laws.

The role of the Court of Justice

In the beginning the court dealt mainly with the problems arising from establishing a customs union. This led, gradually, to common rules on transport, agriculture and an assortment of freedoms such as the right to establish a business anywhere, the right to provide services, and freedom of competition, Increasingly, the work of the court moved into social areas and to the consideration of the freedom of workers, the right to social security and the rights of migrant workers. As with any legal system a number of important cases are quoted as test cases. They have established certain principles which have been accepted as precedents. The American Supreme Court did the same in the first few decades of its existence. In both Europe and America there is a slow evolution over time as cases are brought before the courts.

In principle a court can order an individual, firm or institution to do something it is supposed to do, to stop doing something it should not do, and to do something differently. It can also draw up limitations on the scope of their actions. These various forms of action have precise names:

(a) *Proceedings for failure to fulfil an obligation* There have been several hundred cases under this heading since 1953. Some have been brought by member states against other members because of alleged failure to meet regulations, for example on the free movement of sheep meat or restrictions on fishing. Most cases are initiated by the Commission. Usually the states comply with the court's ruling by modifying their national laws. Occasionally they stall until another action is brought. If the member is desperately keen to continue its policy it may use delaying tactics until the rules are changed. Under the Treaty on Union fines may now be imposed.

(b) *Proceedings for annulment* These are a way of reviewing the legality of Commission decisions and regulations and of settling conflicts over the respective powers of the various institutions of the Community. There have been very few actions brought by member states against the Council of Ministers. There have, however, been about 40 actions brought by them against Commission decisions. These have related to whether national financial help is lawful, to transport, to the free movement of goods and to the settlement of agricultural payments. A few cases have been brought against the European Parliament. It, for its part, once intended to take the Council to the court over a budget dispute but withdrew when the Council gave way. The court has, subsequently, in 1985, had to settle a dispute between the Council and the Parliament. Since 1993 the Court of First Instance has dealt with cases for annulment brought by firms or individuals except where anti-dumping rules are involved.

(c) *Failure to act* These proceedings in the court enable people to punish inactivity which can be damaging. Most of these proceedings have been declared inadmissible, especially those from private individuals and firms. They can only be admissible if the institution in question has previously been called upon to act. In the early 1970s, in a celebrated case, the Parliament brought such an action against the Council of Ministers for failure to act to introduce elections to the Parliament by direct election and universal suffrage, instead of indirect appointment. The court's decision was pre-empted by the 1974 agreement of the Heads of Governments to hold direct elections.

(d) *Actions to establish liability* The court has the exclusive juris-diction to order that the Community pays damages because of its actions or its legislative acts. This is on the principle of non-contractual liability. The Community's contractual liability is dealt with by the individual members' laws and courts.

(e) *Fines* The Union Treaty gave the Court the power, from 1993, to impose fines on member states which did not comply with its judgments or which fail to discharge their obligations. It will be interesting to see how this power is used and the response to its existence. Will member states behave differently? There had been no use of the powers in the period to May 1995.

The Court of Justice acts in the above ways. Thus member states may be brought to observe the law and a greater uniformity of practice is assured. The general long-term effect of the court has been to speed up social and commercial integration.

How do Community law and national law mix?

We tend to hear most about conflicts between Community law and national law because the question of national sovereignty is involved. There is, however, a great area of positive interplay between them where no obvious conflict arises.

The area of interplay is where Community law refers to the members' legal systems in order to complete its own requirements. For example, until the implementation of the Single European Act after 1987, freedom of movement and the right to establish businesses was given only to nationals of the members. It was left to the member states to decide with their own laws who is a national of their state. The Treaty on Union went further and established the concept of citizenship of the European Union alongside national citizenship but there has been little practical effect according to a report of the Commission in May 1995.

Sometimes Community law uses the national law's legal institutions to add to its own rules. This is usual with the enforcement of judgments of the Court of Justice. An article of the Treaty of Rome says that enforcement is to be governed by the rules of civil procedure in the state concerned. In addition, the Treaty sometimes refers to the general principles common to the laws of the members.

Despite the wide areas of agreement or interplay referred to, there are conflicts between Community law and member states' laws because the Community law sometimes creates direct rights and obligations for its citizens. These apply directly to member states and may not be consistent with the rule of the national law. In such instances, one of the systems has to give way. There is no written Community law that resolves this problem. Nowhere does it say that Community law takes precedence over national law. Yet it is obvious that it must if the Community is to survive. It is probably a mistake to think that there are layers of law superimposed upon one another. In practice, the Community legal order and that of the member states are interlocked and mutually dependent.

The issue of conflict is, in practice, resolved by the Community law having precedence, the basis of which is aimed at ensuring the *ability of the Community to function*. The members have given the Community the legislative powers to function and it would not be able to do so if its legislation were not binding on all its members. (The case of *Van Gend & Loos* in 1963 established the direct applicability of Community law.) The Community could not continue if members could annul its laws at any time that it suited their national convenience to do so. The legal consequence of this is that any provision of national law which conflicts with Community law is invalid.

These conclusions have been established over the years by a series of cases before the Court of Justice. The most important of these was the 1964 judgment of *Costa* v. *ENEL*. At the end of the summing up the court said:

it follows from all these observations that the law stemming from the Treaty, an independent source of law, could not, because of its special and original nature, be overridden by domestic legal provisions, however framed, without being deprived of its character as Community law and without the legal basis of the Community itself being called into question.

This assumption of power has been challenged, in early 1995, particularly by anti-Maastricht French MEPs who want a special chamber to be set up to remove the European Court of Justice's exclusive power to review the legitimacy of European law.

Later cases related to national constitutional law. The Dutch have removed any potential problem by writing the precedence of Community law into their constitution. Germany and Italy have constitutional courts which used to make an exception to the principle of the supremacy of Community law where it conflicted with their constitutional guarantees. They argued that any dispute should be settled in favour of fundamental rights. They eventually ended their resistance when they came to consider that the Community had protected fundamental rights sufficiently with guarantees. Thus we now have a situation where Community law is predominant even over the individual members' constitutional laws. The United Kingdom has no separate written constitution and no explicit Bill of Rights, although it does subscribe to the European Convention on Human Rights. The Convention is not written into United Kingdom law despite several attempts by pressure groups, the latest in 1995, to have legislation to that effect passed. It is assumed that United Kingdom citizens have rights unless they are explicitly removed by law. It is clear that many British parliamentarians and commentators have been very surprised at the extent to which Community law has impinged on British law and new legislation. They were, for example, very shocked in 1991 when the European Court ruled that an Act of the United Kingdom Parliament which intended to prevent Spanish fishermen registering their boats in the UK in order to take advantage of the UK's fishing quota, was illegal. As the Single European Act is implemented it is clear that their views of national sovereignty need to be revised to take account of the supremacy of Community law. It is interesting that, in late 1991 and early 1992, the United Kingdom government used the fact that it was awaiting European Court rulings on Sunday trading as an excuse to do nothing about large multiple stores that were flouting what everyone had understood the law to be since the late 1950s. The United Kingdom government has also used reference to European law to explain its inability to act unilaterally over the export trade in live animals. It has also quoted European law as a reason for failing to act to prevent the deaths of young children who are killed in low-speed collisions with vehicles sporting the fashion accessory called 'bull' or 'roo' bars. Most of these vehicles are registered within the M25 motorway London outer-orbital road where free-ranging bulls and kangaroos are not a daily occurrence.

Democracy

In democratic terms the Community is a strange animal. The European Parliament is elected by universal suffrage every five years by proportional representation in every country except Great Britain where the first past the post, or relative majority, system is used. Yet the Parliament is largely a consultative body and has little power of decision, although since the Single European Act was put into force in July 1987 and since the Treaty on Union came into effect in November 1993 it has had extra powers of consultation and approval. The final decisions are made by the Council of Ministers (or Council) which is a meeting of the relevant national ministers for a topic such as transport, finance or agriculture. They make decisions that commit their national governments to policies and to the possible changes of legislation needed to implement them. The assumption is, of course, that these ministers are democratically representative of their people, an assumption that is not always easy to sustain where there are minority governments or minority-controlled coalition governments. In some states ministers do not have to be elected members of any legislative body. As an extreme example, in the USA they are not allowed to be because of the doctrine of 'separation of powers'.

In some countries, because of the way in which their systems of proportional representation operate, the individual voters, once their votes have been cast, are largely ignored and the government which is formed is the result of a complex set of negotiations and compromises between parties as the seats and ministerial posts are allocated. Thus the ministers who make agreements on behalf of their governments at European Union level may be far removed from the original political desires of the electorate. In the case of the United Kingdom the minister may represent a government that has been elected by a minority of the total votes cast or his or her party may even have a majority in the lower house, the House of Commons, despite having fewer votes than the main rival party. This situation arises because of the allocation of seats without regard to the equality or weighting of votes. There is no concept in the United Kingdom of the fully equal distribution of electorate in each constituency. Once elected a United Kingdom government can use the ancient powers of the royal prerogative to exercise powers of patronage, to make treaties, declare war, introduce delegated legislation with the minimum of parliamentary consultation, massage the flow of information to the public under a cloak of secrecy, and choose a date for an election to suit its own party advantage. It is also able to remove, almost at a stroke, the powers of locally democratically elected bodies subordinate to it. Nor is it subject to the rulings of a constitutional court and has shown itself willing to rewrite the law if the decisions of its final court of appeal, part of the non-democratic House of Lords, are not in its favour. It is difficult to credit the idea that, if anyone were given the task of setting up a democratic state in the 1990s, they would follow the United Kingdom pattern.

The Council of Ministers does not, of course, operate in a vacuum. The ministers receive advice and guidance from their national civil servants and diplomats and from the European Commission. Much of the work is done through the Council Working Groups, that is national officials, and through COREPER, the committee of permanent representatives of the member states which is part of the Council. It has become apparent in recent years that Council meetings have become increasingly a formality and that ministers are usually rubber-stamping agreements that have been thrashed out prior to the meetings by the civil servants of COREPER. It can be argued that COREPER is becoming the real seat of power and decision-making in the European Union. The ministers, with exceptions, are defeated by the detail and complexity of their subjects and become heavily dependent on advice.

The Commission is, in theory, the executive body which works on behalf of the Council of Ministers to give it advice, to prepare reports and to implement decisions. It has, however, built up its own authority and has become an important source of ideas and a powerful cohesive force in creating a *European* attitude. Yet its members are not democratically elected but are chosen by national governments. Their appointment must be approved by the European Parliament. The current Commission 1995–2000 was questioned individually by MEPs to see what their attitudes were and whether they were up to the job. The Irish Commissioner for Social Affairs withdrew from the chair of a committee on women's rights when his previous policy of opposing the right to abortion in Ireland was revealed. The Parliament approved the whole Commission despite its lack of confidence in some nominees' abilities because it is not allowed to disapprove of individuals. It can only accept or reject the whole Commission. Critics of the process say that the European Parliament is testing nominees for enthusiasm for the European ideal and not for competence. Once in place the Commissioners have a high degree of independence until their term of office is concluded but they must, by definition, be acceptable to the national government at the outset. The composition and terms of office of the Commission changed from 1 January 1995 as a result of the Treaty on Union. The committees of the Union are not directly elected either. The most established, the Economic and Social Committee with its 222 members representing employers, trade unions and consumers, consists of appointees approved by the Council on the advice of member-state governments although some may be nominated as a result of sectional elections. The Council has created a number of other consultative committees, none of which is elected; rather they consist of appointees from various, often conflicting, pressure groups and sectional interests. It is perhaps as well that they can only give advice and not make decisions. It was decided in December 1991, at the Second European Parliament and Regions of the Community Conference, to call for the creation of an elected independent committee to represent European Regions. Thus the Treaty on Union established a Committee of the Regions with 222 members nominated by the member states. Most of the members are locally or regionally elected representatives but they are still nominated by their governments and not directly elected to serve. It is, therefore, an indirectly elected body but it does help to uphold the principle of subsidiarity.

The Democratic Deficit

The phrase 'democratic deficit' became fashionable in the late 1980s as the proposals for the reform of the political structures of the Community began to be discussed prior to the Maastricht summit on economic and political union. It has two meanings. The main one is how to maintain democratic participation and control if powers are transferred on any significant scale from national assemblies to Community institutions. The second was an idea favoured by supporters of greater powers for the European Parliament; that is, that it should be given far greater powers in accordance with its democratic basis of election. It was assumed that the Treaty on Union would advance the Community towards stronger centralised institutions and that the democratic aspects would need to be underpinned in order to protect them. Those who wanted a much more powerful and influential European Parliament were disappointed by the Maastricht agreement, especially as they had been encouraged by Chancellor Kohl of Germany's demands for greater authority to be given to it on the basis of its democratic nature. Possible methods of tackling the democratic deficit are discussed in Chapter 12.

A Conference of the Parliaments

One idea put forward to make up the democratic deficit was the creation of a 'Congress of Parliaments', that is regular meetings between representatives of the European Parliament and of national parliaments. The Union Treaty agreed at Maastricht contained a declaration saying 'the European Parliament and the national parliaments are invited to meet as necessary as a Conference of the Parliaments'. The Conference 'would be consulted on the main features of the European Union'. Sceptics have expressed the view that the proposed Congress was nothing more than a cosmetic exercise, and that it would be yet another talking shop with no powers. The last Conference of Parliaments (or Assizes) was held in Rome in 1990. Although no General Conference has been held since the Treaty on Union was passed, there have been an increasing number of meetings between different bodies belonging to national parliaments and the European Parliament, 44 in 1993.

The European Parliament

The European Parliament was called the 'Assembly' in the treaties establishing the Community. Until 1979 the members (MEPs) were appointed from their national parliaments. The appointments were, of course, related to party strengths. The original treaties had intended members to be elected but disagreements among the Six prevented this happening until after the accession of the United Kingdom, Denmark and Ireland in 1973. Even so, the first British MEPs were appointed not elected. In the election of 1979, 410 MEPs were elected to the Parliament. This number rose to 518 after the accession of Greece in 1981 and Portugal and Spain in 1986. In 1994 it rose to 567, mainly to adjust for the reunification of Germany, and in 1995, on the accession of Austria, Finland and

Sweden, to 626. The elections are held every five years – 1979, 1984, 1989, 1994 and the next in June 1999. The number of MEPs per country is based broadly on population but not as exactly as, say, the United States electoral districts for Congressional elections. The intention of the European Parliament since 1982 has been that the elections should be by a regionally-based system of proportional representation. This was intended to improve the chances of election of all but tiny parties. The member states did not agree and the 1984 election was held with a mixture of systems according to country. They also failed to agree for the 1989 and 1994 elections. The United Kingdom proved a major stumbling block to agreement and has retained its first-past-the-post system except in Northern Ireland where the single transferable vote (STV) method of proportional representation is used. Britain's main parties have a vested interest in retaining the archaic first-past-the-post method of election. It enables them to exclude other parties, even those with a significant measure of support. The STV is used in Northern Ireland local and parliamentary elections and in Ireland's parliamentary elections. England has 71 MEPs, Scotland eight, Wales five and Northern Ireland three, making a total for the United Kingdom of 87.

Table 11.1 gives the United Kingdom European election results for 1994. The Liberal Democrats entered the Parliament for the first time and the Scottish Nationalists obtained an extra seat. The main change was the shift of seats from Conservatives to Labour. The Table shows clearly the distorting effects of the first-past-the-post system. Nearly half a million Green voters received no representation, nor did 162 000 Welsh Nationalists although a similar number of votes in Northern Ireland where they used the STV did yield seats for three parties.

The overall results in terms of how elected MEPs sit in the European Parliament are shown in Table 11.3, the bottom line of which shows the number of seats allocated to each member state. The figures include Austria, Finland and Sweden who held their elections later. Table 11.2 shown the results of European Parliament elections since 1979.

The issue of seat allocation and the steady rise in the size of the European Parliament raise the problem of the long-term size of the European Parliament as other nations join, especially if the new Union expands to the 25 or 30 nations envisaged by some people. An assembly of 1000 would be unworkable. An additional problem raised in this context is that of the potential increase in the number of languages and the practical difficulties of dealing with translation.

TABLE 11.1
Results of the June 1994 Elections for the European Parliament

GREAT BRITAIN

Party	Votes	%	Seats
Labour	6 753 860	44.24	62
Conservative	4 248 531	27.83	18
Liberal Democrat	2 552 730	16.72	2
Green Party	494 561	3.24	—
Scottish National Party	487 239	3.19	2
Plaid Cymru	162 478	1.06	—
Other	568 151	3.72	—
Total	15 267 550	100	84

Electorate: 42 293 640
Turnout: 36.1%
(Unofficial figures)

NORTHERN IRELAND

Name and party	First Preference	%	Seats
Ian PAISLEY (DUP)	163 246	29.16	1
John HUME (SDLP)	161 992	28.93	1
James NICHOLSON (UUUP)	133 459	23.84	1
Mary CLARK-GLASS (Alliance)	23 157	4.14	
Tom HARTLEY (SF)	21 273)		
Dodie McGUINESS (SF)	17 195)	9.86	
Francie MOLLOY (SF)	16 747)		
Hugh ROSS (Ulster Ind)	7858)		
Myrtle BOAL (C)	5583)		
John LOWRY (WP)	2543)		
Nial CUSACK (Ind Lab)	2464)		
Jim ANDERSON (NLP)	1418)		
June CAMPION (Peace)	1088)	4.07	
David KERR (Ind Ulster)	571)		

TABLE 11.1 *Continued*

Name and party	First Preference	%	Seats
Suzanna THOMPSON (NLP)	454)		
Michael KENNEDY (NLP)	419)		
Robert MOONEY (Const NI)	400)		
Total	559 867	100	3

Electorate: 1 150 304
Turnout: 48.67%
(Unofficial figures)
Elections in Northern Ireland are conducted under a system of proportional representation, using the single transferable vote in a three-member constituency

SOURCE *European Elections 1994*, 'Results and Elected Members', 2nd edn., Directorate General for Information and Public Relations, Central Press Division, July 1994

TABLE 11.2
European Elections: Electorate, Percentage Turnout and Votes Cast in the 12 Member States

Member state		Electorate	Percentage turnout	Votes cast
Belgium	1994	7 211 311	90.7	5 966 755
	1989	7 096 273	90.7	5 899 285
	1984	6 975 677	92.2	5 725 837
	1979	6 800 584	91.4	5 442 867
Denmark	1994	3 994 200	52.9	2 079 937
	1989	3 923 549	46.2	1 789 395
	1984	3 878 600	52.4	2 001 875
	1979	3 754 423	47.8	1 754 850
France	1994	39 044 441	52.7	19 485 953
	1989	38 348 191	48.7	18 145 588
	1984	36 880 688	56.7	20 180 934
	1979	35 180 531	60.7	20 242 347
Germany	1994	60 473 927	60.0	35 411 414
	1989	45 773 179	62.3	28 206 690
	1984	44 451 981	56.8	24 851 371
	1979	42 751 940	65.7	27 847 109

Member state		Electorate	Percentage turnout	Votes cast
Greece	1994	9 485 495	71.2	6 532 591
	1989	8 347 387	79.9	6 544 669
	1984	7 790 309	77.2	5 596 060
	1981	7 319 070	78.6	5 753 478
Ireland	1994	2 631 575	44.0	1 137 490
	1989	2 453 451	68.3	1 632 728
	1984	2 413 404	47.6	1 120 416
	1979	2 188 798	63.6	1 339 072
Italy	1994	47 489 843	74.8	32 923 377
	1989	46 805 457	81.5	34 829 128
	1984	44 438 303	83.4	35 098 046
	1979	42 193 369	84.9	35 042 601
Luxemburg	1994	224 031	88.5	178 643
	1989	218 940	87.4	174 471
	1984	215 792	88.8	173 888
	1979	212 740	88.9	170 759
Netherlands	1994	11 620 300	35.6	4 101 950
	1989	11 121 477	47.2	5 241 883
	1984	10 476 000	50.6	5 297 621
	1979	9 808 176	57.8	5 667 303
Portugal	1994	8 565 822	35.5	2 949 765
	1989	8 107 694	51.2	4 016 756
	1987	7 787 603	72.4	5 496 935
Spain	1994	31 145 446	59.6	18 256 204
	1989	29 283 982	54.6	15 623 320
	1987	28 437 306	68.9	19 173 642
United Kingdom	1994	43 443 944	36.4	15 827 417
	1989	43 710 568	36.2	15 829 054
	1984	42 984 998	32.6	13 998 190
	1979	41 473 897	32.3	13 446 091
Total	1994	265 743 613	56.8	144 960 086
	1989	244 951 379	57.2	137 932 967
	1984	200 505 752	59.0	114 044 238
	1979	191 783 528	62.5	110 952 999

SOURCE *European Elections 1994*, 'Results and Elected Members', 2nd edn., Directorate General for Information and Public Relations, Central Press Division, July 1994

TABLE 11.3
Political Groups in the European Parliament, 10 July 1995

	B	DK	D	GR	E	F	IRL	I	L	NL	A	P	FIN	S	UK	Total
PES	6	3	40	10	22	15	1	18	2	8	8	10	4	11	63	221
EPP	7	3	47	9	30	12	4	12	2	10	6	1	4	6	19	172
UFE				2		15	7	29				3				56
ELDR	6	5			2	1	1	6	1	10	1	8	6	3	2	52
EUL/NGL		1		4	9	7		5				3	1	1		31
GREENS	2		12				2	4	1	1	1		1	1		25
ERA	1				1	13		2							2	19
EN		4				13				2						19
IND	3					11		11			5				1	31
Total	25	16	99	25	64	87	15	87	6	31	21	25	16	22	87	626

The Forza Europa Group and the European Democratic Alliance have joined to form the Union for Europe Group

PES	Party of European Socialists
EPP	European People's Party
UFE	Union for Europe
ELDR	Group of the European Liberal, Democratic and Reformist Party
EUL/NGL	Confederal Group of the European United Left-Nordic Green Left
Greens	Green Group in the European Parliament
ERA	European Radical Alliance
EN	Europe of Nations
Ind	Non-attached

B: Belgium; Dk: Denmark; F: France; D. Germany; Gr: Greece; I: Italy; Irl: Ireland; L: Luxembourg; Nl: Netherlands; P: Portugal; E: Spain; UK: United Kingdom; A: Austria; Fin: Finland; S: Sweden

SOURCE   European Parliament UK Office of the European Parliament 1995

The European Parliament holds plenary sessions, that is the full assembly, in Strasbourg for one week each month, except in August. A new, extremely expensive (probably over £600 million), building is being constructed there to cope with the expected expansion. The French government is adamant that the Parliament should remain in Strasbourg because of its symbolism in terms of

Franco-German reconciliation and also because of jobs and prestige. Moreover, some of the finest restaurants in France are in the Strasbourg area! The Parliament also holds sessions in Brussels for two weeks of each month. The Parliament's 20 main committees also operate in Brussels. The European Parliament itself is eager to settle in Brussels and, after a vote in 1992, has taken a long lease with an option to buy on a colossal conference centre in Brussels. It too is extremely expensive, over £800 million, and has been compared in scale to the Canary Wharf development in London's docklands. Whilst the MEPs and their entourages are constantly shuffling between Strasbourg and Brussels, their administration is based in a third centre, Luxembourg. Some see this merry-go-round as a deliberate plot to keep the European Parliament as an expensive object of derision and to prevent it achieving the status commensurate with its electoral base. Its composition is summarized in Figure 11.2.

The committees of the Parliament

The number of permanent committees of the European Parliament was raised from 18 to 19 in January 1992, and again to 20 in 1994. They are at the root of its work. Their membership is reasonably representative of the strength of the political groupings within the Parliament and their meetings are frequently attended by Commissioners and officials. Public hearings are held at which specialists and experts give evidence; some of these are, of course, pressure groups. The Parliament debates the committees' reports and may amend their recommendations before they are sent back to the Commission which then presents them to the Council for final decision. On most matters it is legally necessary to obtain the Parliament's opinion before legislation can be made. Most of the committee meetings are held in Brussels but some are held elsewhere, even in member countries.

The committees in 1995 were:

- Agriculture and rural development;
- Budgets;
- Civil liberties and internal affairs;
- Culture, youth, education and the media;
- Development and cooperation;

FIGURE 11.2
The European Parliament, Composition July 1995

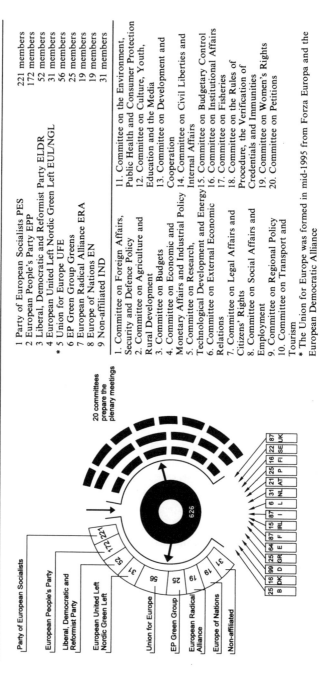

20 committees prepare the plenary meetings

1 Party of European Socialists PES — 221 members
2 European People's Party EPP — 172 members
3 Liberal, Democratic and Reformist Party ELDR — 52 members
4 European United Left Nordic Green Left EUL/NGL — 31 members
* 5 Union for Europe UFE — 56 members
6 EP Green Group Greens — 25 members
7 European Radical Alliance ERA — 19 members
8 Europe of Nations EN — 19 members
9 Non-affiliated IND — 31 members

1. Committee on Foreign Affairs, Security and Defence Policy
2. Committee on Agriculture and Rural Development
3. Committee on Budgets
4. Committee on Economic and Monetary Affairs and Industrial Policy
5. Committee on Research, Technological Development and Energy
6. Committee on External Economic Relations
7. Committee on Legal Affairs and Citizens' Rights
8. Committee on Social Affairs and Employment
9. Committee on Regional Policy
10. Committee on Transport and Tourism

11. Committee on the Environment, Public Health and Consumer Protection
12. Committee on Culture, Youth, Education and the Media
13. Committee on Development and Cooperation
14. Committee on Civil Liberties and Internal Affairs
15. Committee on Budgetary Control
16. Committee on Institutional Affairs
17. Committee on Fisheries
18. Committee on the Rules of Procedure, the Verification of Credentials and Immunities
19. Committee on Women's Rights
20. Committee on Petitions

* The Union for Europe was formed in mid-1995 from Forza Europa and the European Democratic Alliance

SOURCE Updated from Supplement to, *Frontier-free Europe* No. 7/8, 1995 (Luxembourg: Eurostat)

- Economic and monetary affairs and industrial policy;
- Environment, public health and consumer protection;
- External economic relations;
- Fisheries;
- Foreign affairs, security and defence policy;
- Institutional affairs;
- Legal affairs and citizens' rights;
- Petitions;
- Regional policy;
- Research, technological development and energy;
- Rules of procedure, the verification of credentials and immunities;
- Social affairs and employment;
- Transport and tourism;
- Womens' rights;
- There is also a temporary committee on employment.

In 1994 Fisheries was separated from Agriculture, fisheries and rural development to form the twentieth committee. In 1992 the Foreign Affairs and Security Committee replaced the Political Affairs Committee because of the changes agreed at the discussions on the Union Treaty. A new committee was also set up on Civil Liberties and Internal Affairs to cover the new intergovernmental arrangements set up at Maastricht for asylum and immigration. Membership of the committees varies between 25 and 61. There has been some reshuffling of the topics covered over the years but this list gives an insight into the attitude and interests of the European Parliament.

What impact have the MEPs made?

Before the enlargement of the Community after 1972 the European Parliament was a rather innocuous, largely powerless talking shop. Since then the European Parliament and its MEPs have gained in power and influence. Both the Single European Act of 1987 and the Treaty on Union of 1993 enhanced its authority. As a generalisation it is true to say that the United Kingdom MEPs have a more direct relationship with their constituents than most of the other member states' MEPs because of the nature of the regionalised proportional representation system used in many of the other countries. The United Kingdom members 'belong' to a constituency although no one pretends that MEPs are well known, and turnout at the elections is very low – 36.4 per cent in 1994 which was the highest so far. In contrast, the majority of MEPs in the other countries are allocated to a region as a result of the proportionate allocation of seats after the votes are counted. One consequence of this is that distinguished politicians from countries like France, find it easier to become members of the European Parliament and to integrate the work with their other interests, than do their British counterparts.

The British press, rather arrogantly, assumed that the introduction of British MEPs would be like taking the light of the gospel of parliamentary democracy to the benighted heathen. They ignored, of course, the extent to which the United Kingdom Parliament had, in the words of Enoch Powell and Tony Benn, become 'craven' – that is, the feeble rubber stamp to the proposals of the government of the day. Much was made of the introduction of the more extensive use of 'questions' in the European Parliament. This extra use of questions for both written and oral reply by the responsible people has greatly benefited the MEPs in their role as democratic guardians. In 1992 3051 written questions were put to the Commission, 338 to the Council and 137 to Foreign Ministers and there were 785 oral questions to the Commission, 335 to the President of the Council and 205 on political cooperation. Each question is inordinately expensive to answer because of the translation and printing costs associated with replies. In Britain, Question Time, especially on Tuesday and Thursday when the Prime Minister answers a tiny number of questions, is seen as a forum for the gladiatorial nature of confrontational politics. Its impact and effectiveness is grossly overrated except for rare moments of historical importance. The European question sessions are more constructive, genuinely seek information and clarification and usually have less crudely political motivation. This is mainly because the Parliament is not a bipartisan confrontational assembly but a shifting series of alliances. It is also because the 'audience', the electorate, is not usually informed on a daily basis of the doings of the European Parliament and there is no need to play to the gallery of public opinion. The Treaty of Union made formal the right to present petitions to the Parliament. 774 petitions were received in the 1990–91 Parliamentary session and 396 in 1991–92.

One major impact of the advent of the United Kingdom MEPs was the introduction of English as the major language, with French, for communication. English had often been the only common language of MEPs and was in frequent use but its introduction as an official language raised its status, availability and use.

In the 1994–99 Parliament the MEPs represent almost 100 different national political parties and most choose to join one of the political groups in the European Parliament. In order for a group to be officially recognised it needs a minimum of 26 members from one country, 21 from two countries, 16 from three countries or 13 from more than four countries.

National groups of MEPs from the same party have usually operated as fairly tightly disciplined blocks. They consult together, plan coordinated approaches and decide voting tactics and strategies. They try to maintain constant alliances with like-minded groups from other nations. The Conservative MEPs from the United Kingdom, for example, were particularly active in reflecting the wishes of the home leadership of the national party in the issues being debated in relation to the single market. One consequence of their approach was that after the 1989 elections they were almost completely isolated in that the European Democrats in the chamber consisted of 32 United Kingdom Conservatives and two others from Denmark. They naturally tried to make alliances and in the 1994 Parliament the 18 Conservatives and one Ulster Unionist became allied members of the European People's Party Group (the EPP), which is a centre-right alliance dominated by Christian Democrats although that dominance has been weakened by the addition of Scandinavian MEPs. The EPP is both a European Parliamentary group and a transnational party founded in 1976. The British Conservatives are not members of the transnational party but simply allied to it in the Parliament. They are not therefore bound by the EPP's policies, manifestos or declarations when it is speaking as a transnational party. This distinction helps the Conservative Party at home in the United Kingdom avoid embarrassing commitments.

The European Parliament sometimes tends to be dominated by left-of-centre and centre coalitions with a preference for social democracy and interventionism. The United Kingdom Conservative MEPs have been very active in opposing these principles. Occasionally they have been the only group apart from the European right to vote against measures proposed by the Commission. Sometimes the Parliament is dominated by centre and centre-right groups. MEPs sometimes change political groups and in recent years the larger groups have been making more of the decisions. The result has been that the smaller groupings increasingly looked for alliances.

It is difficult to separate the effects of the advent of United Kingdom members and those of the other new members from those resulting from the introduction of elected representatives and the passing of the Single European Act and Treaty on Union which extended the European Parliament's power. On the whole, most of the changes seem to have stemmed from the fact that members are elected instead of appointed. Elections have given MEPs greater confidence and independence and this has been reflected in the growing willingness of Parliament to confront the Commission and criticise proposals of both it and the Council of Ministers. Parliament has begun to propose an increasing number of ideas for legislation on its own initiative. The Commission has acted on most of these. It is evident that MEPs are increasingly concerned at the failure of the Council of Ministers to agree on measures that have already been approved by Parliament. Indeed, the European Parliament has taken the Council of Ministers to the European Court of Justice for failing to implement a transport policy which the Parliament had approved. This event is of very great long-term importance because it shows that the European Parliament could develop into a highly effective and democratic force. Some of the changes made in the Treaty on Union 1993 reflect this growing strength and it can reasonably be anticipated that, after the review of the Community's institutions in 1996, there will be further increases in the European Parliament's powers and authority and probably a simplification of procedures.

The impact of the United Kingdom European MPs has, therefore, been significant but it has not been in the nature of the transformation from darkness to light that was originally predicted. Indeed, over the next few years, especially if proportional representation is adopted throughout the Community, more and more people may see the European Parliament as the true centre of effective democracy and the main protection of individual liberties. A national Parliament such as the United Kingdom's will appear to have diminished in relevance and importance. This may be less true in some European countries where their electoral system, party systems and parliamentary procedures have been updated. The United Kingdom, with its increasingly unrepresentative Parliament, its archaic structures, its executive-dominated legislature, its unelected second chamber and its lack of explicit protection for the individual's rights, will inevitably suffer in comparison.

What are the budgetary powers of the European Parliament?

The Parliament has three budgetary powers in relation to fixing the annual budget. The first is the right to propose modifications to what is designated as 'compulsory expenditure', that is about 60 per cent of the total. The Parliament has considerable influence here if it does not propose an increase of spending. The second is the right to make the final allocation of what is called 'non-compulsory expenditure' but this is subject to a 'maximum rate of increase' fixed annually by the Commission on the basis of economic indicators. Here the Parliament can insist on its proposals being accepted although the Council can try to amend them by qualified majority voting. The third is the right to reject the budget. It has done so twice in 1979 and 1984. The European Parliament's Budgetary Control Committee is also quite effective. It checks the ways in which money is spent and can ask the Court of Auditors to carry out special enquiries. The Court may advise the Parliament to refuse to accept the annual accounts if it is not satisfied. The budget is the joint responsibility of the Council and the Parliament.

The draft budget receives its first reading in October each year and the Parliament may amend the draft proposals for expenditure. The Council considers the amendments and may make further changes before the budget is sent back to the Parliament in December for the second reading. The Parliament can then reject the whole budget and ask for a new draft. The classification of the budget into compulsory and non-compulsory expenditure is not as objective as might be imagined and is subject to political decisions which are usually intended to limit the Parliament's power. The Council has the final say on the classification of 'compulsory expenditure' which is defined as expenditure necessarily resulting from the Treaties or from acts adopted in accordance with them.

Most of this is spending under the CAP. The rest of the budget, about 40 per cent, is 'non-compulsory' and the Parliament has the final say on it although the amount is subject to the maximum annual rate of increase. The application of this maximum is extremely complicated and does not apply to an area of spending called 'non-privileged', that is on transport, energy and fisheries. In practice the maximum rate is much less significant than it used to be. Once the Parliament has approved the budget, the President declares it adopted. At this point a fourth right of the Parliament comes into play because it has the 'right to grant discharge to the Commission', that is it gives its approval of the way the budget is implemented which must be as it has been voted.

The Commission, Guardian of the Treaties

The Commission is the executive of the Union and is, supposedly, independent of the national governments. It has the role of guardian of the Treaties which form the Union. It answers to the European Parliament for its initiation and execution of policy. The Commission has had 20 members since 1995, two each from the United Kingdom, France, Italy, Germany and Spain and one each from the others. The President from 1985 to 1995, Jacques Delors, proved to be particularly dynamic in fostering the single market, the Social Charter and the Treaty on Union. His successor, Jacques Santer was Prime Minister of Luxembourg, a member of the Christian Social Party, and was a compromise appointment after the United Kingdom vetoed the choice of Jean-Luc Dehaene, the Christian Democrat Prime Minister of Belgium, on the grounds that he was too federalist in attitude. In fact there appears to be almost no difference in political attitudes to Europe between the two men. The members of the Commission are appointed for five years by national governments and then distribute their responsibilities among themselves under the President's guidance. In the United Kingdom, the government nominates one and the opposition the other. In practice the opposition's nominee needs to be acceptable to the Prime Minister. Commissioners, once appointed, are intended to be completely independent of their national governments. Indeed, they take an oath of independence from any source of influence. This makes it essential from a government's point of view that the people chosen have attitudes which will not lead to a sacrifice of national self-interest. The Commission has become a vital power base in Europe and its President has an important relationship to the Heads of Government of members. There had been a suggestion at the time of the Maastricht negotiations that the number of Commissioners should be reduced to about 12 but instead the number was raised to 20 on the accession of the three new members in January 1995. The Commission will be too cumbersome to be efficient if the numbers keep increasing with every enlargement of the Union. A new group of Commissioners began work in January 1995 with a five-year period of office to bring them into line with the Parliament's term.

The most important function of the Commission is probably that of initiating new proposals. It consults widely when preparing draft legislation and manages the frequent redrafting of proposals. The final decision on the legislation is, of course, made by the Council, sometimes with a qualified majority vote and sometimes under the codecision procedure with the European Parliament. It is responsible for the execution of legislation once it is in force. The Commission may withdraw proposals if it considers that amendments have produced a bad agreement. It may then produce a new draft, a fact that helps explain why some Directives take years to reach final form.

As guardian of the Treaties its duty is to ensure that members apply European Union law correctly and that all citizens and participants in the single market enjoy a level playing field. It can take legal action via the European Court of Justice against those in the public and private sectors who do not respect their Treaty obligations. It also ensures that any state subsidies are legal and supervises the competition and anti-trust laws. It can fine firms who break the law, sometimes very heavily.

As the executive body of the Union the Commission is responsible for implementing and managing policy. In particular, it manages the budget. It also negotiates international agreements on trade and cooperation, for example the Uruguay Round and Europe Agreements with Central European states. The Commission does have some degree of autonomy in taking decisions in areas where authority has been delegated by the Council or where the Treaties have given it specific powers, for example with agricultural and competition policies.

Some observers say the Commission is endowed with enormous power and often assert that it is undemocratic and malign. This is, on the whole, a figment of the xenophobic or conspiracy theorist's imagination. The Commission's power is very clearly limited by the Treaties and it is the Council and the Parliament who take legislative decisions. That is not to say that the Commission is not very influential and authoritative. It has vast experience and is run by people of exceptional ability. Above all, however, it needs to retain its reputation for impartiality and it must be obviously committed to the common good and not favour sectional interests. It can, in this context, be fairly criticised up to a point for its lack of transparency but probably no more than many national governments. A better case for criticism in this respect is the Council itself which is very unwilling to hold meetings, except of a formal nature, in public. The European Union lends itself to railway metaphors and the Commission is undoubtedly the locomotive pulling and pushing policy towards an objective which it has helped to determine.

The Commission employs about 15 000 people, one-fifth on translation and interpretation services, and its running costs are about 3.3 per cent of the Union's annual budget. The Commission is split into 23 Directorates-general (DGs) together with about 15 specialised services. The Heads of the Directorates-General, who are the equivalent of top civil servants in a national ministry, report to a Commissioner. The Commission meets once a week but may hold extra meetings for special purposes. The meetings adopt proposals, finalise policy papers and make other decisions. Matters of routine are dealt with by written procedures. Decisions may be taken by majority vote and are treated as collective policy. The Commissioners do not rely entirely on the official DG staff because each has a group of seven private officials plus support staff to form something like a personal cabinet. Commissioners may become very heavily reliant on this small group to brief them, to anticipate problems, to ask awkward questions and to smooth their paths.

The Commission is not an isolated body. It is represented at all meetings of the Parliament, the Council and at discussions of draft proposals. It has to be prepared to answer questions on its proposals and policies, especially at the European Parliament. Its management of the budget is subject to scrutiny by the Court of Auditors and it is generally subject to the European Court of Justice.

When critics refer pejoratively to 'Brussels' they usually mean the Commission and they often assert that it is undemocratic. This is rather a nonsensical statement given the nature of the Commission as a civil service and administrative machine. It is like criticising a dog for not being a horse. Moreover, where the Commission is not acting solely as a bureaucracy it is subject to the final decisions being made by a democratically elected Parliament and by representatives of elected governments in the Council.

The Council of Ministers

The Council of Ministers, or Council as it is usually called, sometimes comprises the 15 finance ministers of the members, or the 15 agriculture ministers, or the 15 transport ministers, and so on, plus Commission representatives, so it is democratic at second remove. The Presidency of the Council changes every six months. These meetings lay down the Union's policy, and decisions can be unanimous or by simple majority or qualified majority vote. Certain important decisions must be unanimous although most now may be by a qualified majority of 62 votes out of a total of 87 (a blocking minority is 26 and requires at least three member states). Under the 1994 Ioannina compromise there is a 'reasonable delay' to allow the Commission to reach a solution if the minority vote is between 23 and 26. The topics subject to the qualified majority vote (QMV) are laid down in the Single European Act, which applies QMV to proposals to implement the Single Market, and the Treaty on Union which extended QMV to a limited number of new areas. The reader who would like full details of what policies require each type of agreement is advised to consult Annex 7 of the *Intergovernmental Conference 1996*, Commission Report for the Reflection Group 1995, Office for Official Publications of the European Communities which is reproduced at the end of this book (see Annex).

The ministers are at the Council to act as spokesmen but the real work is done by their civil servants. The meetings have had a reputation for brinkmanship and making decisions only at the very last possible moment. These gatherings usually receive very slender treatment in the press but are frequently of major, long-term importance. The Council has a committee to service it called

COREPER or the Committee of Permanent Representatives. These are the civil servants (Ambassadors) of the members accredited to the Union and their advisers.

In addition, at least twice a year, there is a meeting of the European Council which is attended by the Heads of Government; foreign ministers also attend to give background advice. The President of the Commission is another participant. These so called summits have sometimes had enormous influence in shifting the path of the Union towards new objectives. The system of each member having a six-month stint acting as President of the Council leads to beneficial shifts of emphasis and is also welcomed by the smaller states. Some periods are highly productive in new ideas whereas others largely consolidate past efforts. The meetings are a welcome media event for the national leaders who can be seen acting as their nation's champions, in company with their equals or more powerful neighbours. Such division as occurs is played down by the public relations machine and each leader's point of view is presented in its best light for home consumption. If the divisions have been deep and real the final communiqué will be rather bland and non-committal. It may be couched in what is often called 'eurospeak' which is a mixture of fine-sounding phrases capable of several interpretations, and technical jargon which gives new terminology to ideas and policies. Examples include 'subsidiarity', 'extensification', 'harmonisation', 'set-aside', and a whole range of initials and acronyms. Many of the words are already in the new edition of the Oxford English Dictionary; many, you will have noticed are in this book. There are also dictionaries available of *Eurojargon*. Some of the 'eurospeak' words are simply French words for which there is no straightforward translation, some are acronyms and others are invented. No one has taken much notice of the regularly expressed desire of the Esperanto Society to have esperanto made an official language of the Union although their suggestion makes more and more sense as the membership extends.

In May 1995 the Council moved into a new building in Brussels, the Justus Lipsius Building, so called because it is in a street named after the 15th century Flemish philosopher. The building is referred to as 'The Consilium'. It cost about £300 million and provides for 2500 Council of Ministers officials, delegation rooms and conference facilities for Council meetings and rooms for working groups. The building is about to be modified to accommodate 15 members – it was designed for 12.

The Ombudsman

The Maastricht Treaty on Union gave the European Parliament the right to appoint an Ombudsman to receive complaints from people residing in a member state concerning 'instances of maladministration in the activities of the Community institutions or bodies', other than the Court of Justice and the Court of First Instance acting in their judicial role. The Treaty excludes the possibility of the Ombudsman directly investigating the actions of national authorities even where they are responsible for implementing Community law.

The rules governing the performance of the Ombudsman's duties are laid down by the European Parliament after seeking an opinion from the Commission and with the approval of the Council acting by a qualified majority. The Ombudsman should be appointed after each election for the European Parliament, for five years. There were considerable procedural delays in the appointment which was not made until July 1995 when Jacob Soderman, who had been Parliamentary Ombudsman in Finland, was chosen. Not everyone is convinced that the system will work as well at European level as it has in most national systems and the new institution was criticised by the Vice-President of the European Parliament Committee on Petitions. The Treaty also embodied the right of citizens to bring petitions to the Parliament in the law. This has had little practical effect and the petition process has remained the same as it has been since the early 1970s.

Democracy and the Media

It is very important for the health of a democratic society that its citizens should be informed about the activities of the ruling institutions. This means, in practice, that journalists, academics and ordinary citizens should have very free access to information. Unfortunately, in many governments there are strong pressures to maintain secrecy or to delay the issue of information. A few, such as Sweden have virtually free access to all public information including the content of their Prime Minister's letters on a daily basis. The public good, or the need to prevent unfair financial advantage being taken, is often quoted as the reason for restricted access. On the whole, secrecy merely helps render it impossible to attribute responsibility for decisions. The European Union has gradually begun to adopt a more liberal policy towards information, partly in response to the public disenchantment with the largely secret negotiations leading to the Maastricht agreement. The information services and statistical services of the Union are exceptionally good and very expensive and extensive provision is made for the media in all the new buildings that have been recently erected. They do not apparently take full advantage of it. There has also been a big effort to provide information to the general public through various area and regional centres, for example university and public libraries. There is, however, a caveat. The information tends to be about the decisions that have already been made and very little information is available on the processes involved in reaching them. It is rarely possible to discover the details of voting in the Council such as who supported or opposed proposals. There was a discussion in 1995 about publishing information from the minutes of some Council meetings and an agreement was reached in October 1995 on a new code of conduct to increase the transparency of Council decision-making. This new code has made the criticism less valid and will also restrict the use of unpublished declarations which nations have been in the habit of adding to legislation in Council. These declarations have had the effect of enabling the member to avoid implementing parts of the new legislation and have, according to some lawyers, constituted law of which the citizen is ignorant.

As a symptom of this lack of openness or transparency *The Guardian* newspaper in 1995 was engaged in a lengthy and tortuous legal battle with the Council of Ministers over the European Union's freedom of information policy. At the core of the complaint was the assertion that the Council officials automatically refused to hand over copies of the minutes of Council meetings. The newspaper received support from the European Parliament and from the governments of Denmark and The Netherlands. At the Court of First Instance in July 1995 the counsel for *The Guardian* said 'Only totalitarian regimes legislate in secret . . . For generations, citizens have been entitled to know the arguments used when legislators pass laws that citizens are expected to obey. They are entitled to the same standards when legislation is debated at European level' (*The Guardian*, 6 July 1995).

There is insufficient space to discuss the quality of media coverage of European Union affairs but the British media, even the 'quality press' devotes remarkably little space to such an important topic. It seems to assume that people find the subject boring so they need some sort of 'angle' in order to be persuaded to print a story. The European Commission now employs a few staff on a full-time basis to refute the 'Euromyths' that have sprinkled the pages of the British press. The myths are less prevalent in other countries.

The Future and the Intergovern-mental Conference

12

The future of the European Union depends on two main influences. The first is the accumulated effect of measures put into place in recent years. The most important of these is probably the Single European Act and the developing single market. Others include the reforms of the Common Agricultural Policy and of the Regional Funds, the impact of the Cohesion Fund, the trans-European networks (TENS), the degree of success of the campaign against fraud, Economic and Monetary Union, and the Schengen Agreement. On the political side we could include the effect of the Treaty on Union on the effectiveness of the European Parliament and on the development of a common foreign and security policy and a justice and home affairs policy.

The second factor is the long-term effect of the discussions leading to the 1996 Intergovernmental Conference and the outcome of the IGC itself. The outcome of the IGC will shape the European Union in the early 21st century. Its form will affect the nature of the Union's administrative and decision-making structure and its political nature as enlargement takes place. It will determine whether Foreign and Security Policy and Justice and Home Affairs become genuinely European Union policies, or whether the present ineffective compromise persists. It is likely to determine whether there will be a Union defence policy and a European Union defence force and their relationship to the Western European Union. It will also decide whether there will be a commitment to a guarantee of human rights in a new European Union constitution. The IGC will open officially on 29 March 1996 at Turin and will have monthly meetings.

What Alternative Policies for Development are there?

Some see the future of the Union as an expanding free trade area with the emphasis on free markets, the mobility of factors of production, labour, capital and enterprise, and a legal framework that regulates commerce and trade with the minimum of hindrance. They stress the 'market of 370 million people', economies of scale, the position to influence international affairs and the maintenance of distinctive national customs and culture. They support the policies put forward in the Single European Act because they see the completion of the internal market as realising their hopes. They tend to emphasise the principle of subsidiarity as a means of reducing the influence of the Union on national affairs.

Others see a European Union of the future as one without trade barriers, without hindrance to the mobility of factors, with the economies of scale but with a legal framework that encourages the harmonisation of standards and has a major social dimension. They envisage a more interventionist approach, a more positive direction through regulation, expenditure and taxation to achieve social goals such as lower unemployment or decreased poverty. They see the European Union as essentially an economic union which has a major social role. They are also in favour of the principle of subsidiarity but put greater emphasis on the Union making decisions on both framework policies and detailed applications.

There are others who go further and look forward to a deeper and more far-reaching political union. They see the economic harmonisation leading inexorably towards some more concrete political union such as a federal states of Europe. This concept has already been discussed. Their expectation is that initially there will be greater economic and social cohesion bringing with it a single European currency for those members who meet the convergence criteria, followed at a later date by the other members. It is unlikely that the United Kingdom, if it meets the criteria, will be able to resist the economic pressures to adopt the single currency, despite its Treaty protocol permitting it to make up its own mind over Stage 3 of monetary union. This decision to adopt a single currency will no longer be as early as 1996 as was first intended, but it is a certainty that, assuming the Treaty is adhered to, some members will adopt it in 1999. At the same time, the process begun in 1990 in starting Stage 1 of monetary union has established the European Monetary Institute and will next create a European Central Bank under the supervision of the European System of Central Banks to administer the common monetary policy and to regulate the foreign exchange value of the single currency. They think that even if initially some taxes are not harmonised the long-run pressures will be towards harmonisation. If, for example, France and Germany maintain different VAT rates there will be a tendency to cross- border trade which will force governments into equalising rates. A minor example of these pressures can be seen in the frantic legal and illegal cross-channel traffic in alcohol which arises because of the different tax regimes in Britain and France. This principle of equalisation of tax rates would, they allege, apply in many areas of economic activity if differences are maintained.

A European Union Foreign and Security Policy?

The supporters of deeper political union were probably somewhat disappointed by the Maastricht agreement on the development of a common Union policy for defence and foreign affairs (see below), but the Treaty may provide unexpected scope for change in that it is how the members act that matters, not the wording of generalised statements of intent. The optimists in this field have been encouraged by the development of united foreign policy initiatives in relation to Third World issues, to Namibia and southern Africa, to Iran and the Salman Rushdie affair, Sudan, the Ukraine, anti-personnel mines and to united action against terrorism. Most of the developments in this list took place as a result of the European Political Cooperation (EPC) policy adopted after 1986. The Union is increasingly seeking to put a collective voice in the United Nations and the International Monetary Fund.

There are different interpretations of the role of the Community in the Gulf crisis of 1990–91. Some see it as revealing the deep divisions between the members and call the episode a shambles that augurs very badly for any attempt to create a Union foreign policy. Others see it as part of the learning process and an indication that proper structures are required if common policy is to be formulated. Much of the criticism originated in Britain where there seemed to be little comprehension that countries such as Germany were bound by constitutional requirements not to become involved in military operations outside the NATO area. It may not be altogether a good thing that Germany has amended its constitution to allow its troops to serve outside the Nato area, under a United Nations' mandate, for example, in Bosnia in July 1995. German public opinion is very divided on the change. The Japanese also, for good reason, have a constitution which restricts them to 'self-defence' forces (which are very large), and they too did not send military forces to the Gulf.

The Community had a better experience in dealing with the Baltic States as they broke away from the Soviet Union, largely because the historical background was one of forced annexation by Stalin of states established at the Peace of Versailles. It managed a high degree of agreement over relations with the crumbling structures of the Soviet Union as it dissolved before 1991. There was less unanimity during the period of the attempted coup against Mr Gorbachev in 1991, but unity was regained as the new Commonwealth of Independent States was created. If it survives, which is still by no means certain, it is likely that once again Union foreign policy will be dictated by Germany which is closest to the problem geographically and has most to fear from a flood of economic refugees. Indeed Germany has been most active in supplying economic aid and has paid huge sums for the resettlement of Soviet troops from off the territory of the old East Germany. It has also taken by far the largest share of refugees from Yugoslavia.

The Yugoslavia crisis in the period 1991 to 1992, however, revealed significant differences of opinion, largely on timing of recognition of the independent status of Croatia, between the members of the Community. The episode will probably be seen by historians as marking a watershed in the postwar development of Germany, in terms of it reasserting its traditional role as *the* great power of Europe. Its productive capacity, wealth, and dominance in the ERM and monetary matters, and its enlarged population and area after reunification in 1990 could not be gainsaid. It pushed the other members into fixing a final date for collective recognition in January 1992 but acted before that date to give its own recognition to Croatia. This conflict was occurring at the same time as the negotiations at the Maastricht summit in December 1991. The events in Bosnia-Herzegovina since the German recognition of Croatia are interpreted in different ways. Many blame the chaos and bloodshed on precipitate German recognition. It has certainly been the case that the European Union has frequently appeared very divided in its relations with the United Nations and with the United States over the Bosnia crisis.

The Treaty on Union and Foreign Policy

Foreign policy and security are referred to as the 'second pillar' of the Union, and the Council decided that they would be dealt with outside the scope of the existing treaties by intergovernmental cooperation. The Commission and Parliament receive reports on what is decided and the Commission has the task of maintaining consistency between different areas of policy. Its role may become very important over time but the Treaty does not appear to stress its functions. The wording of the Treaty shows what was decided, but as already stated, it is what actually happens in the future as a consequence of the high-sounding phrases that matters. So far, as a Commission report for the IGC shows, there is a tendency to use pre-Treaty mechanisms rather than those provided for in the Maastricht Treaty (see below). The real, permanent changes may occur after the situation is reviewed in 1996.

The Union and its Member States shall define and implement a common foreign and security policy. [The objectives of these shall be:]

To safeguard the common values, fundamental interests and independence of the European Union;
To strengthen the security of the Community and its Member States in all ways;
To preserve peace and strengthen international security;
To promote international cooperation;
To develop and consolidate democracy and the rule of law, and respect for human rights and fundamental freedoms.

The Treaty allows for common positions and joint actions. The intention of the Treaty was that there should be cooperation between governments who will gradually implement joint action between them. To quote the Treaty again, 'Member states shall inform and consult one another within the Council on any matter of foreign and security policy of general interest in order to ensure that their combined influence is exerted as effectively as possible by means of concerted and convergent action.' This leaves plenty of scope for argument about what is of 'general interest' but the Treaty continues, 'Whenever it is deemed necessary, the Council shall define a common position. Member States shall ensure that their national policies conform to the common positions.' It goes on to require the members to coordinate their actions at international bodies such as the United nations, and at international conferences, and to uphold common positions if not all members attend.

The Council of Ministers decides on joint action by unanimity and lays down the details of timings, procedures and implementation. In this process it also defines which areas in the joint action will be subject to a qualified majority decision. The Presidency of the Council is responsible, during its six-month term of office, for representing the Union in matters coming within the common foreign and security policy. The Commission 'shall be fully associated in these tasks'. The Treaty lays down a procedure for emergency meetings in periods of crisis but policy is usually made at Council of Ministers' meetings, that is by Foreign Ministers, after the Heads of Government have defined the principles and general guide-lines for the common foreign and security policy. The expectation is that eventually there will be European Union embassies and consulates in some smaller countries. The multiplication of states within the Commonwealth of Independent States demonstrates the common sense of this, although it may go against the grain for diplomats who may see their career opportunities reduced if their national embassies decline in number.

One recent policy success for the Union has been the European Stability Pact which was launched in March 1995. It was the product of two sets of discussions for the Baltic region and for Central and Eastern Europe which centred on the nine countries that have been offered membership of the European Union. The Pact includes Russia, the Ukraine, Moldova and Belarus and is regarded as an important step in achieving political stability in Europe.

A European Union Defence Force?

There has been a growing interest, or rebirth of interest, in the idea of a collective European defence force and its possible replacement of NATO. France and Germany have already operated a joint brigade of troops as an experiment and have created a joint army corps that promises to be an extremely powerful force. Spain and Belgium have also contributed to this corps and other members may also join. The Eurocorps was set up in 1993 and has an establishment of 50 000 troops. The main components are a division from each of the four member nations and the pre-existing Franco-German brigade. It is a heavily armoured, mobile corps, consisting of the French 1st Armoured Division, the German 10th Panzer Division, the Belgian 1st Mechanised Division and the Spanish 21st Mechanised Brigade as well as the Franco-German Brigade and the French 21st Transmission Regiment. It has 645 main battle tanks, 280 self-propelled guns, about 1100 armoured personnel carriers and fighting vehicles as well as several missile systems. It is at least as powerful in armour as the British Army. This supra-national Eurocorps is dedicated to the WEU but may also serve NATO and the United Nations.

The United Kingdom, Italy and The Netherlands have also earmarked some of their NATO forces for possible WEU use. In June 1995, the German defence minister spoke to NATO defence ministers and proposed a plan for the future to be put before the IGC. He recommended a merger of the European Union and the Western European Union and supported significant changes in the way decisions are made in the Council. He wants, as does the Commission, an end to the present unanimity rule. The United Kingdom has, in the past, been strongly against this. One of the problems of the proposals is the fact that five of the members of the European Union are not in the WEU. Another handicap is that four of the members are neutral, Sweden, Finland, Ireland and Austria. Sweden's last government was beginning to favour an end to its neutrality but the election of a new government has caused a reversion to neutrality.

Before the Maastricht summit there was considerable pressure to restructure the defence of western Europe under either a Community organisation or to turn the Western European Union into a stronger body. There was, however, very powerful opposition to this from the United Kingdom which wished to see NATO retained as the heart of European defence, and there was even talk of Russia joining NATO. The main attraction of NATO from the British point of view is that the United States bears a high proportion of its financial and manpower costs, and the United Kingdom wants to keep its 'special relationship' with the United States. It received some support from Italy for its line on NATO. The USA has withdrawn large nuclear and conventional forces from Europe and has continued to do so through the early 1990s. Some American experts are wondering why the United States wishes to maintain forces in Europe at all, and there is little doubt that if they were not there already no American President would, in the face of the isolationism endemic in the USA, dare to suggest sending them. The new Republican Congress in power from 1995 is certainly much more isolationist than previous Congresses. The argument is reinforced by the realisation that the USA spends about $36 billion a year on European defence. Economic and political logic will dictate that US forces will eventually be entirely removed, although there may be a rapid response force retained as a gesture. The Maastricht agreement came down in favour of developing the Western European Union.

The Treaty says that the WEU will be developed as the defence component of the Union and as the method of strengthening the European pillar of the Atlantic Alliance. Its decisions 'shall not affect the obligations of certain member states under the NATO Treaty and shall be compatible with the common security and defence policy established within that framework'. In 1992 the WEU moved from London to Brussels and its permanent council now meets weekly. In 1994, NATO supported the strengthening of the foreign and security pillar via the WEU and endorsed the concept of combined joint task forces. In other words it agreed to separable but not separate military capabilities.

In the foreign and security fields the European Parliament is consulted on its main aspects and basic choices and kept informed. The European Court has no powers in this context. The Commission has the role of making sure that the policies do not conflict with the external economic policies of the Union. The Maastricht agreement contains a declaration that a series of other items may be subject to joint action. Some of these are of great significance now that the old Soviet state, after its break-up, has shed its control over much of its arsenals. They include arms control, non-proliferation matters, the export of military technology to other countries, cooperation in the technological fields of armaments, peace-keeping functions for the United Nations, humanitarian ventures, and work under the Conference on Security and Cooperation in Europe (CSCE), now renamed the Organisation for Security and Cooperation in Europe (OSCE). Relations with the United States and the CIS are included here as well. The above points need to be seen against the changing political climate in Central and Eastern Europe. Another factor is the desire of the United States to reduce its colossal balance-of-payments deficit and to cut the costs of its NATO commitment.

The Commission report to the Reflection Group preparing for the IGC concerning the work since the Treaty on Union says in reference to the Common Foreign and Security Policy, in paragraph 150:

It is not easy to measure success in this area, especially in view of the limited experience so far. Nevertheless, the enhanced degree of cooperation and coordination has removed at least some of the incoherence previously evident in the actions of Member States. The value of this should not be underestimated. However, the aim of substantial improvement has not been achieved.

We can expect strong pressure at the IGC to improve the CFSP.

The reader who is particularly interested in the Foreign and Security Policy of the European Union can obtain a detailed insider's view by reading pages 61–8 of *The Commission Report for the Reflection Group*, published by the Office for Official Publications of the European Communities in May 1995.

A Transatlantic Economic Space

In 1995 a series of discussions took place with a view to deepening relations between the United States and the European Union. The Commission produced a strategy paper on the subject which advocated what it called a 'building block' approach to the creation of a Transatlantic Economic Space as a free trade area. The approach would be based on work already undertaken and on consultations about NATO, European security, common humanitarian action and the campaign against drugs and crime. There will probably be a feasibility study on an Atlantic Free Trade Area.

What will be the Effects of the Single Market on the Location of Industry and Commerce?

The answer to this question is a mixture of speculation and extrapolation from past trends. Even these speculative answers depend on what happens as a result of the unification of Germany. The restoration of Berlin as the capital of Germany may eventually shift its centre of gravity further east. If past trends continue there will be a continued concentration of commerce, industry and wealth creation in the central, northern European area of the Ruhr, the Benelux countries, the Ile de France and southern England. This so-called 'power house' of the Union contains the main centres of government and administration, both national and European Union. These naturally generate a large service sector and extensive tertiary employment. The transport and communications networks are geared to exploiting the concentration of population, wealth and employment. An additional area of above-average growth is likely to be the so-called 'southern arc' from North Italy, through southern France to Spain which is proving increasingly attractive for climatic reasons to industry. Over a longer period of time it can be assumed that market forces will ensure some geographical expansion of these areas. Labour and land will become relatively more expensive than on the peripheries. This should create a deterrent effect pushing new firms and the expansion of existing firms to other areas.

Three other major factors will help to counterbalance the tendency to concentration in northern Europe. The first is the European Regional Development Fund (ERDF) which, depending on how it is administered, should put more funds into the disadvantaged, peripheral regions such as parts of Spain, Ireland, Portugal, Greece, southern Italy, Wales and Scotland. Linked to this have been the Integrated Mediterranean Programmes. The ERDF has risen from £5 billion in 1987 to £13 billion in 1995. The plan has doubled the share of these 'deprived' areas and they receive between 60 and 70 per cent of the fund. Portugal has received even more assistance from a special five-year industrial modernisation scheme.

The second factor is the size and application of the Cohesion Fund agreed to at the Maastricht summit as a means of helping Spain, Portugal, Greece and Ireland counter the possible harmful effects of the transition to the Single Market and the movement towards monetary union. The Cohesion Fund was discussed in Chapter 9. It is doubtful if a similar fund could be made available for any future entrants to the Union unless the present beneficiaries are willing to settle for a lot less money so that the savings can be transferred to, say, Poland or the Czech Republic.

The third factor that should offset the centralising tendency will be the development of policy on trans-European networks, that is telecommunications, gas pipelines, transport and electricity grids. The transport improvement programmes, especially the railway modernisation and renovation schemes will create a Europe-wide network of high-speed railways for passengers and freight. Experience in France suggests that this will help to revitalise those areas touched by the new and improved routes. Germany has been changing the orientation of its rail network from East–West to North–South and is going to build an ultra-high-speed line from Hamburg to Berlin. Work has begun on planning a Munich and Berlin to Verona and Milan railway via the Brenner pass. The old network was designed with military considerations in mind so that troops could be easily switched between eastern and western borders. The new orientation is helping to generate economic growth on a more even basis in Germany. Improvements in transport infrastructure are vital to the swift integration of the East German economy into the Union. They are also an essential part of the creation of the EEA, as is demonstrated by the Austrian and Swiss plans to drive three more rail tunnels through the Alps to cope with increased freight, and the proposed Baltic bridge. One feature of the new networks is the intention for some of them to go beyond the borders of the present Union, for example the Budapest to Vienna motorway opened in early 1996.

The great worry for the United Kingdom in this context is that its government has never shown any understanding of the potential of modern railways. Since 1979 it has concentrated on reducing public expenditure on public transport, including the railways, and has insisted, with less and less success, that private funds be used for new developments such as the Channel Tunnel Link or that the money comes from British Rail's or its privatised successors' own resources. These have been, and will probably continue to be, inadequate. European governments heavily subsidise their railways and are increasing their commitment. At the same time, the United Kingdom government has been cutting its allocation for railway subsidies. There is a serious risk that this blinkered approach, which has only been slightly modified since 1990, will leave the peripheral regions of the United Kingdom cut off from the benefits of the continental railway system. These benefits will stop at the London terminals of the Channel Tunnel link and not continue for some years to the north, west or south-west. Some work has begun on northern freight terminals but it is fair comment that lack of government vision and drive have led to serious delays in the essential programmes. Track and rolling stock modifications are needed to operate continental standard trains on British lines. Cheap, fast and efficient rail links are essential if the United Kingdom's outlying regions are to compete in Europe. A general issue arises here, in that it is surely perverse to accept state responsibility for the trunk-road network but not for the railway system.

There is a another element which will affect the location of industry, that is the price of labour. The labour force in some areas of Europe may be regarded as cheap in comparison with others, including Japan or the United States. The concept of 'social dumping' discussed in Chapter 9 is relevant in this context. If the problems of training can be overcome then this makes low-cost labour areas attractive for 'screwdriver' plants which assemble and package products that are designed and researched elsewhere. This has already happened on a significant scale in the United Kingdom with the influx of Japanese assembly plants, and in Ireland, Spain and Portugal with multinationals. They train the workers very effectively for their limited tasks and, using the latest high-productivity technology, produce at low comparative cost. They do not, however, bring sufficient research and development and design employment with them. The machines and technology used, as in the latest silicon-chip plants costing £800 million, are designed and developed elsewhere. These plants, therefore, remain as classic expendable branch factories, easily contracted, expanded, or closed as market whim dictates. If the overall level of costs and wages rise in the 'host country', this type of plant can easily be moved or set up in lower-cost countries within the Union or in the neighbouring countries of Central and Eastern Europe. In this context it is interesting to note that Mercedes Benz, the most profitable vehicle manufacturer in Europe, announced in September 1995 that it was preparing to source 25 per cent of its future production from foreign plants because of its need to keep a balanced mix of labour, material and other costs. It reckoned that it needed a 30 per cent increase in productivity over three years in order to remain competitive. It should be noted that the company was not motivated solely by the concept of lower wage costs.

In the long run, location is supposed to depend upon the overall comparative costs of an area compared with others. In theory, areas are competing with each other for the location of firms, offering them a variety of natural and acquired advantages. Also, in theory, the industries are competing with one another for the factors of production in an area. The most profitable industry can buy more of the factors it needs. In so far as this applies in practice each country must ensure that it has a well-educated, trained, skilled and adaptable labour force and minimum costs of transport and distribution. There are many imperfections in the markets for factors and the location of industry is affected by many influences not covered by the simple theory. Many location decisions for what are called 'footloose' industries where there are no overwhelming locational imperatives, are made on the whim of the entrepreneur for what are mainly social reasons such as family pressures. The Commission needs to be a very effective watchdog preventing governments giving hidden subsidies to incoming investment, or to their own industry.

What are the Gains from Membership?

The economist often talks about 'opportunity cost'. This is the cost, in financial terms of the next-best alternative foregone if a particular course of action is chosen. If a country chooses to spend £15 billion on a nuclear deterrent there is an opportunity cost involved of the other things that could have been bought with the money – roads, schools, hospitals, aircraft or pay rises for government employees.

In the case of membership of the European Union it is very hard to measure the opportunity cost of membership. Nobody can tell accurately what would have happened to an economy if the country had not joined. Some might argue that its future would have been rosier and that like Norway, for example, their country would have done very well outside the Union. They might point to an accumulated net contribution to the Community and Union over the years, especially in the case of Germany, although the exact figure is hard to quantify. They may see that as money wasted. They may also see the Common Agricultural Policy as an unnecessary expense that has placed a considerable extra burden on every household every year. Some place this figure as high as an extra £500 per household per year in the United Kingdom for example in the 1980s, or £350 in the early 1990s.

Against this net outflow, which is not accurately quantifiable, must be set the gains from the Regional and Social Funds. These sums have mainly benefited the areas of high unemployment but not exclusively so. But what is hardest to measure is the gain from trade arising from the large common market. Although not everyone regards the European Union as a true 'single' market despite the 1992 Single Market programme, the gains from specialisation, economies of scale and the incentives to greater competitive efficiency have been very large. The gains to the commercial and financial sectors have also been extensive although they have not been as large as predicted by Paolo Cecchini in his report for the European Commission, *The European Challenge, 1992: The Benefits of a Single Market* (published by Wildwood House for the European Commission). There have, however, been casualties and many firms and individuals have suffered materially from the greater competitiveness of some European firms. The peripheries have sometimes been hardest hit and there is a tendency for the central wealth-generating 'power house' of the Union to lie in the Ile de France, the Benelux countries and north-western Germany with an overlap into southern England. It is also called the Paris–London–Amsterdam–Ruhr quadrangle. See the list of regional incomes in Chapter 9. Economic geographers pay a great deal of attention to monitoring the growth of this region. A new analysis in 1991 found evidence of what has come to be called a 'hot banana', that is a banana-shaped area of higher than average development sweeping from the borders of Spain across to Germany.

There is a major gain to all members in terms of the mutual help given to less-favoured regions and the assistance given to cushion declining industries. This redistributive aspect is not welcomed by all, especially when the needs of Portugal, Greece and Eastern Germany are taken into account. There is also a major gain to all in the fields of scientific and technological research cooperation and education. Although these programmes do not compare in scale with Japanese and American expenditures they are beginning to make inroads into the research backlog and permit competition in selected areas.

On balance, therefore, an individual country may or may not be out of pocket financially as a result of membership. Those who are out of pocket may regard the cost as an acceptable price to pay for political stability and the absence of conflict. There is no doubt, however, that the members are stronger both economically and politically within the European Union than if they had remained outside. Each member has some particular cause to be thankful for in its membership. The people of the United Kingdom, for example, have been increasingly looking to Europe and its Court of Justice for protection of basic rights and freedoms. The idea that some people in the United Kingdom have of leaving the Union is unrealistic nonsense based on a romanticised view of British history and an over-optimistic assessment of the future. There might be a sort of half-way house as an associate member, or in the EEA with little political influence, but they would be less viable positions now the 1992 single market is effective and virtually impossible after monetary union takes place. The parallels that some people draw with Norway and some of the Far Eastern economies are false because of the relative size of the economies and populations.

Europe 2000

One of the admirable qualities of the Union is its forward thinking. 'Europe 2000: Outlook for the Development of the Community's Territory' is an example which applies to the subject of regional development and liaison between regional authorities. Europe 2000 is an initiative launched in 1991 to examine on a Europe wide view, not solely a Community view, the more coherent use of land as the effects of the single market physically reshape the Community by creating new zones of wealth and population. It is not a master plan but is intended to create more systematic transnational cooperation between planning authorities.

The basic premise of the initiative is that the regions must develop harmoniously with equal access to a communications and public service infrastructure. This arises from the recognition that the single market forces the Union to address the problem of regional disparities more energetically. The strategy behind Europe 2000 is to encourage regional and local planners to liaise on development projects that are inherently cross-border. This was helped by the inclusion of trans-European networks (TENS) for transport and telecommunications in the Treaty on Union reforms. It is intended to apply the principle of subsidiarity to the initiative as far as possible to involve local people and not to impose a blueprint from above.

The initiative involves the complex intertwining of a large number of important influences such as energy, transport, telecommunications, water and waste management, pollution, demography, and the special problems of the coastal areas and islands. The aim is to coordinate the work with regions inside the boundaries of states neighbouring the Union. That is why the project was called 'Europe 2000' and not 'Community 2000'. In the same spirit as the initiative are the 'Cooperation Networks' that were set up in 1991 to enhance cooperation between cities and regions of the Community. The scheme was begun experimentally in 1990 and is a sophisticated, and reasonably well-funded, version of town twinning, with an emphasis on linking strong and weak as partners. It is financed under what is called a RECITE programme, under the Regional Development Fund, or 'Regions and Cities for Europe'. A version of it called ECOS is a project to link cities and regions, especially in the less-favoured regions of the Community with counterparts in Central and Eastern Europe. An example of such a network is one formed by the following: Strasbourg (France), Charleroi (Belgium), Coimbra (Portugal), Piraeus (Greece), Malaga (Spain) and Stuttgart (Germany).

Trans-European Networks

The Treaty on Union permits subsidies for trans-European networks (TENS) in transport, telecommunications, gas and electricity. When they are completed they will have changed the face of Europe. In December 1993 the Delors White Paper on *Growth, Competitiveness and Employment* went into much greater detail and was approved by the Council. Extremely large amounts of money are required for the proposed projects. The estimated cost of the

10-year scheme is ECU 400 billion. The Corfu summit in June 1994 discussed 34 large infrastructure projects costing about ECU 64 billion. It agreed to 11 transport and eight energy schemes, but hesitated on information technology proposals. At the Essen summit in December 1994, 14 transport and 10 energy schemes were confirmed. A list of the projects is in Figure 12.1. Four of them apply to the United Kingdom: the London–Channel Tunnel high-speed rail link; modernisation of the West Coast main line from London to Glasgow; an Ireland–UK–Benelux road link; and the Cork–Dublin–Belfast–Larne–Stranraer rail link.

In early 1995 the Finance Ministers' Council discussed the finance of TENS and made three decisions, first that a better regulatory framework was needed to raise private risk capital in the form of equities; second, that the TENS budget would have to be increased because of strong interest from member states; and third, more attention would have to be given to raising long-maturity loans. Much of the money will come from the European Investment Bank (EIB) which does not anticipate any problems in raising the finance for the first group of TENS programmes agreed at Essen. The EIB is now the world's largest international borrower and will fill any gap in the financing requirements because it is committed to supporting the White Paper's growth initiative and to helping small firms.

In 1994 the EIB lent ECU 7 billion to finance capital investment in the networks. This included the upgrading of railways for the Belgian and French Channel Tunnel links. The Vice President of the EIB said that, as a rule of thumb, ECU 1 billion of new investment would create 16 000 new jobs. If this were extrapolated to the whole ECU 400 billion programme over the ten years, in theory, 6.4 million new jobs could be created.

The Schengen Agreements

The Schengen Agreements are an attempt by some members of the European Union to remove their common border controls and to establish a strong external border, along the lines of the USA. The Agreements have been maturing since 1984 and provide an interesting insight into how the European Union members try to reconcile national self-interest with the declared ideals of the Community and

FIGURE 12.1

Trans-European Networks – The First 14 Projects

List of priority transport projects Work begun or to begin by the end of 1996	Countries

1. High-speed train / Combined transport north–south
   Nürnberg–Erfurt–Halle/Leipzig–Berlin
   Brenner axis: Verona–München · · · · · · · · · · · · · · I/A/D

2. High-speed train (Paris)–Brussels–Köln–Amsterdam–London
   Belgium: border–Brussels–Liège–B/D border;
   Brussels–B/NL border · · · · · · · · · · · · · · · · · · · B
   United Kingdom: London–Channel Tunnel access · · · · · · UK
   Netherlands: B/NL border–Rotterdam–Amsterdam · · · · · · NL
   Germany: (Aachen[1]) Köln–Rhein/Main · · · · · · · · · · D

3. High-speed train south
   Madrid–Barcelona–Perpignan–Montpellier
   Madrid–Vitoria–Dax · E/F

4. High-speed train east
   Paris–Metz–Strasbourg–Appenweier–(Karlsruhe) · · · · · · F/D
   with junctions to Metz–Saarbrücken–Mannheim · · · · · · · F/D
   and Metz–Luxembourg · · · · · · · · · · · · · · · · · · · F/L

5. Conventional rail/combined transport: Betuwe line
   Rotterdam–NL/D border–(Rhein/Ruhr[1]) · · · · · · · · · · NL/D

6. High-speed train/combined transport France–Italy
   Lyon–Torino; Torino–Milano–Venezia–Trieste · · · · · · · F/I

7. Greek Motorways: Pathe: Rio Antirio, Patras–Athens–
   Thessaloniki–Prohamon (Greek/Bulgarian border) and Via
   Egnatia: Igoumenitsa–Thessaloniki–Alexandroupolis–Ormenio
   (Greek/Bulgarian border)–Kipi (Greek–Turkish border) · · · GR

8. Motorway Lisbon–Valladolid · · · · · · · · · · · · · · · · P/E

9. Conventional rail link Cork–Dublin–Belfast–Larne–Stranraer · IRL/UK

10. Malpensa airport (Milano) · · · · · · · · · · · · · · · · · I

11. Fixed rail/road link between Denmark and Sweden
    (Øresund fixed link) including access routes for road, rail, air · DK/S

12. Nordic Triangle (rail/road) · · · · · · · · · · · · · · · · FIN/S

13. Ireland/United Kingdom/Benelux road link · · · · · · · · · UK/(IRL)

14. West coast main line (rail) · · · · · · · · · · · · · · · · · UK

---

[1] Ongoing construction – support already provided at Community level

SOURCE *The Single Market* (Luxembourg: Office for Official Publications of the European Communities, 1995)

Union. They also show how progress can be made through the most difficult areas of dispute and how some members are willing to step outside the Union structures to accomplish their aims. The Agreements seek to create a single market within which all persons, whatever their origin, will be able to move freely. The Agreements lie outside the European Union administrative structures but could, one day, become embodied into Union law if some of the non-participating members, especially the United Kingdom and Ireland join the Agreements. The Schengen Convention and the Treaty on Union in Title VI allow for the Union to take over the Schengen system and for European Union rules to have supremacy over Schengen rules.

The Union has been trying for a long time to abolish internal frontier checks along the lines discussed in Chapter 1 but has met with opposition and obstruction from the United Kingdom. Ireland has been forced to follow United Kingdom policy because of the security situation and Denmark, until June 1995, also had great difficulty, for internal political reasons, in abolishing frontier controls. The Agreements have offered a quicker route to the objective of free internal frontiers than the European Union procedures.

In 1984 Germany and France signed the Saarbrucken Agreement to gradually remove their common frontier controls and were joined in 1985 by Belgium, The Netherlands and Luxembourg in signing the Schengen Agreement in Luxembourg. That Agreement came into force immediately and was followed by a Convention in 1990. Since then Italy, Greece, Spain and Portugal have signed. Austria applied in March 1995 and will participate in 1997 when its external borders are fully ready. In June 1995, Denmark, Sweden and Finland joined when they achieved a satisfactory degree of compatibility with their existing Nordic Union agreement with Norway which had already abolished border controls between them. The United Kingdom and Ireland remain fully outside. The system is run by the General Secretariat of the Benelux countries in Brussels. Readers who have travelled across European borders in recent years will have noticed that checks declined into a visual check on vehicles and occupants as they slowed down without stopping. Even that minor check had ceased at many crossings though full checks could be reimposed in emergencies.

In March 1995 the 1990 Schengen Convention came into operation with a three-month trial by seven members, Germany, France,

Spain, Portugal and the Benelux countries. Italy and Greece delayed because of problems with their maritime frontiers and Austria delayed to give it time to erect proper border posts on its 1500 kilometre external border. The three Nordic countries were due to join in July 1995. The members created an external frontier and abolished all internal checks. International airports had to be reorganised so that Schengen nationals could pass unchecked whilst non-Schengen persons underwent the usual, or even more rigorous checks. Citizens from other European Union states who were not participating had to be given special 'Schengen national' status to avoid breaching the European Union's laws concerning free movement. People from outside the European Union had to conform to several requirements, one of which might be the possession of a visa. These visas were for three months only, for tourists, but allowed freedom of movement within all Schengen states once the external frontier was crossed. Long-stay visas remained the responsibility of national governments. The Schengen members had agreed three lists of states, one of countries needing a visa, one of countries which did not, and one of countries where no decision had been made. The result is that an Australian who might have lived in the United Kingdom for many years now required a visa to visit France. Unanimity is required in drawing up these lists. Non-European Union nationals who are illegally in a Schengen state can be expelled from the common territory and the Schengen countries have made readmission agreements with various countries such as Poland, other Central European states and some African states.

The first few months of what has been dubbed 'Schengenland' were not very auspicious. France in particular was very unhappy about its open border with The Netherlands in respect of drug trafficking, which it alleged resulted from a Dutch laxity of approach to soft drugs. It asked for a temporary postponement of the final implementation of the Convention and, when that was refused, used a safeguard clause to replace some of its border controls unilaterally. In August 1995 it reimposed checks at airports because of a bombing campaign in Paris by an unknown group. The French attitude partly reflected the opposition of extreme right-wing groups to open borders through which they allege great tides of illegal immigrants would flow. There were also enormous queues of vehicles building up at the German–Polish borders as the external frontier of Schengen was strengthened. The computerised entry system at Schipol airport at Amsterdam had to be suspended because of the delays it caused. The Schengen visa system should, one day, be replaced by a common visa issued under the auspices of the European Union. The latest attempt to introduce such a visa was vetoed by the United Kingdom in July 1995 because of fears of losing national control of terrorist and drug smuggling activity. The Government was actually succumbing to pressure from its anti-European Union wing. Deep down, the real reason is almost certainly the belief that fellow member states will not exercise proper supervision of the external borders with Poland and ex-Yugoslavia or control the sea-borne migrants from the Adriatic countries and North Africa.

Is a New Police State being Developed?

The Schengen Convention set up the Schengen Information System which has evolved after Maastricht into the European Information System (EIS). This is a very modern data processing system with a central file in Strasbourg (C–EIS) and national files (N–EIS) in each Schengen country. The data is available to customs agencies, to all border posts, to police forces and to overseas institutions that issue visas. The data is on persons and on objects such as weapons, narcotics and stolen vehicles. All this data is subject to the Council of Europe's 1981 Convention on the protection of personal data. Schengen has also tried to develop a high level of cooperation between police forces. There is a common radio communication network in border areas, joint observation of suspects and cross-border hot pursuit of criminals. The French were slow to agree to this last point. The Convention also stresses judicial cooperation on such things as simplifying extradition, searches, seizures and the implementation of judgments. It also encourages the harmonisation of policies on narcotics and weapons. Groups representing refugees and asylum seekers fear that the EIS will be used predominantly to control illegal immigration.

Europol

The Treaty on Union included a decision to set up a European Police Office, to be named Europol. Europol is intended to be an international criminal intelligence agency responding to international crime, terrorism and narcotics trading. The implementation of this part of the Justice and Home Affairs pillar of the Maastricht Treaty required agreement on a Convention which would then be ratified by national parliaments. In mid-1995 the Convention had still not been agreed in full, and once it is it will take up to two years to ratify. The early disagreements were between France and Germany over data-protection systems because the German Constitutional Court was thought unlikely to accept the French plan. By mid-1995 the Convention seemed agreed except for the United Kingdom's obdurate refusal to allow Europol to be supervised via European Union institutions, the European Court of Justice and the Court of Auditors. The British Government regarded this as creeping federalism. The unseemly wrangling looked set to continue and it seemed unlikely that Europol could be up and running officially until late 1997. Fortunately, the Union can be flexible and a Europol Drugs Unit was set up in the Hague on an *ad hoc* basis in late 1993 and about 80 people are employed on establishing the computer systems and databases needed. It has since had its functions extended by the European Council to money laundering, stolen cars, forced prostitution and illegal transfers of nuclear material so a name change is likely in the near future.

There is not likely to be a European police state in a totalitarian sense as long as respect is paid to the safeguards of human rights in the various international Conventions and in national constitutions, but very powerful databases are being created and may lead to serious infringements of civil liberties in individual cases. The present membership of the European Union is heavily weighted in favour of states with excellent records in the field of civil liberties but future extensions of membership will inevitably include several states with poor records in this respect not just since 1945 under communist domination but, in some cases, from the interwar period.

The Intergovernmental Conference of 1996

The Treaty on Union included a decision to set up an Intergovernmental Conference to meet in 1996 to review the Treaty. The IGC and the discussions and negotiations leading up to it will determine the course taken by the European Union in the early decades of the next century and will establish the type of Union into which new members enter. Most observers think that it is a crucial confernece but Mr Hurd, when United Kingdom Foreign Secretary in February 1995, said the 1996 IGC 'will not be the defining event of the 1990s'. The United Kingdom government had a vested interest in playing down the importance of the IGC because of its internal dissensions over Europe, but other nations were taking it very seriously.

In 1993 it was agreed to set up a Reflection Group to examine submissions from the various European Union institutions and from member states in preparation for the IGC. It held its first meeting in June 1995 and consists of a member from each of the 15 members plus two from the European Parliament and one from the Commission. Its Chairman is Carlos Westendorp from Spain so it is often referred to as the 'Westendorp Group'. Most of them are politicians and members of governments but some are ex-Ambassadors and some are bureaucrats. According to a letter containing a questionnaire from Mr Westendorp to the members of the Group they will consider five themes. These are outlined in a *House of Commons Library Research Paper 95/76* as follows:

1. *Principles and objectives*:   The views on the reports of the main institutions; should reform of the Treaties 'reinforce peace, freedom, internal and external security and solidarity between Europeans'; an agreement on three criteria which are greater democracy, greater efficiency and greater transparency; public involvement in the development of the Union; the success of the Common Foreign and Security Policy; flexibility and coherence in an enlarged Union; the future of the single institutional framework; is ratification by all states necessary for reforms to be implemented? should there be a European referendum? This section also asked about the final result of the IGC and whether it should be a Constitution, a Charter or a simplified Treaty. It asked whether the pillared structure of the Maastricht Treaty should be retained.

2. *The institutional system*:   The balance between the institutions; the context for enlargement; the reinforcement of democracy, efficiency and transparency and the modifications required to achieve it.

3. *The citizen and the Union*: The concept and development of European citizenship; fundamental rights; the scope of action in the third pillar of the Treaty.

4. *External and security policy*: External action and the challenge of enlargement; the legal personality of the Union and its external representation; ways to strengthen the CFSP in decision-making and implementation; the examination of defence concepts of the Treaty in the light of the new European security situation; links between the European Union and the WEU and NATO.

5. *Instruments*: Laws, hierarchy of acts and subsidiarity; own resources; budgetary powers; multi-annual programming; solidarity and adequacy of resources; common policies and new areas of action; the impact of enlargement.

The Group proposed to meet twice a month for the remainder of 1995 and to present a report of the Reflection Group to the Madrid European Council in December 1995. A progress report was published at the start of September 1995. It was apparent that the Group had not been 'reflecting' in the usual sense and that the members had been stating their own government's position. The continued opposition of the United Kingdom to incorporating the Social Chapter in the Treaty and to the extension of majority voting was clear. The general thrust of the progress report is towards amending the Treaty on Union rather than wholesale replacement, boosting the importance of action against unemployment, taking stronger environmental action and improving the efficiency, effectiveness and transparency of the Union's administration. It thought that the timetable and criteria for EMU should not be reconsidered though some members wanted the existing content of the Treaty augmented to take account of the economic and social integration of the Union. It put forward the idea of having a European Union figurehead or 'High Permanent Representative' to embody the Union's foreign and security policy. The discussion of qualified majority voting produced new concepts such as super-qualified majority, positive abstention, and consensus less one. They are all possible techniques to avoid 'Eurosclerosis' and achieve progress when one or more members object. The application of the principle of subsidiarity, the development of a common defence policy and the better incorporation of European citizenship were all discussed in detail. The group was agreed on 'the need to maintain the *acquis communautaire* [the mass of Union laws] and to build on it as a basic principle for member states and as a major guide for applicants'.

The European Commission's submission

The Commission's 'Report for the Reflection Group' for the 1996 IGC, published in May 1995, is a very interesting document and has been referred to several times in this book. The report analyses the application of all sections of the Treaty and reaches the following conclusions. 'The finding of this report is that the Treaty is good in parts', a statement that makes it sound like the curate's egg. The good parts have produced substantial benefits such as the keeping to schedule of economic and monetary union and the greater democracy inherent in the enhanced role of the European Parliament. The new codecision procedure working in conjunction with qualified majority voting in the Council is viewed favourably and 'contains the principal ingredients of a balanced legislative regime'. In the preamble to the report it says that 'enlargement and deepening are perfectly compatible'. The report also says that the need for Parliament's approval of the Commission has enhanced the Commission's democratic legitimacy. It argues in favour of the Commission retaining the right to be the sole initiator of legislation and guardian of the Treaties.

The shortcomings of the Treaty take up a great deal more space in the report. They include poor implementation of the concept of citizenship of the European Union and the fact that the Treaty has not brought the citizen closer to the Union. It later suggests that it wants to develop to the full the concept of European citizenship and that this might involve a guarantee of the fundamental rights and duties of citizens in a full text. This sounds like a European equivalent of the American Declaration of Rights, something that many United Kingdom groups have campaigned for over the years. The report expands on the limitations and failings of the Common Foreign and Security Policy. It is aggrieved by the failure to apply the Treaty itself by using the QMV in areas covered by intergovernmental cooperation. It identifies 'some real structural weaknesses' that have rendered the Treaty complex and unclear. They detract from the effectiveness of decision-making and reduce the transparency of the system. It regards the United Kingdom opt-out on social policy as a 'dangerous precedent for the operation and cohesion of the Union'. It says there are 'serious inadequacies of the provisions of justice and home affairs'. It believes that the principle of subsidiarity has not been used for its intended purpose. In one important conclusion it says 'the less than convincing experience with intergovernmental cooperation under the second and third pillars suggests there can be no question of trying to accommodate further enlargements with the present arrangements for their operation'.

The European Parliament's submission

The Parliament's submission was based on amendments and modifications of a report from its Committee on Institutional Affairs. The main points are as follows. The Parliament wants the pillar system of the Treaty to be abolished and wants the three existing pillars to be merged under a single administrative framework. It anticipated a failure of the 1996 IGC to reach unanimous agreement and said 'consideration will need to be given to proceeding without the minority and, possibly, providing for instruments to enable a member state to leave the European Union, subject to meeting certain criteria'. The Parliament wanted an extension of QMV but also wanted to retain unanimity for certain particularly sensitive areas such as Treaty revision and constitutional decisions over enlargement and a uniform electoral system. It recommended a reduction of the present 'very high level' QMV threshold. (This was in direct conflict with United Kingdom policy to raise the level and give the larger members greater weight.)

Much of the rest of its submission comprised detailed policy requirements, some of which, such as a desire to prohibit capital punishment, to have Union control of the sale of arms to third countries and to integrate the Schengen Agreements into Union law, are controversial. The Parliament upheld the right of initiative of the Commission, something that some groups such as the Europe of the Nations Group, have proposed to abolish. It was also in favour of more open meetings with public right of attendance and a Union referendum on new Treaty provisions. Many of the other submissions concerned the working of the Parliament itself. These include a desire for only three decision-making procedures, a simplified codecision procedure, assent and consultation. It proposes the abolition of the cooperation procedure. It wants the distinction between compulsory and non-compulsory expenditure abolished so that the Parliament is an equal partner with the Council in the budget decisions. It makes a bid for greatly enlarged powers by asking for equal status with the Council 'in all fields of European Parliament legislative and budgetary competence', including the right to request opinions of the European Court of Justice and to bring cases before it.

It has been obvious for some time that, once the European Parliament was democratically elected, it would try to assert its rights and become more like national parliaments. The debate leading to this submission and the text itself are evidence of its attempt to gain power and responsibility within the Union.

The Council of Ministers' submission

The Foreign Affairs Council adopted a draft report in April 1995 after it had been examined by COREPER. It consists of rather brief and bland accounts of progress on the implementation of the new areas of activity arising from the Treaty and on the questions of openness and transparency. There is very little analysis or comment except briefly in the initial assessment of the CFSP and the third pillar JHA.

The Court of Justice's submission

The Court and the Court of First Instance submitted proposals. It suggested ways to improve its effectiveness by simplifying procedures in minor cases and wants to be able to change its Rules of Procedure without Council approval. The Court saw no technical objections to the European Parliament's desire to have the right to request an opinion from the Court. It warned against making matters that could be settled in the political field a subject for judicial consideration. It is unusual to hear of lawyers turning down the offer of extra work!

Other submissions

The most important single contribution will be from Germany and the ruling CDU/CSU parties produced discussion documents that indicate the trend of their thinking. They advocate the development of a European state based on the rule of law with national policies on justice and home affairs being brought more into line with each other, that is a progressive extension of European Union competence. They also seek the development of a common border, asylum, visa, refugee and immigration law. They want the Union to progress over the next decade towards being a 'constitutional' community, with a strengthening of the European Parliament. They insist on a strict implementation of the principle of subsidiarity. Chancellor Kohl said in September 1995 that he expected the IGC to culminate in a Maastricht II Treaty. This implies that he does not expect results until The Netherlands Presidency in the second half of 1997, by which time the United Kingdom government might have changed at the general election that must be held before the end of May 1997.

The United Kingdom policy was outlined in a House of Commons debate in March 1995 on an Opposition motion of no confidence in the Government's policy towards the European Union. *The Times* newspaper reported on 27 January 1995, that Mr Hurd, the Foreign Secretary, suffered a strong rebuff in the Cabinet when he presented his recommendations on the United Kingdom's approach to the IGC. The report says that the recommendations were not sufficiently Eurosceptical and did not support British national sovereignty strongly enough. In the debate the Prime Minister, Mr Major, did not believe that the IGC would make huge changes in Europe or that any serious changes would be proposed. The United Kingdom would concentrate on improving the way Europe operated and on developing the CFSP, and on the fight against organised crime and terrorism. It sought a stronger role for national parliaments and more subsidiarity and more action against fraud. The Government would not accept the end of the national veto and wanted larger states to be given more weight under qualified majority voting. It wanted a continuation of intergovernmental cooperation in the second and third pillars. In March 1995 the Government also issued a *Memorandum on the United Kingdom Government's Approach to the Treatment of European Defence Issues at the 1996 IGC*. This showed some recognition of the realities of the changed attitude of the USA to European defence but continued to back NATO and advocate a subsidiary role to the WEU. Mr Major's speech was angled at appeasing his anti-European backbenchers but its general tone boded ill for the success of the IGC unless some equivalent of the Maastricht set of compromises is reached.

French policy under the newly-elected President Chirac had not been clearly stated by September 1995 but he had campaigned with a promise to hold a referendum on the 1996 IGC. Chirac is known to support the strong Franco-German alliance at the core of the Union and supports a common European Union foreign and defence policy. When under attack over France's new nuclear tests in the Pacific he offered the French nuclear deterrent to a European Union and WEU defence organisation. His offer was not accepted. In the Autumn of 1995 the British media were intent on seeing splits in the Franco-German consensus over Europe and a threat to monetary union. Few continental commentators saw it the same way. President Chirac is also in favour of the European Union having its own President. The European Parliament also wants such a President elected by MEPs. It is unlikely that Mr Major would agree.

Other countries have expressed the general approach of their ruling parties to the IGC and some points have aroused great interest. Sweden, for example, wants an amendment to the Treaty on Union to include maintaining high levels of employment as an important objective of the Union, a suggestion that aroused antagonism in some groups in the United Kingdom. Sweden proposes an employment charter which would write effective and compulsory policies, including an employment committee, into the Treaty. One of the intentions behind the idea, which has gathered extensive support, is to ameliorate the effects of the convergence criteria for monetary union. The Netherlands representative on the Reflection Group is reported to have talked of waivers of the convergence criteria for the single currency in respect of government deficits, because his own country and Belgium and France would not qualify in 1999 on the present criteria. The Netherlands regards an overhaul of the decision-making process as essential for enlargement of the Union to take place, and a government discussion paper favoured an extension of the QMV. It also wants, in the long run, to integrate the WEU into the European Union. Spain is also in favour of this integration but wants it to occur as early as 1998.

There were reports, notably in *The Guardian* newspaper of 16 September 1995, that France and Germany were completing a joint minimum programme for closer European Union after 1996. The two countries were said to be moving closer together with the German government and the Bundesbank ready to campaign for a single currency along the lines of the Commission's plan. The two countries' concepts for a common European defence are very similar. Both will support an extension of QMV even into the second and third pillar areas of foreign and security policy and justice and home affairs policy, and an extension of the powers of the European Parliament. They will probably not support the replacement of intergovernmental cooperation in the CFSP and JHA pillars by European Union legal competence and that would reduce the likelihood of a fundamental reform of the European Union on a federal basis.

What is the likely outcome of the IGC?

There will probably be a strengthening of the European Parliament's powers and a rationalisation of the decision-making procedures of the Union. There will be an extension of qualified majority voting and an improvement in the decision-making process for CFSP and JHA. The intergovernmental approach to these two pillars will probably continue. There is unlikely to be a radical reform of the relationships between the five institutions of the Union or a new Treaty which codifies and replaces the existing ones. There may be an extension of the concept of citizenship of the European Union. There is likely to be a reaffirmation of the programme for monetary union in 1999. Decisions about very divisive issues such as budgetary contributions and the redirection of regional funds will probably be referred to other channels or negotiations. The Treaty may be modified to give more priority to employment and environmental policies. There might, however, be much more radical proposals if the United Kingdom government changes by the time the final decisions are made.

There is unlikely to be much joy for those who support the so called *chrysalis principle*. This is the name given by the President of the French European Movement to the federalist idea that the Commission would mutate into the Government of Europe, that the European Parliament would become a lower house and the Council a senate.

Concluding Thoughts

The grand vision of a European Union suffered a set-back in the disputes arising from the negotiating and ratification processes for the Maastricht Treaty on Union. People became disillusioned with an institution which appeared to challenge the prerogatives of governments and interest groups, which requested massive changes in national laws to accommodate the single market programme, and which was used as a scapegoat by national governments to blame for unemployment, recession and an assortment of other ills. The correct lessons may have been learned. The processes for reform and enlargement that will be involved in the 1996 Intergovernmental Conference should be more open and will be accompanied by programmes to inform and educate the general public.

If the intentions of the leaders of the European Union are realised it will maintain its position as the world's largest and richest trading and political grouping. It already has a market 40 per cent larger than that of the United States and three times the size of Japan's. The aim can be achieved whilst maintaining very much the same degree of national diversity as exists at the moment. There is bound to be some trend towards greater uniformity because that is one of the effects of better communications, modern technology and economies of scale. Diversity tends to flourish in isolation. Uniformity tends to be part of the price of knowledge and communication. The hope is that a large degree of this uniformity is based on the adoption of the best standards and practice and not on the second-rate.

A lesson of history is that human society needs ground rules although these may require to be altered over time. Europe is passing out of the phase of the dominance of the nation-state and entering the era of cooperative decision-making. The growth of multinational and transnational corporations and the vast daily flows of capital across international markets highlight the decline of effective national economic sovereignty. The modern European experience in consensus and coalition politics within their own nation-states will enable the transition to be accomplished more easily. A 'Europe of regions' could help to overcome one of the most persistent problems of the modern national state, that is how to combine the strength derived from size and unity with the desires of minorities for self-determination. Nations will be able to obtain strength from membership of the European Union. Minorities will be able to retain their individuality by being a separate region within a member state of the Union. Such a development may solve some of the numerous minority problems of Europe, from the more violent conflicts of the Basque country and Northern Ireland, to the less-troublesome but persistent calls of Northern Italian and Walloon separatists, to the gentler nationalist aspirations of Wales, Scotland, Cornwall and Brittany. Some argue that European Union will nurture self-determination and consequently encourage a return to extreme nationalism but the descent into tribalism which has characterised the break-up of the Soviet empire in Central and Eastern Europe, and in the Balkans, must be avoided at all costs. The growth of right-wing and xenophobic extremism and the events in ex-Yugoslavia are a convincing argument in favour of a more binding unity and a cooperative commitment to economic and social progress. It is reasonable to believe that the European Union holds the potential key to these problems.

ANNEX
Issues on which Unanimity is Required by the Council

EC Treaty

Article 8a	Right of movement and residence save as otherwise provided in the Treaty
Article 8b	Right to vote in European Parliament and municipal elections
Article 8e	Additional rights of citizenship
Article 45(3)	Compensatory aid for imports of raw materials
Article 51	Social security (coordination of arrangements)
Article 57(2)	Amendment of principles laid down by law governing the professions in a Member State
Article 73c	Measures which constitute a step back as regards liberalization of capital movements
Article 93	State aid
Article 99	Taxation
Article 100	Approximation of laws for the common market where Article 100a is not applicable
Article 100c	List of countries whose nationals require visas (until 1996)
Article 103a	Financial assistance for a Member State and economic measures in the event of severe difficulties

ANNEX *Continued*

Article 104c(14)	Excessive deficits
Article 105(6)	Tasks for the European Central Bank
Article 106(5)	Amendments to the Statute of the European System of Central Banks
Article 109(1) and (4)	Agreements on an exchange-rate system
Article 109f(7)	European Monetary Institute
Articles 109k (5), 109l(4) and (5)	Economic and Monetary Union: institutional provisions
Article 121	Social security for migrant workers: assignment to the Commission of powers for implementation of common measures
Article 128	Culture
Article 130	Industry
Article 130b	Specific action outside the Structural Funds
Article 130d	Structural Funds and Cohesion Fund
Article 130i and o	Adoption of the framework research programme and setting-up of joint undertakings
Article 130s	Certain environmental provisions
Article 136	Overseas countries and territories
Article 138(3)	Adoption of a uniform electoral procedure for the European Parliament
Article 145	Conferral of implementing powers
Article 151(2)	Appointment of the Council's Secretary-General
Article 157(1)	Alteration to the number of Members of the Commission
Article 159	Non-replacement of a Member of the Commission
Articles 165 and 166	Increase in members of the Court of Justice and Advocates-General
Article 168a (2) and (4)	Increase in actions heard by Court of First Instance and approval of Rules of Procedure
Article 188	Amendment of Title III of the Statute of the Court of Justice and approval of Rules of Procedure
Article 188b	Court of Auditors: appointment of members
Article 189a	Amendment of a Commission proposal
Article 189b(3) and c(d) and (e)	Second reading in co-decision and cooperation procedure

Article 194	Appointment of members of the Economic and Social Committee
Article 198a and b	Committee of the Regions: appointment of members and approval of Rules of Procedure
Article 201	Provisions relating to the own resources system
Article 209	Financial Regulations
Article 217	Rules governing languages
Article 223	Trade in arms
Article 227	Overseas territories
Article 228(2)	Conclusion of certain agreements
Article 235	Objective of the Community without provision for the necessary powers
Articles 238 and 228(2)	Association agreements

Common foreign and security policy (Declaration No 27 annexed to the Treaty on European Union)

Article J.3 in conjunction with Article J.8	Adoption of joint action
Article J.2(2) in conjunction with Article J.8	Defining of common positions
Article J.11	Decision to charge operational expenditure to the Community budget

Justice and home affairs

Article K.3 (in conjunction with Article K.4)	Adoption of common positions, or joint action
Article K.8	Charging of operational expenditure to the Community budget
Article K.9	Crossover to Article 100c

Protocols (ref.Article 239)

| Articles 12 and 45 (see Article 165 EC) | Protocol on the Statute of the Court of Justice |

ANNEX *Continued*

Article 41(1)	Protocol No 3 (Statutes of the European System of Central Banks and of the European Central Bank)
Article 2(3) and Article 4	Agreement on social policy (between 14 Member States) annexed to the Protocol No 14
Article 6	Protocol No 6 on the convergence criteria referred to in Article 109j of the EC Treaty

Final provisions of the Treaty on European Union

Article O of the Treaty on European Union	Accession of new Member States

SOURCE *Intergovernmental Conference 1996, Commission Report for the Reflection Group* (Luxembourg: Office for Official Publications of the European Communities, 1995)

Bibliography

Beharrell, A. *Unemployment and Job Creation*. London: Macmillan, 1992.

Cecchini, P. *The European Challenge 1992: The Benefits of a Single Market*. Aldershot: Wildwood House, 1992.

Canzoneri, M. B. and Rogers, C. A. 'Is the European Community an Optimal Currency Area? Optimal Taxation versus the Cost of Multiple Currencies', *American Economic Review*, 80, 1990, 419–33.

Central Statistical Office. *Social Trends 95*. London: HMSO, 1995.

Commission of the European Communities. *One Market, One Money*. European Economy 44. Luxembourg: Office for Official Publications of the European Communities, 1990.

Commission of the European Communities. *The New Regulations of the Agricultural Markets*. Green Europe 1/93. Luxembourg: Office for Official Publications of the European Communities, 1993.

Commission of the European Communities. *Support for Farms in Mountain, Hill and Less-Favoured Areas*. Green Europe 2/93. Luxembourg: Office for Official Publications of the European Communities, 1993.

Commission of the European Communities. *Intergovernmental Conference 1996: Commission Report for the Reflection Group*. Luxembourg: Office for Official Publications of the European Communities, 1995.

EFTA. *Annual Report 1994*. European Free Trade Association. Geneva, 1995.

European Monetary Institute. *Annual Report 1994*. Frankfurt: European Monetary Institute, 1995.

Eurostat. *Basic Statistics of the Community*. 31st edn. Luxembourg: Office for Official Publications of the European Communities, 1994.

Eurostat. *Basic Statistics of the Union*. 32nd edn. Luxembourg: Office for Official Publications of the European Communities, 1995.

Eurostat. *Europe in Figures*. Luxembourg: Office for Official Publications of the European Communities, 1995.

Eurostat. *A Social Portrait of Europe*. Luxembourg: Office for Official Publications of the European Communities, 1991.

'EU Ministers withhold tapes in secrecy case', *The Guardian*, 6 July 1995, p. 14.

'EU's top two plan for more unity', *The Guardian*, 16 September 1995, p. 14.

HMSO. *Memorandum on the United Kingdom's Approach to the Treatment of European Defence Issues at the 1996 IGC*. London: HMSO, 1995.

Morris, Boehm, and Geller. *The European Community: a Practical Guide for Business, Media and Government*. London: Macmillan, 1990.

Mundell, R. A. 'A Theory of Optimum Currency Areas', *American Economic Review* 51, 1961, 657–65.

Nevin, E. *The Economics of Europe*. London: Macmillan, 1990.

OECD. *Economic Outlook*. Paris: Organisation for Economic Co-operation and Development. Bi-annual June and December.

Pilbeam, K. *International Finance*. London: Macmillan, 1992.

The European Commission has set up a network in the United Kingdom to provide information on its policies and programmes. The network consists of EURO INFO CENTRES (EICs) and EUROPEAN DOCUMENTATION CENTRES (EDCs). EICs serve their local business community with up to date information on funding and legislation. EDCs cater mainly for students and academics by maintaining a stock of all major official publications for consultation. The Information Services Unit of the European Commission at 8 Storey's Gate, London SW1P 3AT publishes a leaflet giving the location of the network centres.

There is also a complete catalogue of EC publications and documents available on CD-ROM. It is called EUROCAT and contains records from 4 official databases. It is co-published by The Office for Official Publications of the European Communities, Chadwyck-Healey and ELLIS Publications.

If you want to fathom the meaning of the endless acronyms and titles such as JOPP, THERMIE, CEDEFOP, LEDA and so on, there is a comprehensive list in a booklet *Sources of European Community Funding*, 2nd Edn. London: Representation of the European Commission in the United Kingdom, 1995.

Index